UNIVERSITY OF NORTH CAROLINA AT CHAPEL HILL
DEPARTMENT OF ROMANCE LANGUAGES

NORTH CAROLINA STUDIES
IN THE ROMANCE LANGUAGES AND LITERATURES

ESSAYS; TEXTS, TEXTUAL STUDIES AND TRANSLATIONS; SYMPOSIA

Founder: URBAN TIGNER HOLMES

Distributed by:

UNIVERSITY OF NORTH CAROLINA PRESS
CHAPEL HILL
North Carolina 27514
U.S.A.

NORTH CAROLINA STUDIES IN THE
ROMANCE LANGUAGES AND LITERATURES
SYMPOSIA
Number 5

SAMUEL BECKETT
THE ART OF RHETORIC

SAMUEL BECKETT
THE ART OF RHETORIC

Edited by
EDOUARD MOROT-SIR,
HOWARD HARPER,
DOUGALD McMILLAN III

CHAPEL HILL

NORTH CAROLINA STUDIES IN THE ROMANCE
LANGUAGES AND LITERATURES
U.N.C. DEPARTMENT OF ROMANCE LANGUAGES
1976

Library of Congress Cataloging in Publication Data

Symposium on Samuel Beckett: the Art of Rhetoric,
  University of North Carolina, 1974.
  Samuel Beckett, the art of rhetoric.

(North Carolina studies in the Romance languages and literatures:
Symposia; no. 5)
Includes bibliographical references.
  1. Beckett, Samuel, 1906-   — Criticism and interpretation — Congresses.
  I. Morot-Sir, Édouard. II. Harper, Howard M. III. McMillan, Dougald. IV. Title. V. Series.
PR6003.E282Z489   1974   848'.9'1409   75-29183
ISBN: 9780807891711

DEPÓSITO LEGAL: V. 752 - 1976
ARTES GRÁFICAS SOLER, S. A. - JÁVEA, 28 - VALENCIA (8) - 1976

CONTENTS

                                                                                Page

INTRODUCTION   9

I. ON BECKETT'S PHILOSOPHY
  1. DAVID H. HESLA: *Being, Thinking, Telling, and Loving: The Couple in Beckett's Fiction*   11
  2. EDOUARD MOROT-SIR: *Samuel Beckett and Cartesian Emblems*   25

II. ON BECKETT'S RHETORIC
  1. RUBY COHN: *Warming Up for My Last Soliloquy*   105
  2. RAYMOND FEDERMAN: *Samuel Beckett: The Liar's Paradox.*   119

III. ON BECKETT'S POETRY
  1. MELVIN J. FRIEDMAN: *Introductory Notes to Beckett's Poetry*   143
  2. LORI HALL BURGHARDT: *The Bawds of Euphony: Images of Women in Beckett's Early Poems*   151
  3. STEPHANI POFAHL SMITH: *From Poetics to Anti-poetics* ...   157
  4. DOUGALD MCMILLAN III: *Echo's Bones: Starting Points for Beckett*   165

IV. ON BECKETT'S NOVELS
  1. MARYSE J. LEISURE: *Murphy, or the Beginning of an Esthetic of Monstrosity*   189
  2. WILLIAM TRITT: *Statistics on Proper Names in* Murphy.   201
  3. RUBIN RABINOVITZ: *The Addenda to Samuel Beckett's* Watt.   211
  4. ANGELA B. MOORJANI: *A Mythic Reading of* Molloy ...   225
  5. HANNAH CASE COPELAND: *The Couples in* Comment c'est.   237
  6. HOWARD HARPER: *How it is*   249

V. WORKING WITH BECKETT, by ALAN SCHNEIDER   271

INTRODUCTION

THE essays collected here are papers given or written on the occassion of the Symposium on Samuel Beckett: The Art of Rhetoric held at the University of North Carolina at Chapel Hill, April 4-6, 1974. We have chosen the title of that symposium as the title for this book because the essays reflect the major concerns of the symposium. Our purpose in placing the emphasis on rhetoric was not to examine or enumerate the formal rhetorical figures used by Beckett, or to compare his rhetorical techniques with those of other modern writers, but to look at him as a man who has had a very intense and personal concern with words and their literary organization. Our interest was in Beckett as a man who has experienced the limits of language, has put words on trial, forced them to confess their failure, and refused to exonerate them through any illusory triumph. Our concern was with Beckett as a man for whom rhetoric — a response to the possibilities and the demands of language — is a deeper and more urgent problem than the usual philosophical or philological problems of form and meaning.

We have arranged the essays in four groups which represent significant perspectives. First there are two essays which deal with the relation of Beckett's language to philosophy as a universal language of truth; then, two studies of recurrent forms of language in Beckett — the soliloquy and the "liar's paradox" — and their attendant problems. The remaining studies are presented under the headings of the two genres which were emphasized at the symposium: poetry and fiction. We think that these essays illuminate not only the specific works themselves, but also the themes and concerns of the work as a whole.

We have not tried to draw conclusions or to provide a summing up. Discussions during the symposium were wide-ranging, well-informed, and cordial. We feel that they were guided by the single principle of fidelity to Beckett and his work. We wish to thank all of the participants — not only those whose work is published here, but also those who enlivened the discussion and created a special ambiance.

We also wish to express our gratitude to James Gaskin, Dean of Arts and Sciences; Jacques Hardré, Chairman of the Department of Romance Languages; and William Harmon, Chairman of the Department of English, for their generous support of the Symposium. We would like to thank also the Department of Dramatic Art for its friendly cooperation and the Extension Division for its efficient help in the organization of the Symposium.

EDOUARD MOROT-SIR
HOWARD HARPER
DOUGALD MCMILLAN III

BEING, THINKING, TELLING, AND LOVING: THE COUPLE IN BECKETT'S FICTION

by David H. Hesla

I

THE theme and motive force, as it were, of Beckett's first novel, *Murphy*, is desire. The desires of some characters are simple, of others more complex. Cooper has apparently only one — the desire for strong drink in unlimited quantities. Wylie desires Miss Counihan, partly for her body, partly for her money. Miss Counihan and Celia desire Murphy. The former sees him as only a means for setting her up in middle class respectability, and while the latter wants him for the same purpose, she has a certain appreciation of Murphy in and for himself. Neary, whose name is an anagram of "yearn," desires first Miss Dwyer, then Miss Counihan, then Murphy as a means, then Murphy as an end (as "friend"), and finally Celia. Murphy himself, asyndetic and contradictory as he is, desires both the pleasures of the body (Celia, for example, or ginger cookies) and the pleasures of the mind (as described in section six of the novel).

The life lived according to the dictates of desire is, however, a life of frustration and vanity, and this for four reasons. For desires can be unfulfilled, fulfilled, changed, or in mutual opposition to one another. While he is yearning for Miss Dwyer, Neary is miserable: "All is dross, for the moment at any rate, that is not Miss Dwyer" (Mu, p. 5).[1] In course of time Neary's desire is fulfilled, but he is no less miserable, for "No sooner had Miss Dwyer... made Neary as happy as a man could desire, than she became one with the ground

---

[1] New York: Grove Press, 1957. Hereafter references will be given in the text.

against which she had figured so prettily" (Mu, p. 48). The narrator tells us that Neary wrote to Herr Kurt Koffka and demanded an immediate explanation of the phenomenon; but Neary would have done better to apply to the author of *Proust,* for there he would have found what he was looking for. "The aspirations of yesterday were valid for yesterday's ego," writes Beckett in that essay, "not for to-day's. We are disappointed at the nullity of what we are pleased to call attainment. But what is attainment? The identification of the subject with the object of his desire. The subject has died — and perhaps many times — on the way." [2] The ego named Neary that yearns for Miss Dwyer is not the same ego that attains her.

The same is true of Celia. She has her heart set on Murphy's finding a job. Murphy protests strenuously, but finally capitulates, and hires out as a male nurse at the Magdalen Mental Mercy Seat. When he reports to Celia that he has fulfilled her heart's desire, she responds with an unenthusiastic "Oh" (Mu, p. 137). The Celia that wanted Murphy to get work has died, partly as a result of learning the joys of Murphy's rocking-chair, and partly as a result of the suicide of the "old boy."

Murphy's desires correspond to the two parts into which he is so neatly split. His body rejoices in the ecstasies of music, *music,* MUSIC, but his intellect delights in the three-storied pleasure palace of his mind. Since the two kinds of pleasure weigh about the same, they keep him in a reasonable balance. But when he takes his rocking chair from the room he's been sharing with Celia, thereby indicating that he is leaving her for good, he upsets the balance. He is fascinated by his patients, and thinks of them as "the race of people he had long since despaired of finding" (Mu, p. 169). He supposes that since they are, to all appearances, "immured in mind," they must dwell continually in the peace and freedom which he enjoys only intermittently and with the aid of his rocking chair. He is especially fascinated by Mr. Endon, "a schizophrenic of the most amiable variety," and he seeks to enter into a relationship with the patient. His effort is doomed to fail, however. After their catastrophic chess game, Murphy analyzes the situation in these words: "The relation between Mr. Murphy and Mr. Endon could not have been better summed up

---

[2] New York: Grove Press, 1957, p. 3. Hereafter references will be given in the text.

than by the former's sorrow at seeing himself in the latter's immunity from seeing anything but himself" (Mu, p. 250). That is to say, Mr. Endon is impenetrable, as far as Murphy is concerned.

Mr. Endon's impenetrability is not merely a function of his mental condition, however. It is rather a fact, a truth, about the self as such. The self is impenetrable by any other self. Writing in *Proust*, Beckett says:

> No object prolonged in this temporal dimension tolerates possession, meaning by possession total possession, only to be achieved by the complete identification of object and subject.... All that is active, all that is enveloped in time and space, is endowed with what might be described as an abstract, ideal and absolute impermeability [Pr, p. 41].

From the fact of impermeability Beckett draws the only possible conclusion: "We are alone. We cannot know and we cannot be known" (Pr, p. 49). Two images in Murphy illustrate the best that can be hoped for: the tug and its barge, coupled abreast, and two kites in tandem, flown by a child. The two pairs are sustained by water and wind, ancient symbols of the flow of time.

The impermanence and impermeability of the self, together with its consequent unknowability and isolation, become the themes of Beckett's second published novel, that Kantian caricature, *Watt*. Mr. Knott's physical appearance is typical of Watt's epistemological plight, "For one day Mr. Knott would be tall, fat, pale and dark, and the next thin, small, flushed and fair, and the next sturdy, middle-sized, yellow and ginger, and the next..."[3] Because the impermeability of the self denies any access of one to another, friendship can be illustrated as the dance of synchronized robots:

> Then I [Sam the narrator] placed his [Watt's] hand on my shoulders, his left hand on my right shoulder, and his right hand on my left shoulder. Then I placed my hands, on his shoulders.... Then I took a single pace forward, with my left leg, and he a single pace back with his right leg (he could scarcely do otherwise). Then I took a double pace back.... And so, up and down, up and down, we paced between the fences, together again after so long, and the sun shone bright upon us, and the wind blew wild about us [Wa, p. 163].

---

[3] New York: Grove Press, 1959, p. 209. Hereafter references will be given in the text.

In the seventh and last of his inverted speeches to be recorded, Watt describes the best that friendship has to offer: "Two men, side by side" (Wa, p. 168).

Given the impermeability of the self, communication can be reduced to a matter of stimulus and response, as when Molloy programs his mother. "I got into communication with her by knocking on her skull. One knock meant yes, two no, three I don't know, four money, five goodbye. I was hard put to ram this code into her ruined and frantic understanding, but I did it, in the end." [4]

Or more brutally in *How It Is*:

> table of basic stimuli one sing nails in armpit two speak blade in arse three stop thump on skull four louder pestle on kidney
>
> five softer index in anus six bravo slap athwart arse seven lousy same as three eight encore same as one or two as may be [5]

Enduring love is a statistical impossibility, if not a simple contradiction in terms. Celia and Murphy may love (or at least desire) one another in their room at Miss Carridge's on Brewery Road, but when Celia begins to appreciate the pleasures of the mind in consequence of taking a rock in Murphy's chair, she is not the Celia she was. Since she is not, she cannot love Murphy — not, at any rate, in the same way she loved him before — and Murphy cannot love the changed Celia — not, at any rate, in the way he loved her before. If Murphy's universe were Leibniz' universe, ordered by the system of the preestablished harmony, all would be well. But of course it is not. As Beckett writes in *Proust*, "When it is a case of human intercourse, we are faced by the problem of an object whose mobility is not merely a function of the subject's, but independent and personal: two separate and immanent dynamisms related by no system of synchronization" (pp. 6-7). So in the poem "Cascando":

> terrified again
> of not loving
> of loving and not you
> of being loved and not by you

---

[4] *Molloy, Malone Dies, and The Unnamable: Three Novels* (New York: Grove Press, 1959), p. 18. Hereafter cited as TN, with references in the text.

[5] New York: Grove Press, 1964, p. 69.

II

In Beckett's later work the theme of the couple appears more prominently in the drama than in the fiction. Beckett's famous couples are Didi and Gogo, Pozzo and Lucky, Hamm and Clov, Winnie and Willie. Nonetheless, there are two aspects of the theme in the trilogy that I want to treat, one in *Molloy* and one in *The Unnamable*.

Molloy and Moran form a certain kind of couple. The fact that Moran at the end of his adventures looks a good deal like Molloy at the beginning of his has led some critics, notably Hugh Kenner, to speculate that Molloy is in some sense a continuation of Moran.[6] The fact that the two characters are also very different, however, has led other critics, notably Edith Kern, to suppose that Moran and Molloy are two aspects of one self, perhaps Nietzsche's Apollonian and Dionysian selves.[7] I have suggested that Molloy is a Character in search of his Author ("mother"). Molloy fails to find him (or finds him and kills him), and is forced himself to turn author and tell the story of his search. Moran is the Author in search of a Character. He too fails to find him (or finds him and kills him), and returns home to write the story of his search, thereby becoming his own Character. Both stories are autobiographical, and an autobiography is by definition a story in which the author is the chief character.[8]

The novel abounds with allusions to other narratives of travel and quest. There are more or less overt references to the *Aeneid*, the *Odyssey*, Jesus' entry into Jerusalem and his subsequent passion, *Pilgrim's Progress*, *Through the Looking-Glass*, and Goethe's *Faust*.[9] To these I would add the following story, narrated in Plato's *Symposium*

> On the day when Aphrodite was born there was a feast of all the gods, among them the god Poros or Plenty, who is

---

[6] *Samuel Beckett: A Critical Study* (New York: Grove Press, 1961), p. 65.

[7] "Moran-Molloy: The Hero as Author," *Perspective*, XI (Autumn, 1959), 187 ff. Prof. Kern elaborates her interpretation in her *Existential Thought and Fictional Technique: Kierkegaard, Sartre, Beckett* (New Haven: Yale University Press, 1970), pp. 194-208.

[8] *The Shape of Chaos* (Minneapolis: University of Minnesota Press, 1971), pp. 86-128, 181-83.

[9] Michael P. Decker has pointed out to me that Molloy's travels correspond point for point with Alice's.

the son of Metis or Sagacity. When the feast was over, Penia or Poverty, as the manner is on such occasions, came about the doors to beg. Now Plenty, who was the worse for nectar... went into the garden of Zeus and fell into a heavy sleep; and Poverty considering that for her there was no plenty, plotted to have a child by him, and accordingly she lay down at his side and conceived Love.... And as his [Love's] parentage is, so also are his fortunes. In the first place he is always poor, and anything but tender and fair, as the many imagine him; and he is rough and squalid, and has no shoes, nor a house to dwell in; on the bare earth exposed he lies under the open heaven, in the streets, or at the doors of houses, taking his rest; and like his mother he is always in distress. Like his father too, whom he also partly resembles, he is always plotting against the fair and good; he is bold, enterprising, strong, a mighty hunter, always weaving some intrigue or other, keen in the pursuit of wisdom, fertile in resources; a philosopher at all times....[10]

The descriptions of the two aspects of Eros are, to my mind, pretty good descriptions of Molloy and Moran. Molloy seeks his mother not simply because he is an avatar of Aeneas or Faust (though he is that too), but because he is an Author who is almost completely impoverished, who, in Beckett's own words is "working with impotence, ignorance."

In Plato Eros is not simply a semi-divine being but a function of the human soul. In the *Phaedrus* Plato elaborates his doctrine of the soul under the figure of the charioteer and his two horses, one of them noble, the other base. The noble element seeks to fly up to the Plain of Truth, the ideal world, but the base element seeks after the things of this transitory world. Plato tells us the law of Destiny which governs the fate of those souls in which the base element predominates. When the soul fails to behold the truth and "sinks beneath the double load of forgetfulness and vice, and her wings fall from her and she drops to the ground," then the law ordains that she pass into a man. There are nine orders of man available to the soul, the first order being that of the philosopher, the ninth a tyrant, and the sixth "a poet or some other imitative artist." Moreover, ten thou-

---

[10] *Symposium* 203B-203E. The translation is Jowett's in *The Dialogues of Plato* (4 vols.; Oxford: Clarendon Press, 1953), I, 535.

sand years must elapse before the soul can regrow her wings and ascend to the divine world.[11]

All of the characters in Beckett's trilogy are ancient souls doing penance for the sin of having been born. The major images are therefore taken from the literature of suffering and purgation — the Hades of Odysseus, Plato's world of appearances, Dante's *Purgatorio*, Christian's progress to the Celestial City. The hope of eventual salvation from suffering, a hope common to both the Platonic and Christian traditions, is, however, all but extinguished. One of the most poignant images of the soul condemned to human existence is only just hinted at by Beckett in the story of Worm stuck in his jar. Worm here is the Cumean Sibyl, and this is Ovid's version of her story.

> While Apollo still was hopeful,
> Seeking to bend my will with gifts, he told me
> *Choose what you will, O maid, and you shall have it.*
> I pointed to a heap of sand and uttered
> The foolish prayer that my years might be as many
> As there were sand-grains in that mound. I should have
> Asked that those years should be forever young,
> But I forgot. He granted me the years,
> And promised endless youth if he could have me,
> But I refused Apollo, and no man
> Has ever had me. Now my happier days
> Are gone, and sick old age comes tottering on,
> And this I must endure, for a long time.
> I am seven hundred years of age; I have
> Three hundred still to go, before I equal
> The tally of those grains of sand. The time
> Will come when I shall shrivel to almost nothing,
> Weigh almost nothing, when no one, seeing me,
> Would ever think a god had found me lovely.
> .... To such change
> I am borne onward, till no eye can see me,
> And I am known by voice alone; my voice
> The Fates will leave me.[12]

In the *Satyricon,* Petronius reports that the Sibyl was contained in

---

[11] *Phaedrus* 246A-249C; *Dialogues*, III, 153-56.
[12] *Metamorphoses,* Book XIV. The translation is by Rolfe Humphries in *Ovid: Metamorphoses* (Bloomington, Ind.: Indiana University Press, 1955), pp. 342-43.

a vessel or jar, and when asked what she wanted, she replied, "I want to die." [13]

III

In these last comments I have strayed from the topic of the couple in Beckett's fiction. I return to that matter now, but I must do so by way of Descartes and the *cogito*.

You will remember that in the *Discourse on the Method* Descartes tries to discover the bedrock of truth on which he can build philosophy. He therefore rejects "as absolutely false everything as to which I could imagine the least ground of doubt," including the facts supplied by the senses and the truth derived from reasoning. Having eliminated all facts, truths, opinion, information, and experience from his mind, he finds that there is still something left. "Whilst I thus wished to think all things false, it was absolutely essential that the 'I' who thought this should be somewhat, and remarking that this truth, '*I think, therefore I am*' was so certain and so assured that all the most extravagant suppositions brought forward by the sceptics were incapable of shaking it, I came to the conclusion that I could receive it without scruple as the first principle of the Philosophy for which I was seeking." He then continues, "From that I knew that I was a substance the whole essence or nature of which is to think, and that for its existence there is no need of any place, nor does it depend on any material thing; so that this 'me,' that is to say, the soul by which I am what I am, is entirely distinct from body...." [14]

Now the fact of the matter is that Descartes was wrong. He was wrong not in separating mind from body — for our purposes that is irrelevant — but wrong in his description of what remains when the contents of the mind are eliminated. For if I perform the Cartesian epoche or doubt, what I have left is not the *cogito*, not the "I think," but *cogitationes* or thoughts, or even better, *cogitans*, thinking. That is to say, when I reflect upon my thinking, I find nowhere behind or under my thinking an ego or "I" or soul which is the agent of thought. What I find is simply thinking.

---

[13] Petronius, *Satyricon*, 48.8.
[14] "Discourse on the Method," Pt. IV. The translation is by Elizabeth S. Haldane and G.R.T. Ross, in *The Philosophical Works of Descartes* (2 vols.; New York: Dover Publications, 1955), I, 101.

William James knew this, and said it very well.

> The first and foremost concrete fact which every one will affirm to belong to his inner experience is the fact that *consciousness of some sort goes on.* "States of mind" succeed each other in him. If we could say in English "it thinks," as we say "it rains" or "it blows," we should be stating the fact most simply and with the minimum of assumption. As we cannot, we must simply say that *thought goes on.* [15]

Descartes' language is wrong, and James's is right. It is not the case that "I think." It is rather the case that "thought goes on." The "I" or ego or self is not then the agent or subject of thinking but its "occasion" or "locus." Thinking, or consciousness, is impersonal.

At the same time, thinking or consciousness is personal, in the sense that what I am thinking about or what I am conscious of is determined by my body (including of course my brain), my past experience, my projects for the future, and my immediate environment.

I want to bring to bear two of these terms — "immediate world" and "past experiences" — on the intentional act called "reading *The Unnamable.*" I am sitting in my living room. It is night, the children are asleep, the house is quiet, except for all the little night noises. I pick up the book and begin the act of reading. I concentrate on the text. Immediately the house, the children, and even the little night noises disappear from my consciousness. There is left only the steady flow of the words. They enter my consciousness, they are what I am conscious of, they and only they constitute my consciousness. They are no longer Beckett's words or the Unnamable's words but my words. For as long as I read, these words are my immediate world, and they are as well the total content of the past experience called "reading *The Unnamable.*" In the act of reading I am nothing other than "being conscious of the words."

There are then two reasons why the Unnamable can have no name. The first is that the Unnamable is that impersonal consciousness which simply "goes on" thinking and speaking, and which, as such, is always an instant ahead of the namable self which is constituted by its being conscious, as the slug is always an instant ahead of the trail of its slime, or the comet of its tail. But insofar as the words

---

[15] *Psychology: Briefer Course* (New York: Collier Books, 1962), p. 167.

in which that impersonal consciousness expresses itself become, in the act of reading, the total content of the consciousness of the reader, they become also the reader himself. So the Unnamable is also every reader who allows himself to be hypnotized by the words, who allows himself to be constituted by the words, whose consciousness is an edifice raised up by the words.

Hence the ultimate couple in Beckett's fiction is the couple formed by the impersonal consciousness of the unnamable one who is speaking the words and the impersonal consciousness of the unnamable one who is reading them. His words are my words, his story my story, his consciousness my consciousness, his being my being. In the communion of the written word, writer and reader become one. Thus Beckett overcomes the solipsism and isolation which are the conditions of the existence of the changing and impermeable self. By means of his art he possesses all of me there is to possess — my consciousness; and he and I are one as no two mortal lovers, separated from one another by their bodies and their different histories, can ever be one.

In this sense, *The Unnamable* is an act of love in which writer and reader are united in the words and in the story the words are telling. Indeed, from my experience of Beckett's work I must conclude that he is best understood as the poet of love. It has been his theme from first to last. But what the word means for him is certainly not what it meant for Yeats or D. H. Lawrence or Eliot, or for Proust or Goethe or Dante. The difference between Beckett and the Romantic tradition in general, whether Christian or neo-pagan, is that the Tradition holds that the being of the lover is more or less stable, permanent, and identical with itself through time, while for Beckett it is impermanent, changing; and the Tradition holds that in the act or process of love two persons become one, whereas for Beckett the self is finally impermeable to any other.

Hence love is futile, for its ideal — the total possession of the beloved — is an impossibility. Strictly speaking, it is absurd, for it is a human need or demand or value which cannot be satisfied by the conditions of human existence.

So love too joins the list of the great absurdities. Being itself is absurd, contradicted by death, yet we find in ourselves the compulsion to be. Thinking is absurd, contradicted by the limitations of our knowledge and the errors of our reasonings and interpretation. Yet thinking goes on, and we are condemned to thinking for as long as we are condemned to being. Telling our stories to one another is absurd, for I cannot tell you who I am, partly because I do not know who I am, partly because there are no words for telling you, partly because the words I must use or try to use are not the words that you can understand, and partly because my being is constantly changing, and what I tell you about me then is not true of me now. And yet we find ourselves under the compulsion to tell our stories — we are saddled with the absurd "obligation to express." Loving too is absurd, contradicted by the impermanence and impermeability of the self, and the absence of any "system of synchronization," yet we find ourselves under the compulsion of loving. The great absurdities — being, thinking, telling, and loving — are all impersonal forces which set me going to and fro on the earth, and walking up and down on it,

> peering out of my deadlight looking for another
> wandering like me eddying far from all the living
> in a convulsive space
> among the voices voiceless
> that throng my hiddenness
> ("Four Poems")

IV

Propelled by these impersonal forces, I seek the place where my being can come to rest, "The place, I'll make it all the same I'll make it in my head, I'll draw it out of my memory, I'll gather it all about me" (TN, p. 572). There the thinking that goes on in my head "will tell me everything, tell it to me again, everything I need, in dribs and drabs, breathless, it's like a confession, a last confession, you think it's finished, then it starts off again, there were so many sins, the memory is so bad, the words don't come, the words fail, the breath fails, no, it's something else, it's an indictment, a dying voice accusing, accusing me, you must accuse someone, a culprit is indispensable, it speaks of my sins, it speaks of my head, it says it's mine, it says that I repent, that I want to be punished, better than I am, that I want to go, give myself up, a victim is essential, I have only to listen, it will show me my hiding place, what it's like, where the door is, if there's a door... quick now and try again, with the words that remain, try what, I don't know, I've forgotten, it doesn't matter, I never knew, to have them carry me into my story, the words that remain, my old story, which I've forgotten, far from here, through the noise, through the door, into the silence, you don't know, perhaps it's the door, perhaps I'm at the door, that would surprise me, perhaps it's I, perhaps somewhere or other it was I, I can depart, all this time I've journeyed without knowing it, it's I now at the door, what door, what's a door doing here... (TN, pp. 573, 576).

The being of the Unnamable is a penance for the sin of having been born, his thinking is a penance for the sin of his being, and his talking is a confession of the sins of his being and thinking. He is torment incarnate, and he seeks the repose that comes when his being shall have been enough, when his thinking shall have become thought sufficient, when his telling shall have been thought sufficient penitential confession to atone for his sins of being and thinking, when he shall have arrived at the door opening onto his peace.

So too another great sinner concluded his confessions of sins with the image of a door:

> By the gift of your grace some of the works that we do are good, but they are not everlasting. After them we hope that we shall find rest, when you admit us to the great holiness of your presence. But you are Goodness itself and need no good besides yourself. You are forever at rest, because you are your own repose.
>
> What man can teach another this truth? What angel can teach it to an angel? What angel can teach it to a man? We must ask it of you, seek it in you; we must knock at your door. Only then shall we receive what we ask and find what we seek; only then will the door be opened to us. [16]

Unlike St. Augustine, however, the Unnamable is not trying to teach us that God is goodness itself, and that the human heart is restless until it finds its rest in Him. For his last words are those of the proud Christians on the first cornice of Purgatory, "piu non posso," "I can't go on," and these words are immediately contradicted by the last words of all his words, "I'll go on." [17]

---

[16] *Confessions*, XIII, 38. The translation is by R. S. Pine-Coffin, in *Saint Augustine: Confessions* (Baltimore: Penguin Books, 1961), p. 347.

[17] Dante, Commedia, Purg. X. 139.

Like being, thinking, telling and loving, this disembodied intelligence, this devilish angel will go on and on and on and on. For the being of the human is precisely thinking, telling, and loving in spite of the carelessness of all that is not human. What counts is being human, what counts is the human being, not for any good reason, not for any traditional reason, but for no other reason than that it is *human* being. The human being is not to be validated by the image of God, not by some future being more than human, not by the project of being for-itself-in-itself, not by heroic rebellion against all that is not human, but by the immediate "being-with" another human being here and now.

If we may call this impulse to be with another anything at all we may call it love, if that word still means anything at all. The goal of love is to be one with the other, but this goal is defeated by the facts of the impermanence and impenetrability of both the one and the other. Loving is therefore as absurd as being, thinking, and telling, but one is condemned to loving, or the effort at loving, as one is condemned to being, thinking, and telling. And yet for all its absurdity, loving is being human, and "being with" is better than "being there."

Or, to use the words of Koheleth, the preacher, "two are better than one."

> Two are better than one; because they have a good reward for their labour. For if they fall, the one will lift up his fellow; but woe to him that is alone when he falleth; for he hath not another to help him up. Again, if two lie together, then they have heat: but how can one be warm alone?[18]

---

[18] Ecclesiastes 4:9-11.

SAMUEL BECKETT AND CARTESIAN EMBLEMS [1]

by Edouard Morot-Sir

I

IN its generalities as well as in its analyses in depth, literary criticism develops in a sort of separate history that grows and progresses with its ups and downs, according to the organic rules of a very special game and in great part independently of the quite different history of the works and authors which it takes for its critical pretexts — a relation analogous to that which brings together the meadow and the digestive system of the ox, or the lazy barge and the busy stream. Of a like nature is my excuse for saying that I do not know and do not have to know what Mr. Samuel Beckett personally thinks of Descartes, Cartesianism and the Cartesians, great and small. But I know well that Beckett's so-called "Cartesianism" or "anti-Cartesianism" has inspired a unique body of thoughtful criticism that has grown up in the '60s of the present century. There exists an original phenomenon, a sort of cultural isle, a pure critical situation with its own set of problems, as an integral part of our literary criticism: Can Descartes and Cartesian ways of life and thought become literary crafts and techniques? If so, in what way?

Let me add a subjective note which may justify in fine the present enterprise. The only adjective I can discover to describe adequately

---

[1] Beckett's works will be referred to by their initial title, whether in English or French. Quotations and pages will be cited from the English Grove Press edition and from the French Éditions de Minuit.

I would like to express my deep gratitude to my colleague, Professor Alfred Engstrom, who has kindly accepted to read this text in its final form, and has suggested many stylistic corrections and improvements.

my feeling before this problem of Beckettian criticism is "irritating" — in the direct and proper sense of causing irritation, like itching in its actual itch, because I am unable to get rid of all those explicit or implicit Cartesian allusions and references, and because I cannot see clearly the difference between a "Cartesian Beckett" and a "Beckettian Descartes." And I must keep this Cartesian semantics in harmony with a well-known statement of Beckett: I am not a philosopher; I do not understand philosophers and their linguistic habits!

This set of Cartesian themes related to Beckett's works is a specific aspect of a more general set of postulates. First, it is often said that the literature of our century — especially that of the mid-century years — has been invaded by philosophical problems, methodologies and vocabularies. The relations between philosophy and the literary genres (novel, play, poem, essay) have clearly raised important technical questions for Sartre and Camus — but even before them for Proust, Claudel, Valéry, Joyce, *et al.*, and after them for the New experimenters of the '60s. I do not mean that the solution of Beckett is analogous to the solutions of Sartre and Camus. Each of these writers has his personal problems and his way of solving them.

A fortiori Beckett's problem belongs only to Beckett. I am even tempted to say that Beckett's approach to the connection between philosophy and literature is deeper and more original than that of any of the others, who do not go beyond a more or less sophisticated act of translation from language X to language Y. The ultimate *raison d'être* of the present study could well be the demonstration of Beckett's rhetoric — the search for it at the confluence of contradictory languages.

It seems naïve to pretend that literatures of our time are fated to be more philosophical than those of any other time. I fear that there is a universal dimension to our problem. There can be no literature without an awareness of this problem and its more or less happy resolution. I am convinced that all the histories of literature should be reread with those prerequisites in mind. Philosophy is an attempt to give " the last word" in any language, and the philosopher is the vocal actor who plays at one and the same time the First and the Last Adam! Literature has this same finality. It borrows inevitably some of its tricks from philosophy — especially the devices which transform a linguistic closing-up into an eternal promise of reality. The opposition between truth and beauty is often cited to "explain" the differences in the two languages. But this duality is perfectly ambiguous. Everyone supposedly knows that for a classical writer beauty is truth, and that for a romantic truth is beauty. Yet these clear-cut distinctions are misleading, and let us not forget that those two words (*beauty* and *truth*) must play their rôle here in a lively ballet with goodness and reality!

Is it possible to offer a precise and technical formulation for our problem? Let us recognize that creeping disease of any literature in any genre: the *allegorical sin*. Let us also remark that there can be no literary criticism without an implicit recognition of literary language as allegory, and this for a very simple reason: if there is justification for a critic's adding a new projection to a given language, is it not because he thinks that the first language contains within it another hidden language which it is his responsibility as a critic to extract from and expatiate upon? This is why I risk saying that allegory is more than a second-rate instrument of rhetoric, that it is the pitfall of any literary enterprise — something ideally to be avoided, and yet something that is inevitable! To seek a meaning for a group of phrases is to accept the fact of allegory. Some writers, as we may recognize — is this not the fault for which Beckett reproaches Baudelaire when he denounces the "intellectual symbolism" of *Les Fleurs du Mal?* — lightheartedly assume this risk and play out their games at this level, considering philosophy merely as a spice for their literary repast. But there is another perspective from which to view this question — the lexical one concerned with the problem of how to combine words relating to philosophy with words of any other specialized vocabulary.

As early as 1929 young Beckett saw Philosophy and Philology as "a pair of nigger minstrels out of the Teatro del Piccoli," or as "a carefully folded ham-sandwich" (thus anticipating Belacqua's sandwich in *More Pricks than Kicks*). The petulant young Beckett pays tribute to Giambattista Vico for his understanding of the problem's technical aspect: "He [Vico] insisted on complete identification between the philosophical abstraction and the empirical illustration, therefore annulling the absoluteism of each conception — hoisting the real unjustifiably clear of its dimensional limits, temporalizing what is extratemporal." Needless to say, those texts belong to the first paragraph of *Dante ... Bruno. Vico .. Joyce* — a paragraph that ends with an astonishing premonition, a protest in interrogative form: "Must we wring the neck of a certain system in order to stuff it into a contemporary pigeon-hole [which announces the "niches" of *Le dépeupleur*], or modify the dimensions of that pigeon-hole for the satisfaction of the analogy-mongers? Literary criticism is not book-keeping."

We — the book-keepers and analogymongers — are warned of the dangers and possibilities of ridicule in our language. But it is permissible for us to drag along with us willy-nilly a reluctant Beckett for the first step in our research — for there is, indeed, beyond all other possible dualities, the basic duality of Philosophy and Philology. The literary problem is not how to *trans*-pose abstraction into illustration, or the reverse — or how to *juxta*-pose them in the artificial unity of a language — but how to -*pose* them together (waiting meanwhile, at least until the end of the present article, to decide whether the right particle even exists).

To sum up, Beckett's references to Descartes and Cartesian themes correspond to a specific and fundamental literary problem with extensive overtones. There is no literary development possible without the use, explicit or otherwise, of philosophical vocabulary and patterns, so that the actual problem is not whether philosophy is a possible part of literature, but just how its intervention or interference comes about. We know that Beckett was conscious of the need for a critical solution of this problem as early as 1929 when he raised the issue under the lofty aegis of Vico by introducing a double duality — that of *Philosophy* and *Philology* and that of *abstraction* and *illustration*. It is thus clear that the problem does not stem exclusively from the period in which certain teachers of philosophy took it into their heads to storm out on the Parisian literary scene and steal its spotlights. I have no intention of presenting Beckett as the precursor of Existentialist maxims. Far from it! I merely suggest that this Cartesian interrogation in Beckett's works exemplifies one aspect of a permanent problem of literature, whose solution affords the perennial phenomenon of literary renewal. It relates to the dynamic imperative of novelty. The underlying duality in this literary *becoming* is not revolution versus tradition, but rather novelty versus allegory, if it is true that allegory is merely an aspect of the literary process, a permanent force pervading every genre and making academism for the writer either a prospect of anguish or something to which he can turn for a soothing relief.

II

To launch our investigation, let us turn to Federman and Fletcher's bibliography,[2] which has entries down to 1966. A superficial examination of the two indexes shows that, in the section entitled "Criticism of Samuel Beckett's Works," there are 10 entries for Descartes, 8 for Geulincx, 2 for Malebranche, 3 for Leibnitz, 1 for Spinoza, and 2 for Berkeley (for evident reasons, in a Beckettian perspective, the Irish bishop can be put among the Cartesians) — and this in comparison with 14 entries for Kafka, 12 for Sartre (mostly dealing with the theatre and only one concerned with philosophical problems), and 11 for Camus. Other philosophical references are rare: among Greek philosophers, for example, Aristotle, Democritus, Empedocles, Epictetus and Pythagoras have only one entry each. Plato is not even mentioned. There is only a single entry for Saint Augustine. In modern philosophy we find 2 entries for Pascal, 2 for Vico, 2 for Diderot, 1 for Schopenhauer, 2 for Kierkegaard, 1 for Dostoievski, 3 for Bergson, 4 for Heidegger, and 4 for Wittgenstein. Gabriel Marcel is cited 6 times, but only as a critic of drama. We may be sure that the picture will change with an up-to-date edition of this excellent bibliography; but at first glance and for the period of a decade (1958-1968) criticism of Beckett in its philosophical aspects has tended to concentrate on Descartes and the Cartesians on the one hand and on the other on the thinkers of the nineteenth and twentieth centuries more or less connected with Existentialism. The absence of any reference to Plato is quite remarkable, as is the rarity of entries for the pre-Socratics. The period of the Gnosis and the Church Fathers is all but ignored, and there is no entry for medieval times or for Hermetism in its various forms.

From its inception, criticism of Beckett has been international, although the most important part of it has been written in English and French. The French criticism has emerged slowly, and it was not until the late '60s that one found much more than articles in which writers like Blanchot and Robbe-Grillet pay homage to Beckett. Up to the present, "French" critical reaction can be characterized under

---

[2] *Samuel Beckett: His Works and His Critics* (University of California Press, 1970).

two headings: 1) Beckett's works are discussed in Existentialist language — not specifically through any technical vocabulary of methodology inherited from Sartre, but in the sort of *koiné* that has been the Parisian post-war cultural language; and 2) the Cartesian references are played down or, if they are discussed, are interpreted as clear evidence of Beckett's *anti*-Cartesianism.

In the criticism of this period two dates deserve special mention: 1966 and 1969. In 1966 appeared Ludovic Janvier's *Pour Samuel Beckett*, a general presentation in French of Beckett's works. In his introductory pages, Janvier protests against any forced pigeon-holing, cites certain examples of this, and condemns any attempt to reduce Beckett to a narrow perspective: Beckett is not a "soft pessimist" ("un pessimiste mou," as Sartre nicely phrases it); nor is he merely an "Oblomov *redivivus*," an "Ecclésiaste bis," "a philosopher of nothingness," "a son of Descartes," "a yes-man for Dante," "a great humorist." He is all these last and something more — a writer who has achieved an exceptional linguistic success ("avant tout réussite d'un langage exceptionnel" [p. 107]). References to Descartes and Geulincx serve merely to underline one aspect of Beckettian research. Descartes does not beget Beckett. Initially, Beckett uses Descartes as a sort of prop or springboard. But all existence cannot be locked into the Cartesian "poêle," and Janvier clearly prefers to fall back on Existentialist patterns, whether they originate in Pascal, Hegel, Kierkegaard, Artaud or others of similar persuasion. Yet Janvier is fair to American and English critics and pays due tribute to the writings of Ruby Cohn, Hugh Kenner, and John Fletcher.

Of greater significance because of its aggressiveness and its influence on more recent critical studies in French is Olga Bernal's *Langage et fiction dans le roman de Beckett* (1969). Here in a great cultural hodge-podge occur all the names familiar to the Parisian intelligentsia, from Hegel and Marx to Merleau-Ponty and their current followers. Descartes is quoted a few times (see pp. 69, 73, 93); but there is not a single reference to possible Cartesian patterns or attitudes in Beckett's works, and none of the Cartesians, not even Geulincx, is so much as mentioned. Bernal attempts to define Beckett's postulates entirely in terms of contemporary philosophies with all current tendencies represented. On page 163 of her book one comes upon a sort of declaration of war (it is worth noting that the author in her bibliography cites only Martin Esslin's *Samuel Beckett* for the English or American side of the controversy): "La critique anglo-saxonne voit dans Beckett un écrivain cartésien dont l'œuvre répète la vieille équation entre penser et être. *Un pareil contresens* est d'autant plus incompréhensible qu'*il suffit de jeter le regard le plus superficiel* sur ce roman [here the context is not clear, for the author could be referring to Beckett's novels in general or to anyone of his individual novels — perhaps to *Murphy* or, more likely, to *L'Innommable* (they are both cited on p. 162)] pour voir que Descartes y aurait reconnu *le travail de la déraison incapable d'idées claires et distinctes*" (italics mine).

We shall see in a moment whether this is a justifiable and consistent statement; but, in my judgment, it is only fair to remark that Bernal, in the last paragraph of her book, has offered one of the most perceptive insights ever proposed on the ultimate meaning of Beckett's works: "L'œuvre de Beckett est une tentative démesurée, tant elle est difficile, *d'échapper à la fatalité de la lumière*. Aussi est-elle écrite dans le noir, seul capable de modérer, sinon *d'arrêter cet incœrcible tropisme vers la lumière qui est terreur de l'obscurité*, exigence de sens et de clarté. Mais cette lumière que la littérature du passé considère comme 'nature' n'est aujourd'hui qu'éclairage variable distribué par un sujet toujours changeant..." (p. 230 — italics mine).

Finally, it may be of interest to note that in a more recent volume, *Beckett* (1972), a rather general introduction for use in the schools, the author Gérard Durozoi follows the lead of Olga Bernal with a brief polemic against "la critique anglo-saxonne" (which, moreover, is not represented in the well-ordered and selective bibliography, except by a few articles that have been translated into French). This criticism is given short shrift: "... la critique anglo-saxonne... voit dans Beckett un héritier lointain de Descartes.... En fait tous les textes de Beckett sont une constante négation du cartésianisme" (p. 184). Durozoi's proofs are rather puzzling: the body disappears in Beckett's works and Man is reduced there to a head or a mouth... Beckett defers indefinitely any revelation of the thinking subject and denies man any possibility of knowing his world... in the minds of Beckett's characters there is not discoverable a single clear and distinct idea... the very concept of man's being able to think is challenged in his work... and there is no God anywhere to vouch for anything. Thus Cartesianism, which was responsible for the renaissance of the Western world, is seen at the opposite pole from the Beckettian novel, which ends in the disappearance of the thinking subject (p. 185). Finally (p. 197),

Beckett is pigeon-holed in an affiliation with Breton, Artaud, and Bataille.

In brief, French critics, courteously or otherwise, with or without knowledge of "Anglo-Saxon" criticism, view Beckett primarily through the recent evolution of French literature — more precisely, in the light of Existentialist semantics. Up to now the methods applied in Beckettian criticism have been those of the so-called "Nouvelle critique," and they have been applied in a very impressionistic way. Biographical justification for critical pronouncements is rare indeed. Critical analyses are generally thematic or stylistic with greater emphasis on content than on form, in spite of Beckett's own early admonition that literature is born only when form and content are one. There has been no noticeable evolution in this criticism. In my judgment, the best critical synthesis on Beckett in French is (with Janvier's book) Jean-Jacques Mayoux' introduction to the bilingual edition of *Words and Music, Play, Eh Joe*, which is comparable with the recent syntheses in English by Cohn, Kenner and Fletcher.

Now, granting the existence of such a monster, let us turn to the so-called "Anglo-Saxon" criticism. Here chronology is of interest, and we can recognize two rather distinct critical periods. In the first of these, roughly the period from 1958 to 1967, a series of important studies have a common theme: if Beckett is analyzed and interpreted within his own *Weltanschauung*, some of his novels and the overall unity of his works can be explained by reference to Descartes and Cartesian themes, even while one grants the importance and significance of his connections with Dante, Joyce and Proust. One's selection is more a matter of emphasis than of denial.

In the late '60s the critical mood changes slightly, as if in response to a necessary shift in orientation for greater breadth and depth of understanding. The Cartesian connection is not abandoned, but Beckett's work is considered in relation to the entire scope of its allusions and possible contexts. This marks a new effort to put Descartes and Cartesian devices in their proper light, transcending the oversimplified duality of Cartesianism/anti-Cartesianism, in order to obtain an intuitive and synthetic view of the work in its totality and its uniqueness.

This story begins, then, in the Fall of 1959 with a special issue of *Perspective*, edited by Ruby Cohn. An article by Samuel I. Mintz on "Beckett's Murphy: A Cartesian Novel" presents a persuasive and very well documented proof that *Murphy* is a novel of ideas and should be read against the background of seventeenth-century intellectual history (p. 156). Its hero, Murphy, is not an idealist-Berkeleyan type of character. He is an orthodox Cartesian, a true dualist, obsessed with the problem of communication between the two substances of body and mind. Mintz cites by name those Cartesians who call on God's omnipotent and miraculous intervention to solve the problem (Cordemoy and Malebranche and, of course, Geulincx [p. 158]). All interactions are seen as under God's control... only pure mental activity is free within the distinctions of the great and the little world, interpreted as referring to the opposition between the outer and inner worlds (*ibid.*). Mintz emphasizes the ethical consequence drawn by Geulincx: asceticism is the only legitimate solution for man — what can he do but cultivate his inner life? It is the now-famous *Ubi non vales, non velis* (a very anti-phenomenological and anti-existentialist rule!) which Beckett recognizes as one of the leading principles of his entire work. Such is the meaning of the many images of isolation in *Murphy*. The general conclusions of Mintz's interpretation are clearly stated: *Murphy* is an exploration of the human Self refracted through the medium of Cartesian ideas (p. 165), and Beckett throughout his works will be committed to this theory (p. 164). Beckett's irony is seen by Mintz as "a defensive gesture" to avoid any accusation of metaphysics by a logical analyst (*ibid.*). Thus Beckett uses Descartes and his accomplices "to give his novel structure, action and meaning, and not merely to exercise his own intellectual ingenuity" (p. 156).

In the same issue of *Perspective* Hugh Kenner's brilliant essay, with its often-quoted title, "The Cartesian Centaur" (later reprinted in Kenner's *Samuel Beckett: A Critical Study* [1961, revised edition, 1968] and in Esslin's *Samuel Beckett: A Collection of Critical Essays* [1965]), introduces the Beckettian bicycle and proposes the now well-known hypothesis that "the Cartesian centaur is a man riding a bicycle, *mens sana in corpore disposito*" (p. 54 in Esslin's book). It is the perfect machine as described in *Le Calmant*: "fulfillment of young manhood." Is not Godeau the name of a veteran racing cyclist? But Kenner notes that Beckett goes further than Descartes in exploring the relation between mind and body: "... the Cartesian body seems not subject to loss of toes or arthritis of the wrists" (*ibid.*). If the bicycle appears in *More Pricks than Kicks* and is the dominant moving motor in *Mercier et Camier* and in *Molloy*, it is no longer present in *L'Innommable*, "for *The Unnamable* is the final phase of a trilogy which carries the Cartesian process backwards.... [Mahood] is a Descartes cursed by the dark of the moon. At rest in the jar, he peruses the *Cogito* sufficiently to think of demanding proof that he exists" (p. 59). Kenner's final comment is that at the time of *L'Innommable* "the bicycle is long gone; the Centaur dismembered; of the exhilaration of the cyclist's progress in the days that he was the lord of things that move, nothing remains but the ineradicable habit of persisting like a machine.... The Cartesian centaur was a 17th-century dream, the fatal dream of being, knowing and moving like God. In the 20th-century he and his machine are gone, and only a desperate élan remains..." (p. 61). We can already see the meaning and limits of the so-called Cartesian interpretation of Beckett. For Mintz, Cartesianism is a pattern (a structure and a meaning) within which Murphy develops his personal adventures, which are not necessarily Cartesian! Kenner goes further: without saying so specifically he suggests an anti-Cartesianism with Beckett's works showing the contemporary doom of the Cartesian expectations.

In 1962, Frederick J. Hoffman's *Samuel Beckett: The Language of Self* cites Kenner's "brilliant essay" as "an indispensable beginning" (p. 61). In his introduction Hoffman interprets this Cartesian point of departure along the following lines: Beckett's work is the meeting-place for the "adventures of rational proof and the language of a disillusioned (or a largely inoperative) rational assertion.... [where] rationalism detached from metaphysics diminishes to an epistemological inquiry." From this point of view, Murphy's death is due to "an accident which occurs to the mechanism of the Cartesian W. C." (p. 113)... Watt's peculiar rationality is "a stuck-needle Cartesianism in which the possibilities of language and reason are exploited nervously and feverishly" (p. 114)... and "Moran begins in the full Cartesian confidence" (p. 126), his list of questions is "a parody set of principles, directed against the rational order of statements and answers to questions found in Descartes" (p. 117). Then, in a discussion of the dramatic necessities of theater, Hoffman defines Beckett's rhetoric as a "residual Cartesianism." More specifically (p. 73) he makes the interesting suggestion that Beckett "has deliberately mixed Cartesian geometry with the consequences of two centuries and more of scepticism to come up with a mélange of rationality, introspection, brooding over bodily corruption." This Beckettian rhetoric marks a shift from metaphysics to epistemology in which Cartesian certainties are direct and principal causes of obscurity (p. 79). However, Hoffman sees in Beckett, along with Dostoievski and the Russian novelists at the end of the nineteenth century and with Kafka, the last phase in the destruction of the human self: "... the significance of the Underground man as a symbol of the marginal self achieves its final position in the non-heroes of Samuel Beckett's novels and plays" (p. 48).

The same year (1962) sees the publication of the important study by Ruby Cohn, *Samuel Beckett: The Comic Gamut*. Here there is a clear statement of the Beckettian ambivalence toward Descartes and the Cartesians which had already been noticed in earlier studies. All Beckett's work is seen as "an extrapolation of the Cartesian definition of man as 'a thing that thinks' " (p. 13). Ruby Cohn enumerates the Cartesian objects that are present all through Beckett's novels, short stories, and plays. The early Beckettian heroes imitate Descartes and his trip through Europe. The garret at M. M. M. in *Murphy* "is specifically linked to Leibnitz and the stove is a cogent Cartesian reminder" (p. 50). Watt is a latter-day Cartesian (p. 69). Cohn remarks of *Mercier et Camier* that Camier "by rejecting M. Conaire's company, may be performing a symbolic 'conarectomy,' removing any possible meeting ground for mind and body" (p. 98). Moreover, "a sentence in Book IV of *Le discours de la méthode* seems to foreshadow the *Unnamable*: 'I could suppose that I had no body, and that there was no world nor any place in which I might be' " (p. 17). This novel is a battle against solipsism. "Like Descartes the Unnamable begins in doubt — aporia" (p. 159). In *Comment c'est* the only real proper name refers to Malebranche, "who carried Cartesian dualism of mind and matter to its most extreme form, so that any action of the one upon the other was the occasion for divine intervention" (p. 198). But all this and many other references still do not make Beckett a follower of Descartes. For Beckett's heroes "doubt does not, as in the *Cogito*, lead to a certainty of existence; doubt leads to more profound doubt" (p. 102). Beckett is no longer an indirect Cartesian by way of his fellow-Irishman Berkeley. His heroes are not idealists! Murphy "accepts the mental fact and the less pleasant physical fact" as he accepts "collusion between his body and his mind" (p. 57). Murphy, according to Cohn (and I would add that the same is true for all Beckett's characters), "has small interest in the crucial question of the 17th century — how mind and body communicate" (*ibid.*), and "Beckett carefully disclaims for his hero any concern with the 'ethical yoyo' to which both Descartes and especially Geulincx were drawn" (*ibid.*). In discussing Mintz's article Ruby Cohn makes a comment that is decisive for any possible interpretation of Beckett's works: "Subsequent Beckett heroes will, like Murphy, find themselves reluctant to accept the absolute cleavage between body and mind; instead the two will be attracted to A. Geulincx, the 17th-century Cartesian, who emphasized the delight of the mind" (p. 49). In conclusion, to follow Ruby Cohn's analysis, Beckett's attitude toward Descartes is ambivalent and ironic. And this is the meaning of the last statement in this basic book for Beckett scholarship: "... introspectionists who descend from Descartes, [Beckett's] protagonists show how miserably the line has deteriorated" (p. 295).

Two years later (in 1964), in her article on "Philosophical Fragments in the Works of Samuel Beckett," Ruby Cohn reminds us that by his own admission Beckett is not a philosopher. But she reaffirms the continuous presence of Descartes throughout his work. Writing of *Whoroscope,* she notes that "although Descartes himself does not reappear in Beckett's subsequent works, Cartesianism echoes sound through that work" (in Esslin, *Samuel Beckett,* p. 169). The true Beckettian problem concerns "that thing which thinks" — in other words, its consciousness, not in itself and its glorious power of self-awareness, but in its precarious link with the body and the latter's successive "stages of decay." Ruby Cohn makes the very important comment, which deserves further exploration, that this motif of decay may originate in Descartes' idea on the infinite divisibility of the body as opposed to the indivisibility of the mind (p. 171). Then comes this further perceptive statement: "*The Unnamable* reminds one not only of the Cartesian Geulincx but of Descartes himself, for his monologue is virtually a Discourse on lack of method, on the impossibility of method.... Like Descartes the Unnamable postulates a malevolent divinity" (p. 172). But Ruby Cohn raises a problem for future Beckett criticism when she notes Beckett's familiarity with Logical Positivism and Existentialism, and she advances the following hypothesis: "When Beckett turned from English to French as a writing language, his protagonists turn from a kind of Logical Positivism to a kind of Existentialism. The French work is Existentialist in conveying human dread and despair, as a world of unreconstructed absurdity" (p. 175). She mentions also the influence of the "stream-of-consciousness writing" and of Heidegger's *andenkendes Denken,* echoing Cartesian introspection (p. 176).

Ruby Cohn's suggestive remark on Existentialism will be developed in many ways. In this same year (1964), in *Samuel Beckett: Configuration Critique,* edited by M. J. Friedman, the reference to Kierkegaard is cited by Edith Kern and Robert Champigny, while Germaine Brée thinks that *Watt* could be a parody of the preestablished harmony and monadology of Leibnitz. Martin Esslin, in his introduction to *Samuel Beckett* (1965), ignores the Cartesian connection, but remarks that the parallel between Descartes and Kierkegaard is striking, though there is no evidence that Beckett had in fact been directly influenced by Kierkegaard's thought and writings.

Finally, along the same vein of critical explanation of Samuel Beckett's Cartesianism, in 1967 we come upon *Samuel Beckett's Art* by John Fletcher, which presents a greatly elaborated restatement of this irritating problem. Fletcher distinguishes three different aspects of the problem: Descartes's life, Descartes's philosophy, and Cartesian philosophers. "We may wonder why Descartes's life held such *fascination* [italics mine] for Beckett.... Whatever the reason, Beckett not only admired the thinker's life, but read deeply in his philosophy and traces of Descartes's influence can be found, as critics have not been slow to notice, in nearly all his writings" (p. 129). Fletcher insists on the central problem of duality and union of mind and body, with the difficulty it raised for the seventeenth-century Cartesians and the solutions they were induced to take. "In Beckettian as in Cartesian man, the body is utterly distinct from mind and mind is free to ignore the body's mishaps with the serenity of one who knows that they occur as it were on another planet" (p. 131). I am not at all sure that Descartes would subscribe to that statement! The philosopher who said that man lives only a few minutes a year as a pure mind was conscious of the difficulty of uniting the duality of mind and body, while for Beckett the true catastrophe is the very fact of this union. I shall consider this question hereafter. For the moment I am pleased to be in full agreement with Fletcher in his emphasis upon the deep significance for Beckett of the doctrine of dualism.

In Fletcher's study, the Cartesians are cited with well-documented references: Geulincx (pp. 131-135), whose *Ethics* Beckett read in Dublin before reading Baillet's *Vie de Monsieur Descartes*; Spinoza, in relation to the epigraph in Chapter VI of *Murphy*; Malebranche, who is cited in *Murphy* and reappears in *Comment c'est*; Leibnitz, who is referred to more frequently than Malebranche (Fletcher considers part III of *Watt* an attack on Leibnitz); and, finally, Berkeley, whose influence upon *Watt* (along with that of Hume) Fletcher considers more significant that that of Wittgenstein, though he confesses that "it is difficult to decide exactly where Beckett got those ideas" (p. 136).

If one attempts to sum up the general attitude in all these English and American studies on Beckett, one easily arrives at a consensus. No one sees Beckett as a twentieth-century Cartesian. On the contrary, Beckett's ultimate word to date makes his identification with Cartesianism all but impossible. If he is "fascinated" by Descartes and his life and main ideas, if there is recurrent in his writings use of Cartesian behavior, objects and semantics, it is not for Cartesian purposes. Is it for moral or aesthetic reasons? The answer is not clear. It is not even certain that the problem of Cartesian influence has been well posed.

Among the numerous books and articles published on Beckett after 1967 I shall consider only those that seem to me most significant for my present research and for effecting a possible change of direction or emphasis in Beckettian criticism. After 1967, two typical trends deserve mention: 1) the emphasis on Cartesian influence lessens, while that of Beckettian anti-Cartesianism is increasing; and 2) in a parallel way, the philosophical dimension, far from being neglected, is explored more and more from the viewpoint of the history of ideas, and Beckett is thus integrated into the world literatures and philosophies.

In 1970 Laurence E. Harvey published *Samuel Beckett: Poet and Critic*. A glance at the index shows how extensive are the references to philosophers, although these are mainly Cartesian or belonging to philosophies in a similar tradition. (One notes, however, the surprising absence of Malebranche.) As Beckettian scholars well know, Harvey's book affords extraordinarily rich biographical data, unpublished texts of Beckett, and documentation or clarification of Beckett's numerous allusions. Like his predecessors, Harvey notes Beckett's early "fascination" with Cartesian dualism. He refers to Beckett's lasting espousal, both in his life and in his writing, of a general dualistic point of view. This is not from mere intellectual conviction. It should be linked with "deep tendencies in [Beckett's] nature" (p. 204). In a long analysis of *Whoroscope,* Harvey identifies and locates most of Beckett's allusions or borrowings from Baillet. He observes that Descartes (along with Geulincx, Berkeley, Schopenhauer, and many others [p. 267]) is at the origin of Beckett's distinction between the macrocosm and the microcosm. I intend hereafter to discuss this duality. For the moment let us note merely that the words "macrocosm" and "microcosm" are not precisely the terms employed by Beckett, who usually refers, rather, to "the big" and "the little" worlds, though these terms may well relate to Descartes's dualism, where mind and body are both infinite.

In general, Harvey insists upon the distance between Descartes and Beckett; and he interprets the Cartesian duality of mind and body in a sort of Existentialism mood — for example, it springs from "an anguished revolt against life in society and from a rueful defense of solitude" (p. 203). The true Beckettian *Cogito* is "I need, therefore I am." (For me, the final Beckettian *Cogito* could very well be, rather: "It is always spoken in me, therefore perhaps I exist from time to time.") Harvey rightly recognizes the non-Cartesian accent of revolt in *Whoroscope* (p. 41); and he sees Beckett as a realist, far from the Cartesian temptation of idealism. Beckett's Descartes is more Beckett than Descartes (p. 53). Finally, Descartes's influence or prestige is so reduced that it is seen as being at the same level as that of Proust (p. 403) or Schopenhauer. (Harvey is the first critic to examine in detail the presence of Schopenhauer's themes in Beckett's works, and he remarks that "Schopenhauer's view of both ethics and poetry helped to affirm central tendencies in Beckett's thought" [p. 76]. I regret only that Harvey, who refers us to Schopenhauer's important study on "The Two Fundamental Problems of Ethics" and mentions his use of the Buddhist concept of *nirvana,* does not explore the Schopenhauerian hierarchy of human virtues, with the final superiority of pity over charity.) [3]

If Harvey's comments on Geulincx add nothing to what had been said in earlier studies, his remark on Leibnitz raises a question of very great interest. Contrary to one's expectation, Leibnitz is cited, not in reference to Beckett's allusions to the pre-established harmony or monadology, but in reference to Kant. In a beautiful poem in French, "Ainsi a-t-on beau," Beckett shows "sur Lisbonne fumante Kant froidement penché." The Lisbon earthquake of November 1, 1755, which motivated Voltaire's attack against Leibnitz's *Theodicy*

---

[3] See also a very interesting study by Rubín Rabinovitz, "Watt *from Descartes to Schopenhaner,*" *Modern Irish Literature,* 1972.

with its concept of the best possible world, is also for Kant (still Leibnitzian at that time), the inspiration for writing an essay on fire (*De igne*). Harvey' states that "the monad of Leibnitz was an isolated, self-contained microcosm reflecting the world with more or less clarity from a particular point of view. The poet's [Beckett's] negative reaction to reason and implicitly to Leibnitz-Kant monadism is a measure of his own dissatisfaction with life in the 'little world'" (p. 409). A note on the same page refers briefly to a problem which has never received much attention: "Kant's mature position as the founder of German idealism and in particular the limits he sets upon pure reason are much closer to views expressed by Beckett in his discussion of the theory of art in articles on the Vam Velde brothers in 1945, 1948 and 1949" (pp. 210-211). Finally, Harvey is correct when he says on page 271 that "the metaphysical problem that plagued the young Beckett [and, may I add, the problem that is present throughout Beckett's works from 1929 to the present] is the central problem of any theodicy: 'How can an all-loving and all-merciful God permit the existence of pain and suffering in the world?'" Here we are very far from Descartes, who refused to become involved in theological problems of this sort and saw the so-called problem of final causes as a matter beyond the reach of human understanding.

David Hesla's *The Shape of Chaos* (1971) is an ambitious and successful attempt to integrate Beckett's work into the broad current of Western culture since the time of the pre-Socratic philosophers. Hesla's book is a fine amalgam of precise erudition and deep insight. In its extraordinary forum of philosophers one can hardly fail to notice the neglect of two great figures: Freud, who is not cited at all, and Vico, who is mentioned only in passing ("The extent to which Beckett has employed Viconian theory in his own work is a matter yet to be investigated, and I do not mean to go into it here, but there seems a possibility that this scheme helps shape the structure of the trilogy" [p. 159].).

At the very beginning Hesla observes that Descartes' influence is obvious and pervasive (p. 14) — and more specifically that the duality of mind and matter in Beckett's work is "one of the fundamental polarities" (p. 16). But immediately thereafter Hesla insists on the anti-Cartesian use of that polarity: "We shall return to Descartes from time to time, but it suffices for now to remark that... he thought mind and matter worked together in sweetest harmony. In Beckett's view, however, they are joined in mortal combat" (p. 17). This explains, for example, why Beckett constructs in *Murphy* "a Cartesian cosmos with Proustian inhabitants" (p. 41) and why Murphy himself is a "Cartesian catastrophe" (p. 36). It is the same with Descartes' doubt: with Beckett it becomes an uncontrollable instrument; initial Scepticism leads to Solipsism — not to the realization of the Cartesian dream of making man "master and owner of the universe." Watt is unable to realize the Cartesian program, and the application of Cartesian rules collapses in intellectual confusion (pp. 78-79).

In the same spirit, Hesla, with a remarkably rich documentation, addresses himself to the Cartesians. Geulincx and Malebranche are considered "significant" (p. 14), and Leibnitz is recognized as the philosopher of the "impermeability of the self" (p. 50) and of the non-communicability of monads. The thematic unity of the Cartesians is seen in their common effort to refer to God instead of the pineal gland (*conarium*) to explain the liaison between mind and body.

Hesla opens wide avenues through Beckett's work. He does not leave Beckett an isolated prisoner in the Cartesian stocks. The philosophers most frequently cited in his book along with Descartes are Hegel, Kierkegaard, Sartre and the Sceptics, with special attention to Saint Augustine, Bergson, Husserl, and Schopenhauer. Hesla's central idea is that a theory of consciousness has evolved in our modern times through these thinkers identified as "dialectic philosophers" (mainly, Hegel, Kierkegaard and Sartre) (p. 211). Such is the fate of the Absolute Ego. Hegel splits it. Kierkegaard counters its positive qualities by equivalent negations. Bergson sees a succession of states of consciousness. Sartre sees consciousness as nothingness, but like Camus manages to transcend the condition of the Absurd. As for Beckett, he sees absolutely nothing and recognizes the domain of the Absurd as his permanent home. In Hesla's view, the "dialectic philosophers" along with the philosophers of the stream-of-consciousness help Beckett to "replace the Cartesian concept of mind as place with the Bergsonian or Husserlian concept of mind as the continuous living process of consciousness" (p. 177). Consequently, Beckett is identified not only as an anti-Cartesian struggling on the rack of Cartesian thought-patterns, but as a thinker in the idealistic contemporary current for whom consciousness is not a splendid indivisible unity but a dialectical process punctuated by negations and negations of negations.

Hesla knows that Beckett is not a philosopher — or at least that he is not using the languages of philosophy with purely epistemological aims. Hesla considers Beckett's philosophy an aesthetic vehicle and Beckett himself an artist seeking to free art from realism and expressionism. With such aims, Beckett is seen as turning for help first of all to Descartes and the Cartesians and then to Hegel, Husserl and Sartre, among others. In the last paragraph of this grandiose perspective Hesla quotes Beckett's remark to Tom Driver ("Where we have both dark and light, we have also the inexplicable."), and he seems to suggest that Beckett finds an ethical-aesthetic solution in the Greek ideal of moderation and balance: "Master dialectician and ontological funambulist [Beckett] knows how far he can lean toward the dark of Nothing before he must right himself toward the light of Something." So the ultimate Beckettian answer could be: perhaps! In fine, does Hesla suggest that Beckett the artist relies on Beckett the Sceptic? Does this mean that beyond Descartes or Cartesianism — beyond the dialectic idealism where the great philosophers of the nineteenth and twentieth centuries meet in their various efforts to explore human consciousness — Beckett finds his secret force and inspiration in the Greek pre-Socratics and Sceptics? Hesla leaves that question unresolved.

But Hesla raises another question: Is it possible to go still further in the criticism of Beckett? Can it be through pure chance that in 1973 both Hugh Kenner and Ruby Cohn, scholars who have played decisive roles in the first period of Beckett criticism, provided important critical summations (in *Samuel Beckett* and *Back to Beckett*) with various sorts of temporary conclusions, as if in response to a current need for reflective pause before the opening of new critical avenues? Is it a significant observation that the Cartesian connection or influence, if not ignored or underestimated, has become a low-keyed affair? The former creator of a brilliant metaphor (the Cartesian Centaur) now avoids any general statement as to Beckett's Cartesianism or anti-Cartesianism. Descartes is explicitly quoted only three times and each time only for a limited specific purpose: in *Murphy* the *conarium* has "shrunk to nothing," and there is no comment on the importance of its shrinking. A second reference to the *conarium* is accompanied by a rather puzzling coyness in the phrase "if we are to adopt the Cartesian terminology" (p. 63). Finally, there is reference to the Cartesian *ergo* (therefore) which serves to link thought to existence and, according to Kenner, is the Unnamable's problem: can I come into existence? There is no Cartesian — not even Geulincx — in the general index. Kenner warns us, however, against any hasty conclusion about a change of interpretation, and he makes a point of remaining loyal to his Beckett of the early '60s: "... meanwhile I have not changed my mind in any important particular" (p. 18).

In Cohn's synthesis there seems to be an emphasis upon distanciation from Descartes. Murphy (p. 38) is said to find the Cartesian problem of how mind and body communicate of little interest. He is passionately interested only in his mind and its three zones; and in the dark zone alone "the mind approaches the will-lessness differently dear to Geulincx and Proust" (*ibid.*). The trilogy is seen as "Beckett's Pocket History of the Western Thought from Homer to the Unnamable" (p. 119). Descartes and Geulincx find their place with Homer, Democritus, Aquinas and Dante. As with Kenner, though through a quite diferent process, philosophical vocabulary is reduced to a secondary role. In her comment on Beckett's early works, Ruby Cohn enunciates a critical principle that could be applied to all his writings: "Beckett's sophistication cloaks his metaphysical uneasiness and compassion" (p. 28). It should be the critic's responsibility to remember that "explanation risks exorcism" (p. 270) — but not to conjure away the Beckettian spirits, or to destroy the haunting force of that unique language, or to forget that through "phrases that resist paraphrase" (p. 272) one can dig up "the residue of basic human experience" (*ibid.*).

Is this not the final moment of those fifteen years of Cartesian criticism applied to Beckett? Two new distanciations are proposed from Descartes and the Cartesians: 1) Descartes is only one among the many philosophers Beckett has read and used — tongue in cheek; and 2) Beckett's philosophical apparatus is merely a cloak that we are invited to look through.

Before leaving this historical review of Beckettian criticism, I should like to raise one final question: Are there important aspects of Descartes's philosophy that have not been considered? Save for a very few indirect allusions, Beckett's critics have failed to discuss the problem of Cartesian methodology and the possible impact of the "four rules" as exposed in the second part of the *Discours* or as developed in the *Regulae ad directionem ingenii* — especially the first rule, often called "the rule of evidence," where Descartes defines his criterion for truth, the clear and distinctive ideas with their mathematical model, and inveighs against the confusion and obscurity that result from the union of mind and body; and the fourth rule, called "the rule of enumeration" ("the last [step] was in all cases to make enumerations so complete and reviews so general that I should be certain of having omitted nothing"). In *Back to Beckett* (p. 27), Ruby Cohn reminds us of Beckett's aesthetic statement in 1938: "... art has nothing to do with clarity." Can we identify the basic and ultimate reason for Beckett's anti-Cartesianism as a sort of "fascination"-in-reverse? It is not so simple as that! We know well that for Beckett the duality of clarity and obscurity does not coincide with the battle of light and darkness, which itself has very little to do with the distinction between body and mind. We know also — and Beckett can be our teacher — that there is an ontological obscurity (or clarity) and an epistemological one. For example, the statement quoted by Ruby Cohn is a perfectly *clear* negation of the value of clarity — and thus a clear principle of aesthetic obscurity! For me, especially as it occurs in his French language, Beckett's phrase is an extraordinary achievement of rare and formal clarity.

However it would be unfair to pretend that this question of clarity-obscurity has been ignored by Beckett's critics. We have even noticed that some of them refer ultimately to the duality of light and darkness. But I cannot find any systematic approach to this aspect of Beckett's work to explain how duality could play the role of a "regulative principle," except in the recent brief essay of James Knowlson, *Light and Darkness in the Theatre of Samuel Beckett* (1972): "There can, however, have been few, if any, writers, who, while not aiming to expound a strictly theological or cosmological system based upon contrarieties, have used light and dark imagery as consistently or as interestingly as has Samuel Beckett" (pp. 11-12). Among Beckett's critics, Knowlson quotes only Robert Harrison for his study on *Murphy* (1968), an unpublished thesis by John Pilling on the "Conduct of the Narrative in Samuel Beckett's Fiction," Ludovic Janvier's article on "Le lieu du retrait de la blancheur de l'écho" (1967), and Lawrence Harvey for a few references. For Knowlson, the origin of these themes and images is to be found in *Murphy*, most clearly in Chapter VI with its distinctions between the three zones of light, half-light and dark. This view, however, should not be attached to the Cartesian distinction between mind and body: "The tripartite zoning of Murphy's mind is, I believe, far more likely to be Beckett's own highly original version of a vision which has certain affinities with that of Dante, although there is no direct form of correspondence, for a zone of darkness that recalls the 'eternal darkness' of Dante's hell is considered by Murphy to be the most desired of states to which he can aspire" (pp. 16-17).

After this important suggestion Knowlson concentrates his analysis on *Krapp's Last Tape*, with allusions to *End Game, Play, Film, Happy Days* and *Godot*. On page 38 one finds indication of a possible junction between Berkeley's principle "*Esse est percipi*" as used by Beckett and Sartre's concept of the regard: "... throughout Beckett's novels and plays there is a desperate need to be observed and, in Sartrian terms, to be witnessed by the Other." Moreover, "the fear of darkness and silence ... is balanced there by a thread at the prospect that there should be no 'eye' to observe one" (*ibid*.). "The eye stands at the meeting point between two worlds. It projects outwards and it regards inwards" (p. 39).

These quotations suffice to show the complexities and multiple facets of this Beckettian duality. In a discussion of the most recent texts Knowlson evokes Dante's Hell and Milton's cosmology, but he insists on the absence of any direct relations between the three poets. The most significant image is that of the little world which is a "last refuge" ("a refuge created by a dying imagination that will obstinately refuse to die" [p. 40]) combined with the two key-images of light and dark, heat and cold, mind and mindlessness, being and non-being.

Finally, without meaning to diminish in any way the great interest of Knowlson's essay, I must call attention to what seems to me the most important part of his book — a two-page photo-facsimile from Beckett's notebook (written in Berlin on October 5, 1969, on the occasion of the production of *Krapp's Last Tape*) comprising his notes on "light emblems" and "dark emblems." Can it be simple coincidence that the last phrases of Knowlson's essay are extracts from the *Unnamable* dealing with "this stuff about light and dark" and the image of "a big talking ball"? "And after all why a ball, rather than something else, and why big? Why not a cylinder, a small cylinder? An egg, a medium egg? No, no. That's the old nonsense...."

Does this conclusion imply that the Cartesian reference that has been so important now for fifteen years is *passé*? Has it faded, of its own accord, in a sort of self-effacement and with the common consent of all? Everyone seems tired of it, and it is as if all the critics were saying in unison: "Now, let's talk about something else!" Perhaps. But this critical re-examination has also taught us something new: following some of Beckett's signposts or clues, a Cartesian criticism has been of late so fascinated by the collusion between the two dualities of mind and body and of the big and the little worlds that it seems more or less to have forgotten that Descartes is also the philosopher of clarity and light; and it has thus underestimated the symbolic significance of the duality of light and darkness with its possible moral and aesthetic overtones. This is my only excuse for probing once again into these Cartesian waters. But there is need for caution. Literary critics at one moment or another tend to fall, willy-nilly, into the allegorical trap — i.e., they consider a work of art the illustration of a concept. I merely seek possible enlightenment on this critical question: What is involved technically from the point of view of his art when someone who feels the compulsion to be a writer borrows significantly from philosophers and from the specific semantics of their discipline?

III

"Whoroscope" re-examined

> "A statement of itself drawn across the tempest of emblems." — *Alba*.

Critics have almost unanimously belittled the literary merits of this poem. Even when they recognize its unique significance as a prophetic indication of the works to come, they fail to give it the credit it deserves. The same story is told of it again and again with recurrent details: It was the product of a chance occasion. Beckett, in need of money, heard by accident of the House Press poetry competition and, after working all night and into a Parisian Sunday morning, he walked through the city to deliver his poem before the deadline for submission. He added the notes at the request of Nancy Cunard. He ended the poem at verse 98 in order to satisfy the prescribed limit of 100 lines, and he finally won the contest, etc., etc. There is no need to rehash all these well-known biographical data. Let me add one small detail: It seems that Beckett's research on Descartes had no relation with any formal academic obligation. Mr. Jerome Lindon, whom I consulted on this matter, very kindly replied that for *Whoroscope* Samuel Beckett utilized notes taken in the course of his studies in Dublin, but that he never wrote any school paper on the topic. However, before going to Paris, when he was about to leave Dublin, in order to obtain a study grant Beckett, who was then interested in Pierre-Jean Jouve, did write a paper (now lost and forgotten) on the Unanimists.

Whoroscope has aroused a rather remarkable variety of critical comment. Fletcher finds it "not very interesting" and "one long, intellectual 'dare' — written in an elliptical and queasily hearty style after Browning and Eliot." For Hoffman, it is a "mock ceremony of creation and immortality." Janvier considers it "a clownery Joyce type." For Durozoi it is "an intermingling of culinary phantoms under the patronage of Descartes himself." Hesla appears to limit the poem's Cartesian themes to "Descartes's bifurcation of substance into mind and matter." And Ruby Cohn remarks with no very great enthusiasm that, "in spite of its vexingly erudite allusions, the poem is worth reading aloud." All Beckett scholars should clearly be grateful to Lawrence Harvey for his analysis of *Whoroscope*, in which he has located and interpreted almost all the allusions to Descartes' life and works (mainly the *Discourse of Method,* the *Metaphysical Meditations,* the *Principles of Philosophy* and the correspondence) as they are related with Adrien Baillet's *La vie de Monsieur Descartes*. It is fair to remark also that Harvey has done justice to the literary qualities of the poem and has shown the presence of its themes throughout Beckett's works, and that he has quite rightly opposed the true Descartes to the Descartes seen by Beckett. Harvey adds a further comment that seems to me to deserve greater elaboration: "This is perhaps one reason Beckett abandoned the biographical poem and sought other literary forms to recreate essentially the same human experience inscribed here" (*ibid.,* p. 8).[4] This raises a problem of paramount importance: *Is the Descartes of "Whoroscope" the first character created by Beckett?* Moreover, is not this poem in its concentration

---

[4] We may note that Ruby Cohn claims that the poem can be enjoyed without erudition and contends (*Back to Beckett,* p. 28) that probably at the time he was writing *Whoroscope* the young poet "had almost too much to say and was afraid to say it without guidance from authors in several languages and several centuries."

at one and the same time a novel and a play? It is with these two questions in mind that I should like now to reconsider *Whoroscope,* looking back at it from two perspectives — from that of its structure (the problem of *the egg*) and from that of its coherence (the problem of *Descartes*).

The allusions — puzzling for the non-specialist in Cartesianism — are all, in every detail, polarized around proper names of real persons, most of them men. Of these last, fourteen (including Jesuits and Rosicrucians, but excluding the Pretender and Henry the Fourth) are enemies, competitors and rivals of Descartes. (There is not a single friend — only a valet.) Of the four girls, two are innocent children, one is an innocent victim of philosophers and theologians, and one is Christina the ripper, the girl who kills, a living incarnation of death (is she not responsible for the *W* added to *horoscope,* this "Rahab of the snow"?). I do not see the proliferation of characters in this mini-tragedy as resulting from young Beckett's awkwardness or overconfidence, but rather as a very curious (if unsuccessful) literary device — precisely the one that will be employed in his first attempt to write a novel. Look at *More Pricks than Kicks* and, even more particularly, at *Murphy* with its fictional characters and proper names of real persons. In *Watt,* this proliferation is restrained, and in the French period it is limited to a small number of names and allusions; but Beckett still succeeds in communicating to us a strange sense of possible expansion in beings who are more or less obliterated by excessive brightness or deep dark — a sense of promising beings, like the lost beings in Dante's Hell, who may at any moment break through the impenetrability and indivisibility of proper names! The name of Descartes is dominant and real, and around it the other names, like many other mysteries of nothingness, take their meaning and play their occasional roles. Here we stand at a deeper layer of literary creation. Would it be a far-fetched hypothesis to suppose that this systematic use of proper names, this choice of an illustrious name as the central character for a first experiment in linguistic creation, is Beckett's solution for the most difficult problem of novelistic genesis — a problem "admitted solved" by the greatest novelists of the nineteenth century, whether English, French or Russian, but a very real problem for Proust and Joyce, Beckett's immediate predecessors, who both saw the necessity of inserting real proper names within a purely fictive universe?[5] Would it be absurd to consider *Whoroscope* Beckett's first attempt to answer such a problem?

Recent criticism, in an effort to give the so-called "New Novel" a juridical or transcendental status, has collectively insisted upon the fall or disappearance of the omniscient novelist-God, and it has described our new novelists as playing the role of the ignorant and stupid father or mother. But this epistemological emphasis has blunted the New Critics' awareness of the fundamental problem for any novelist — the ontological decision of responsibility for the birth of numerous Adams and Eves. The device of the Proustian Narrator could be a sort of alibi — a trick to avoid taking direct responsibility for all the ghosts. Beckett, on the contrary, from the very beginning has recognized this responsibility as paramount for a writer; and his first solution was to choose Descartes as the hero of the tragedy of life.

"Descartes," then, as a real name, is the hidden unity for *Whoroscope*. It does not appear in the poem. It plays hide and seek with the first person "I," except for one unique parenthetical moment of self-pity in the antepenultimate line "(René du Perron...!)" — and even here Beckett does not use the name "Descartes."

The introductory "notes" in three phrases give us clues to the poem's structure: 1) Descartes sees his life as an omelette made of eggs "hatched from eight to ten days" (a complex image of *the egg* — hatched, broken and cooked). 2) Descartes fears astrology because, as he says in a letter to Mersenne, a known horoscope can influence one's life — and the clue is the image of *the horoscope*, in its double meaning of life's fatality and man's efforts to penetrate and predict the unknown future. 3) In the third phrase Beckett combines the two preceding images of *egg* and *horoscope* into the new image of the shuttle ("the shuttle of a ripening egg combs the warp of its days").

As all critics have noticed, the thirteen stanzas of *Whoroscope* describe the play of the shuttle. May I add that the formal structure itself provides the essential projective force of this play? *Whoroscope* is composed of alternating interrogations and exclamations (I consider the last line of stanza 9 ["How's that, Antonio?"] an exclamatory apostrophe rather than an interrogation) — a language for the shuttle

---

[5] There are nineteenth-century examples of this technique in novels by Stendhal and Balzac; but one does not sense there any realization by their authors that they are dealing with a capital problem of literary creation.

and a language for the warp. There are five stanzas to designate the movement of the shuttle and seven to show its effects in the warping process (a successive recurrence of "What's that?" or "Who's that?" separated by life's fragments, personal or intellectual, private or public). Then comes the last stanza (the thirteenth) with shuttle and warp in a unique final action where interrogations and exclamations converge into an ultimate prayer opening with the query "Are you ripe at last?" It is the beginning of the end, the moment when all the threads are finally interwoven, the moment of death expressed in the form of a prayer — the only moment of praying in the poem. After all the outbursts of revolt and angry action there is this final release of tensions as life's aggressiveness gives way to a timidly stated hope: "... and grant me my second starless inscrutable hour."

The central image is that of the egg, with its astrological overtones. I do not mean to imply that Beckett refers us directly to Hermetism or the alchemist's tradition. But astrological patterns are present in the poem. The allusion to "the Rosicrucians" is more than casual, in their implicit fight against Christianity. Beckett may not have known that Queen Christina, at the end of her life in Rome, was connected with the Rosicrucians; but it might throw some light on Descartes's still highly puzzling decision to go to Stockholm. The egg is not a vague and ironic image of life maturing into an abortion (i.e., an omelette). It is evidently the ovary; but as such (and Beckett will never forget or undervalue this biological dimension of its imagery) it is the image of the little world of men and of the universe itself. The presence of the egg in alchemical or hermetic treatises is well known, and I need not insist on its polyvalent semantics. Any dictionary of mythological symbols will tell us that the egg is "chaos," the "cosmic germ of the universe," "creation," and "sun." It belongs to all sorts of cosmological folklore. It can be a symbol for initiation and consummation. In Greek myths it is Night from which Love issued. Dreams of broken eggs mean misfortune, or quarrels when the eggs are scrambled. In the alchemical tradition the egg is assimilated into the alchemical vase wich contains the compost of the *Œuvre* (the Great Work by which other chemical elements are transmited into silver or gold). The transmutation process is compared to the incubation of the egg.

In Dom Pernety's *Dictionnaire mytho-hermétique* (1787) one finds a special paragraph on the *philosopher's egg*. Is not one tempted to apply this image to the Descartes of *Whoroscope*? Dom Pernety observes that many chemists have mistakenly thought the *Sages* have called "philosopher's egg" the vase in which they enclosed their matter to cook it. But this was wrong: the egg was not the container, but the content, which is properly the vase of Nature, as it is during the period of putrefaction. The philosophical power is embodied in the compost; the internal fire of the egg is excited by the heat of the hen; it gives life to matter of which it is the soul; and such is the birth of the *philosopher-child* who will make his brothers rich and perfect. There is an engraving of the Philosopher's Egg in *Atalanta Fugiens* edited in 1618 by Jehann Theodore de Bry, in which a philosopher wearing a cuirass holds an uplifted sword as he prepares to strike an egg standing upright on a table. In the background of this extraordinary engraving there are a fire with high flames and a tunnel with indefinite perspective like that in a Chirico painting of the Surrealist period. (There is an excellent reproduction of *The Philosopher's Egg* on page 97 of Frances A. Yates's *The Rosicrucian Enlightenment* [1972] and in J. Van. Lennep's *Art et Alchimie* [1966].) Van Lennep, on page 54, mentions the hermetic relationship between the egg and the vase which gives birth to the androgyne. (One recalls here the intentional vulgar pun on the concierge in stanza 12 and the recurrent apparition of the androgyne theme all through Beckett's work.) On page 59 Van Lennep evokes still another hermetic image — that of the muddy man — as symbol of the alchemical putrefaction, also related to the ripeness of the egg. Finally, the egg is the Saturnian symbol of the Dark; and it is hard to deny a Saturnian dimension to the last lines of *Whoroscope,* with its ultimate appeal to a "starless inscrutable hour."

I do not pretend that the rich semantics of the egg is clearly present in Beckett's poem. This is a personal problem for any reader — one that allows him to pursue a writer's dream. But it is an undeniable fact that the combination of egg and shuttle gives the poem its formal structure and unity. In itself the egg's image is neither Cartesian nor anti-Cartesian. The Cartesian substance — whether *causa sui* or *ens creata* — is the opposite of a finite, perfect and closed world. It is infinite in the sense of the infinity of God — geometrical infinity — the infinity of the human will (see the fourth *Metaphysical Meditation*). Moreover, this image of the egg belongs to a cultural tradition much older and more universal than the one we call Cartesian!

One might object that coupling the image of the egg with that of the shuttle provides different overtones from those provided by the image of the egg alone. In the first place, the shuttle image belongs to a more general and vague tradition, almost incarnated into the common metaphorical stuff of any language. The image of weaving is a most outworn cliché. Anyone with a background in Western culture will think at once of the Greek Fates — and especially of Clotho, seated behind her spinning-wheel and inexorably weaving human or other destinies. Is Beckett, consciously or otherwise, playing with the two meanings of the word "shuttle"? According to Webster's dictionary a shuttle is a wooden device used by weavers for "passing the thread of the wool between the threads of the warp" — a movement that is analogous to the Cartesian movement described in the second stanza of *Whoroscope* (a "come and go" or "back and forth" movement). Thus the shuttle is Cartesian! But a shuttle is also (according to Webster) "a spindle-shaped device holding the thread that one manipulates in tatting, knotting, netting," and it has usually the form of an egg. I know that Beckett, in his notes, refers explicitly to the first meaning. But the egg image makes a connection with the second meaning. The "compost" of a life is at the same time the ripeness of an egg and the movement of a shuttle.

Here three trends of images come together: the vague symbol of the weaving, the more specific symbol of the egg, and Descartes' view of relative movement in his first effort to define modern mechanism (the second and more successful attempt is that of Newton, and *Murphy* is a definite defense of the Cartesian principle of quantity of movement against the Newtonian [and Leibnitzian] concept of quantity of energy). Beckett substitutes the egg for the weaving machine, thus avoiding the development of clichés and (more important) basing his irony and humor on the opposition between astrology and the modern mind, with Descartes as its first hero — the true adversary not only of horoscope-readings but, more seriously, of those false and superstitious sciences which he attacks in the first part of the *Discours*: "Et enfin pour les mauvaises doctrines, je pensais déjà connaître assez ce qu'elles valaient pour n'être plus sujet à être trompé ni par *les promesses d'un alchimiste*, ni par *les prédictions d'un astrologue*, ni par *les impostures d'un magicien*, ni par les artifices ou la vanterie d'aucun de ceux qui font profession de savoir plus qu'ils ne valent" (italics mine).[6] Here we have a supreme irony bursting into a duality of two conceptions of life and two versions of the universe — two human dreams! There is a difference between Descartes and Murphy as Beckett's heroes: when Murphy manipulates his horoscope that has been brought by Celia, Descartes is making his as a succession of significant moments of his life and thought.

To sum up, *Whoroscope*'s formal structure is not Cartesian; it is the projection of Hermetism in its two aspects denounced by Descartes — alchemy and astrology. But the purity of this form is troubled by the secret equivocality of the shuttle-spindle, and finally by the duality of the egg and the shuttle. In my judgment, this confusion is not a weakness in the poem. It is part of an ironic protest against being forced into existence!

The shuttle comes and goes through the lines; the spindle turns and makes the weaving more and more tight and consistent; the egg is finally ripe, after many unhappy efforts. We must not forget the general duality in structure: 12 stanzas where shuttle and warp are distinct from each other and the egg is not ready — a full poem of life which is finally realized with this metaphysical proclamation: Who am I? Not this nor that, "but the chip of a perfect block that's neither old nor new, / the lonely petal of a great high bright rose." But it is not the end: that would be too good to be true! Against this poetic culmination comes stanza 13 and the definite end, when, in an ultimate act of consent and resignation, the "climbing up the bitter steps" is, at death time, converted into salvation by a return to Nothingness.

There are five reactions to the question of the egg's ripeness, and seven images of life (with none of these included in the last stanza [13], when the shuttle stops its movement). Are these thoughts, then, carefully selected, only to be presented in random order? I do not believe so. Behind the façade of unrelated allusions one can detect a strong coherence in the order of images. Let us summarize the topics

---

[6] The English translation by E. S. Haldane and G. R. T. Ross is as follows: "And finally, as to false doctrines, I already knew well enough what they were worth to be subject to deception neither by the promises of an alchemist, the predictions of an astrologer, the impostures of a magician, or the artifices or the empty boastings of any of those who make profession of knowing that of which they are ignorant."

considered, in their successive order: theory of relative movement... importance of mathematics and dioptrics... family difficulties... military earnings... (leading to) "the hot-cupboard" and the revolt against Jesuit education... the two loves... two girl children... biology (theory of blood circulation — the true illustration of the relative movement) and the heart in the crypt... Descartes's dreams... pilgrimage... Rosicrucians rejected... the theological compromise for transubstantiation and the problem of the union of mind and body... Ann Shurman (a possible love for Descartes, but she turns into a poor theological "parakeet")... then the climax of Cartesian metaphysics, the spiritual road and ascension, leading from doubt to the subjective certitude of the *Cogito*, and from there to the discovery of the presence of God in human consciousness and, consequently, of human mind as part of the divine Absolute.

This thematic succession shows a skillful intermingling of Cartesian theories with incidents from the most important moments of Descartes's life. The choice and succession of themes are not accidental. Important aspects of Descartes's philosophy are included. Two of Descartes's great errors are cited (but with a hint that he might finally be right): his theories of relative movement and of the permanence of the quantity of movement — the heart as a heat center. There are two remarkable omissions: there is no direct reference to the Cartesian ethics — that "code of morals for the time being" with its three rules, as they are justified in part III of the *Discourse*; and there is no word on the famous Cartesian method and its four rules. Such omissions cannot be explained as simple oversight. Allusions recur throughout Beckett's work to the second rule of ethics (when one is lost at a crossroad in the midst of a forest and has no reason to choose one path over another, the only solution is to choose one of them and stay firmly on it until one at last finds his way out). The "rule of evidence" is shown only through its first application to metaphysics; it becomes the "bright rose."

Thus Beckett deliberately disregards Descartes's practical theories and so changes him as scientist and philosopher into a purely theoretical thinker. Beckett chooses also to ignore the thinker who, in part VI of the *Discours*, dreams of making man the master of the universe and affirms that medicine can extend the duration of human lives, including his own. Beckett is not an historian of philosophy. But there is artistic significance in his choice of Descartes for transformation into a literary character — the model of human destinies.

The succession of themes and facts does not, then, follow the chronological order or any other kind of logical order devised to present Descartes and his philosophy. Yet I disagree with the critics who see in this succession either pure fantasy or incoherent reminiscences. It is quite possible that Beckett intended to give us a sense of apparent disorder, as if Descartes were to be evoked jumping from one situation or thought to another with no perceptible link between them. We are introduced first to Descartes's theory of movement in its connection with the explanation of the earth's movement around the sun and in opposition to the theory of Galileo. In the second part of his *Principles of Philosophy* (section 26), Descartes affirms that movement and rest are merely two differing modes, and in the following sections (27-30) he justifies the relativity of that distinction, which is ultimately a matter of viewpoint. Then in part III (sections 24-31) he explains that the skies are liquid and transport with them the bodies they contain; thus, although the planets and the earth are moving, they cannot be said to be in motion (*en mouvement*), since they are, in fact, merely carried along by the movement of the skies. (This theory of movement is related to mathematics and to the theory of light.) Thus stanzas 2 and 4 are concerned with Descartes as scientist. But in the second group (stanzas 5 and 7) Beckett suggests events in Descartes's private life (the famous night of November 10, 1619 and Descartes's acceptance of Harvey's recent explanation for the circulation of the blood). The dominant details are Descartes's temperament as an influence on his life, his military experience, and his loves. In the third group of stanzas (9, 11 and 12) Descartes is presented as the theoretician of the Incarnation and of pure mind. — Thus three aspects of Descartes are evoked: the scientist with his concept of illusory motion, the life of the body with its liver and its heat, and the life of the mind — first at the level of its union with matter, then in its pure existence in the divine Spirit. Within those three levels, coherence is obtained by a double duality: first, in the opposition between relative movement and real movement, and second in the opposition between material and spiritual lives; and the unity is to be found in the passage from the form of movement (which is relative) to the reality of the body — and from the reality of the body to the reality of the mind and its culmination in God. Then another duality opposes the first twelve stanzas to the last one (the thirteenth), where life becomes death, brightness darkness, illusion reality, and being nothingness.

Thus far we have examined only the skeleton of the poem and seen its fundamental tensions and unities. But the poem's reality results from its images, and these can be grouped under three separate headings: 1) images signifying movement: boat, horse, rider, boatman, walk, dance, avalanche, sun-drowning, ripening, rise; 2) images of the body: liver, blood, heart, sensory organs (ear, nose, eye, mouth, faecal outlet), foetus, skin, tonsils, ovaries, womb, blooming-withering; and 3) images of the mind: pebble, syllogism, cupboard, skylight, yellow key, dance, kiss, drinking, eating, love crucified, chip of a block, petal of a rose, and the adjectives great, high, bright, starless, inscrutable. It is not a systematic enumeration. It merely suggests how the three levels of the poem are folded up with concrete words which are put together and attached to each other by the poet's shuttle. And all these words take their places and their full meanings around the egg, which plays the role of semantic coordinator. Any reader of Beckett will have recognized in this listing the most important images that he will develop in his future works.

If my analysis is correct, the true critical problem is not whether *Whoroscope* as a poem is Cartesian or anti-Cartesian. It is a deeper matter — the possible choice of Descartes as *an exemplary character of literature*. If one admits this possibility, the Cartesian attitudes, the pros and cons of the matter, the borrowings of Cartesian ideas and images all take on meaning in the light of that single hypothesis. Any literary language must be polarized around a character. Is it possible that Descartes may here be that character — after the contemporary (1930) failure of a century of novelistic or other creations and after the illusory conversions of failure into success by the Proustian Narrator or Joyce's linguistic auto-creations?

Whoroscope is Descartes put to the test for his possible literary adaptability. As an experiment, the work transcends poetic genres and those of all literature. It is simultaneously lyricism, epic poetry, burlesque. Its various characters swarm around a central figure as in a traditional novel. It is a dramatic monologue interrupted by interrogations without answers — a true anticipation of *Krapp's Last Tape*. The following note by Beckett on Krapp could be applied as well to Descartes and could supply a secret key for *Whoroscope*: "Krapp decrees physical (ethical) incompatibility of light (spiritual) and dark (sensual) only when he intuits possibility of their reconciliation intellectually as rational-irrational" (see J. Knowlson, *op. cit.*). We may note that Lawrence Harvey (*op. cit.*, pp. 78-79) has an explicit presentiment of this interpretation, but with no further development, so that it amounts finally to little more than an incidental remark on Beckett's interest in "the tradition of the troubadours": "... there is little doubt that the hypersensitivity to suffering so characteristic of Beckett the man and the poet is psychologically congenial to a philosophy like the Manichean, which deifies the principle of evil. One is even tempted to associate with the Cathar cult of sterility Beckett's avowed sympathy toward those who, either for similar philosophical reasons or simply because they are unwilling to add to the potential suffering in the world, refuse procreation." (I may observe that one of the main aims of the present study is to give full credit to this aspect of Beckett's thought and art.)

The young Beckett, passionately serious, protected against his culture by wild irony and merciless humor, and knowing that he cannot repeat Proust and Joyce, themselves victims of their success, tries desperately to break out of his own literary solitude by simultaneously exalting and mocking the solitude of a great figure of another age. I dislike deriving hypothetical inferences from the relations of a work to its author, but I cannot be blind to the fact that, for a young man of 24, Beckett's Cartesian scholarship is quite remarkable[7] — not exceptional, but surely at the level of that of a very good advanced student of philosophy at the Sorbonne! But why should Beckett do this? He was not one of those "khagneux" that he mentions in *L'Innommable* and that he had surely met when he was "assistant d'anglais" in Paris. We know that he had a pile of notes that he had taken from Adrien Baillet's *La Vie de Monsieur Descartes*. Again I ask: Why? There is some truth in the legend of the Nancy Cunard contest; but, in my opinion, it conceals more than it reveals. Whatever the truth may be, the examination of a single poem, *Whoroscope*, shows the seriousness of the literary search involved: Descartes fighting for brightness with enormous efforts implying mathematics, physics,

---

[7] It might be of interest to examine in this regard the state of Cartesian studies in the '30s, with the capital research done by Brunschvicg, Gilson, Gouhier, Laporte, *et al.* Such research might well afford material for another paper written from the viewpoint of a French cultural historian.

biology, theology and metaphysics under the frail guidance of those pure and innocent Beatrices; Descartes ultimately failing under the influence of Christina-Rahab and making of his death the true solace, the return to the womb of darkness — is not that Descartes the portrait of the artist, the portrait of the only possible character as a proxy for the "I" — the portrait of Everyman as sign-consumer?

But why Descartes? Why not Dante? Why not a Proustian or Joycean puppet? Here again I do not believe in pure chance, and I contend that the entrance of this Descartes on Beckett's stage is final — with no exit, even for a moment — and for this reason, which I repeat: the choice of Descartes is the answer to the critical literary problem par excellence — who is the speaker or narrator?

I see two main reasons for Beckett's choice of Descartes: First, among the indefinite possibilities offered by human cultures (living or fictive) Descartes had been conscious in a very new way of the epistemological problem of abstraction related to illustration (as formulated by Beckett in his *Dante*. . . .). He rejected Scholasticism and medieval realism based upon an Aristotelian principle often quoted by Beckett in later works: there is nothing in intelligence which has not been first in the senses — a principle implicitly adopted by the novelists of the nineteenth century. Descartes rejects also any Platonic interpretation of the connection between abstraction and illustration (i.e., abstraction proposing an exemplary model for illustration as imitation of an ideal reality). Descartes' absolute refusal to admit a liaison between rational and sensorial ideas, clear and obscure ideas, distinct and confused ideas, condemns realism as well as idealism and thus becomes a true challenge to the writer — for *if there is no contact between abstraction and illustration, how is literature possible?* In brief, selection of Descartes as a character marks a notable beginning towards abolishing the dead-ends of the past and going beyond Descartes himself, or at least learning whether that is possible.

Moreover, this multi-dimensional dualism has another function, at once ethical and aesthetic. In *Dante*. . . , Beckett notes a decided difference between Dante and Joyce: "A last word about the Purgatories. Dante's is conical and consequently implies culmination. Mr Joyce's is spherical and excludes culmination. In the one there is an ascent from real vegation — Ante-Purgatory, to ideal vegetation — Terrestrial Paradise: in the other there is no ascent and no ideal vegetation. In the one, absolute progression and a guaranteed consummation: in the other, flux-progression or retrogression, and no apparent consummation." This last paragraph of Beckett's article should call for detailed analysis. For my purpose, we must heed the duality ascent/no ascent, as based upon two opposed literary structures: the ascensional movement in a straight line and the folding up of the circle (the kitten trying to catch its tail, to use another of Beckett's images); and Proust goes here along with Joyce in an attempt to transform the language-world into a finite world of its own — not one suspended from an ideal world, but the Ptolemaic world in itself, with no promise that it will become a Paradise, lost and regained!

Yet, with the circle, the possibility of unity persists — the unity of the literary vase or egg, which allows the cooking-putrefaction of reality. *The only way to be sure of avoiding a complacent unity is through absolute refusal of any unity in disguise.* Is not radical dualism the very essence of this refusal? This is why we can identify *Whoroscope* as "Descartes on trial." To use a formula of Beckett's from *Dante...,* Descartes is at the same time content and form; but he is not the unity or fusion of the two!

Thus Descartes may be seen as anti-Dante and as serving to exorcize the ghosts of Joyce and Proust. But it is not quite so simple as that for anyone with the scrupulous, intellectual sophistication of Beckett, who has already found in Belacqua an anti-Dante in the no-man's land between Hell and Purgatory! There are two anti-Dantes, one outside and one inside: that one who dares (like Descartes) to go beyond and the one (like Belacqua) who remains within — the active one and the lazy one. To pursue my hypothesis: In his critical conclusion Descartes fails the test; and *Whoroscope* affords Beckett neither an aesthetic nor an ethical solution for his problem. "Tranches de vie" and the figure of intellectual prowess are still separate, like oil and water in the same vessel, or like the white and the yellow in the egg. Descartes is not all men or Everyman, and we have the challenge of Belacqua! Thus we may pose this new question for Beckett in the early '30s: Is not Belacqua the true literary hero, the one with the right to speak in the name of the writer, precisely because he has the gift and refuses to use it?

This new trial was then the still unpublished *Dream of Fair to Middling Women,* though some aspects of it were also in *More Pricks than Kicks,* where fragmentation of the narrative is the anti-technique employed to avoid the temptation of unity, whether ascensional or circular! And thus we arrive at *Murphy* — the so-called Cartesian novel or novel of ideas, the pure intellectual novel, etc. After a second failure (in the sense of that word in Beckett's later works), Belacqua is given up, dead, and Descartes gets a second chance. *Murphy* is more than a novel on Cartesianism (particularly as it concerns the problem of the separation/union of mind and body). It is a new trial for the literary hero. Murphy is Descartes transposed, with his travels, his garrets, his friends, companions and loves — with a rocking-chair experiencing relative movement as neutralization of physical movement, and with an astrological background. But there is something new. Murphy is a Descartes with a Belacqua temperament! He is in a dual situation with all the other characters, so that the novel is a proliferation of oppositions. But there is one duality that is basic: Murphy-Descartes against Murphy-Belacqua. This internal polarity is not strongly emphasized as are the conflicts with external characters. Perhaps this is why it has passed unnoticed. But it is certain that the Murphy of the clear zone is not the Murphy of the grey zone, though both are united in the darkness of zone three. Misleading also has been the emphasis upon the image of the "conarium" and the duality of mind and body. On the other hand, the brightness-darkness duality has not been sufficiently emphasized (one critic even refers to chapter VI of *Murphy* as merely a sort of metaphysical potpourri). But from *Murphy* on, Descartes and Belacqua will be present in all of Beckett's works — novels, short stories or plays; and this *persona* duality, which contains in itself all the other abstract dualities, will be transposed into the diverse couples which will become more and more inseparable in Beckett's soliloquies.

IV

THE CARTESIAN EMBLEMATIC

I am about to study the evolution of the Cartesian images in Beckett's works from *Whoroscope* to the most recent texts such as *not I, Sans, Bing,* etc. If my earlier analyses are correct, the philosophical problem of whether Beckett is Cartesian or anti-Cartesian is an artificial concern. But there is in Beckett's writings an ever-recurrent use of Descartes and Cartesian themes; and if there has been any perceptible evolution in this phenomenon it has been a matter of emphasis upon certain themes or images rather than of any significant overall change in attitude. Even the shift from the English language to the French might have been virtually anticipated from the beginning by anyone noticing Beckett's critical awareness of the language problem in English (see *Dante*...), or his multiple references to other languages in his first prose texts. For the moment I shall limit my research to a systematic (though not exhaustive) inventory of Cartesian emblems.

May I propose the following semantic convention and agreement? I take the word *emblem* as synonymous with *image,* and I shall use the word *emblematic* as a noun to mean a certain grouping with a virtual or actual theory justifying a coherent assemblage of emblems. This definition concurs with the usual definition of *emblem* as "a visible sign of an idea," or "a symbolic object, figure, device used as an identifying mark." But if an emblem is an image, what is an image? We enter a very confused semantic field, because any known definition of the word *image* implies a full theory of knowledge — whether it be Platonic, Aristotelian, Thomist, Cartesian, or what you will! I can adopt the convenient opposition of *idea* and *image*; but then I immediately fall into a cascade of philosophical antinomies, like rationalism/empiricism, or the opposition between *abstraction* and *the empirically concrete* or that between *image* and *sensation* — and each time I encounter an epistemological confusion of theories. I propose, therefore, to hold to a minimal definition at the rhetorical level: *an image is a device to illustrate a given language*. I follow Beckett himself, who in turn was following the postulates of Vico: a language is the relation of two functions — abstraction and illustration. Here let us avoid two slippery roads, one leading from illustration to model, the other regarding the passage from image to abstraction as an irreversible step in human knowledge.

My decision to avoid any sort of theoretical implications is both practical and provisional. Like everyone else, I shall have to make a theoretical jump on occasion. But, for the moment, in view of this Cartesian inventory, the most elementary caution should restrain any philosophical flights, especially when one is concerned with philosophers and their stock of concepts. Such "semantic suspension" affords still another very definite advantage: it withdraws us from the Cartesian/anti-Cartesian dilemma.

An emblem, then, is an image in the rhetorical sense of the word — i.e., an illustration. Thus a writer, as user of language, is a sort of emblematist, and the verb *emblematize* is entirely appropriate for his daily activities. In adopting the semantic conventions outlined above we avoid the dangerous swamp in which the New Criticism has floundered for a decade — the duality of metaphor and metonymy. An emblem is not necessarily a metaphor; and an illustration is not necessarily a metonymic transfer. For example, to say that a poet is using metaphors is going beyond a mere stylistic indication. As Proust has shown, such a statement implies a theory of literature; and Beckett does not ignore this when, in his *Proust*, he opposes the intellectual symbolism of *Les Fleurs du Mal* to the auto-symbolism of *A la recherche du temps perdu*. Thus we shall avoid the rhetoric of metaphor with its nice allegorical seesaw between proper and figurative meanings and take the word *emblem* as meaning image and as a definite rebuff to the employment of the word *metaphor*.

I apologize for this long and rather awkward attempt at clarification. But we need at least to know where we stand and what rhetorical vocabulary should be used for a writer whose deep methodological doubt is brought to bear upon two thousand years of Western philosophies of language and, more immediately, upon the culminating points of a century of Romantic aesthetics in the two castles of Realism and Symbolism. In accordance with this semantic consideration I shall call "Cartesian emblem" any sort of illustration which refers to Descartes, Cartesians and Cartesianism.

Cartesian emblems can be grouped under two headings: 1) those in which we find Descartes or Cartesians as literary characters, modes of behavior or decors; and 2) those in which we find Cartesian themes or what is called generally Cartesianism in a very broad or vague sense.

As is well known, specific reference to Descartes, his name or his life is rare in Beckett's works after *Whoroscope*; but names of Cartesians are recurrently cited with or without definite allusion to their philosophies. More often Cartesian themes are developed without reference to any specific philosopher. But proper names, in their uniqueness, play the role of emblems, and Beckett relies on their magic power. They are like mysterious, inscrutable milestones. Descartes's name disappears after *Murphy*, and so does that of Leibnitz. Only Geulincx is cited more than once (one remembers the oft-quoted passage in *Molloy* evoking the old Dutch philosopher); and Malebranche makes a striking appearance in *Comment c'est*. It seems that, after an excessive use of proper names in the English works from *Dream* to *Watt*, Beckett has decided against such frequent reliance on that easy magic. But he has never wholly renounced exploiting the emblematic power of the Cartesian proper names, and the rarity of their appearance makes them even more strange, secret, enigmatic! One may wonder why Descartes's name is not mentioned after *Murphy*. If my interpretation of *Whoroscope* is correct, the answer may be not that Beckett has become less Cartesian, but that Descartes has come to be identified with one aspect of the writer and his life, in the bright zone of light. Geulincx and Malebranche, on the contrary, recur here and there as envoys from nowhere, sometimes with an intellectual halo, sometimes with only the opaqueness of their names.

Except in a reference to the Hanover garret of Leibnitz in *Murphy*, Beckett never alludes to the private lives of Cartesians. But it is just the contrary with Descartes, whose life gives form and behavior-patterns to the Beckettian heroes. There is a significant difference in Beckett's treatment of Belacqua and Descartes. If the name of Dante's character has a particular value and his attitude of incurable indolence is evoked a few times, Belacqua himself, after *Murphy*, is never a model for a life-pattern. On the other hand, two aspects of Descartes's life acquire an emblematic power: his personality and his general life-style. There is no reason for us to consider the adequacies or inadequacies of Beckett's version of Descartes in comparison with the real philosopher. It is enough to ascertain that Beckett's knowledge of Descartes's life and thought is far superior to that of the average student in Philosophy, but (as we have seen earlier) clearly not that of a specialist in French thought of the 17th century. For our present purpose it should be of interest to show how Beckett understands his character René Descartes and how he selects for his own use some of Descartes modes of thought.

The Descartes of *Whoroscope* is temperamental, with alternations of violence and tenderness; he has on the whole a strong and self-contained emotional power, but with bursts of anger; he is self-centered and aggressive; he thinks of others only in relation to his own experiences or desires; to the very end, even when addressing Weulles, the Queen's doctor, he maintains a challenging attitude, always retaining his superiority; he is constantly reckless, insecure, without poise, and suffering from a very real and deep anguish which turns to bitter pessimism. But this temperament is dominated by an absolute intellectual passion. In spite of his intermittent and irrational explosiveness, Beckett's Descartes strives hard to control his life by intellectual patterns. He is a mathematician as well as a metaphysician. He raises very abstract problems. Finally, he has a definite tendency to soliloquize. Considering these facts, is it absurd to say that this Descartes is the first character conceived by Beckett and that his later characters will borrow from him, with nuances and variations, their psychological singularities? In my opinion, Descartes as he appears in *Whoroscope* is, for Beckett, the image of man and the image of the writer. All such characters as Murphy, Watt, Molloy, Moran, Malone, Macmann, Mahood are direct inheritors of Descartes. Their likeness is striking. This does not mean that Beckett's works are simple variations or repetitions of the *Whoroscope* tragedy. Each work has its own problems and corresponds to a specific movement in Beckett's personal literary adventure. But these movements are always referred to a basic human character.

Let us recapitulate briefly what has been stated above: Descartes's personality contrasts with Belacqua's: intense restlessness against indolence, total emotional involvement against perfect indifference! The Belacqua hero of *More Pricks than Kicks* is actually a Descartes who would like to be a Belacqua and never succeeds! Is it man's fate to be a furor of the heart and a restless consciousness? This could be man's basic personality problem: a duality between what man cannot help being and what he might be — between life and sleep, action and contemplation, passion and indifference. It is clear also that Beckett's Descartes has taken some of his character from the Schopenhauerian will-to-live.

A duality of this sort leads to still another duality when one passes from Descartes's character to his life. Descartes' life may be divided into two parts: the one devoted to moving from place to place, with the final move to Stockholm, where Descartes meets with death and night — and the other devoted to solving theoretical problems quietly at home, even in bed. The projective image of this duality is the opposition of *the road* and *the room*, an opposition that is permanent in Beckett's work. But the contrast road/room, with all its possible varieties, becomes more important after *Whoroscope*, where one can find two images of travel (the rider and the seaman) that Beckett will never use except in allusion to Geulincx and his power to walk the opposite way from the direction his boat is going. The bicycle, as everyone who reads Beckett knows, will replace the horse. The boat represents the dream of travelling or, reduced to a small craft, it becomes the vehicle of love or death (as in *Malone Dies* or *Krapp's Last Tape*). When the bicycle is abandoned as a means of transportation, men (normally in poor anatomical or physiological condition) walk with the assistance of two adjuvant instruments — a stick and crutches. The road can become a ditch, walking is transmuted into crawling, and there is a possible limit-situation when the ditch (a place for slow motion) can be assimilated to the bed (a place for little motion or no motion at all). The duality road/room is then transposed into the final opposition of word and silence.

The image of the room is at the origin of similar emblems such as the rotunda, cylinder, circle, and sphere. The road in Beckett is always related to a room which is at the end of the road (see *Molloy* and *Film; The Expelled* is a little more complex with the relation from one room to the street to another room). Unlike the road, the room can exist by itself and be a possible source of imaginary travel or evocation of past roads. The inventory of all the possibilities of the duality road/room should be made. Here it is enough to establish, without further proof, that Beckett has explored its literary power. But I repeat: those two images do not signify Cartesian philosophical influence or a Cartesian state of mind. They mean only that Beckett recognizes in Descartes's character and life certain features of literary significance. I would even go further and say that Beckett's vision of humanity is dominated by those two couples (Descartes and Belacqua, the road and the room), which organize his order of meanings (in the sense of the 17th-century expressions "order of nature" and "order of grace"). In consequence, all Beckettian events derive from them as from their occasional and material causes. The different elements (sky, sea, swamp, forest, plain, mountain, etc.) take and make sense from the room or/and from the road. The room is the center of perspective (is this why Beckett's characters look for the center of the room?); the road is the bridge (one knows the special value of bridges in the *Poems* and in *More Pricks than Kicks*). The objects also derive from the same semantic source. They are means of transport or parts of the room (the shoes are already present in *Whoroscope*).

One might object that *the hat* does not belong in this lineage; but two remarks should be added to the already numerous comments about these Beckettian hats. First, their form assimilates them to the form of the room; and I believe it may safely be said, without straining my interpretation, that the hat may be seen as the analogue of a sort of Super-ego cover-up and, thus, of a protective device for the head and its content, much as the room is a protective envelope for the body. Second, Beckett often associates the hat with the coat or cloak (as he does in *Malone Dies*). Both are emblems of recognition for humanity. Has not Descartes himself raised the difficult problem of human recognition in these very terms at the end of the *Méditation Seconde*? After the forceful declaration "I am a thinking thing" ("Qu'est-ce donc que je suis? une chose qui pense.") and the famous analysis of the piece of wax, he asks himself, "How do I see this wax? through my eyes or only by the intuition of my mind?" Then he considers the following example: if I look from a window at pedestrians in the street I do not hesitate to say that I see men, as I say that I see wax. Then comes this passage: "And yet what do I see from the window but hats and coats which may cover automatic machines? Yet I judge them to be men." [8]

Most critics, as shown in the second part of this article, have insisted on the influence of Cartesianism on Beckett's work as a rationalistic or idealistic philosophy. But it is too general and, moreover, too debatable to consider Descartes from this point of view — and it is not in accord with Beckett's mood. I should prefer to study Cartesian themes one by one and seek their proper place in Beckett's work and, once and for all, dispel the false problem of his Cartesianism or anti-Cartesianism. We already know that from the beginning of Beckett's literary adventure he identified his Descartes as a typical characterization for the hero of a novel — i.e., as the necessary heroization for the literary language. *He is the hero with an exemplary character and a permanent life-pattern.* Then, by way of his philosophy, Descartes introduces other literary devices which form a sort of Cartesian kit or trophy. I shall present the main objects of this panoply in a non-systematic, non-exhaustive, non-chronological enu-

---

[8] Translation of Haldane and Ross. The French text says: "... et cependant que vois-je de cette fenêtre, sinon des chapeaux et des manteaux, qui peuvent couvrir des spectres ou des hommes feints qui ne se remuent que par ressorts?"

meration; but I shall attempt to define for each of them its principal function.

The Cogito. This is Beckett's most important borrowing from Descartes: I think, therefore I am a thinking thing. The reference in *Whoroscope* to the Augustinian phrasing *Fallor, ergo sum* does not mean that Beckett champions Saint Augustine in the discussion about the originality of the Cartesian *Cogito*. He simply reminds us that error is the chronic state of thought. It does not suffice to say with Descartes: *Dubito, sum* (I doubt, I exist). In doing so Beckett condemns in advance Cartesian dogmatism and nips in the bud any optimistic impulse in the conquest of truth. For Descartes the *Cogito* is the first and absolute certitude — the rock which will support the building of the sciences. Beckett refuses this epistemological conversion of error into doubt and of doubt into truth because from the time of *Whoroscope* he rejects the parallel aesthetic effort to change failure into success and decides to remain loyal to failure as failure. Such would be, contrary to Descartes, the first lesson of the *Cogito*. But there is another. The *Cogito* is the act by which I become conscious of myself as "I" (I think that I think). It is not "thought in general" (*cogitatum est*). It is *I* who think. Thus the *Cogito* raises the most difficult problem of modern logic: any statement implies an "I" to state it; any language requires "I" as its origin and warrant. Thus the *Cogito* is at the origin of a permanent set of Beckettian postulates: who speaks when I write and when I am forced to select characters as "my" proxies? The Beckettian *Cogito* becomes, then: it is spoken "in me"; therefore, may be, "I" exists. But how is it possible to pass from the statement " 'I' exists" to that of "I exist"? No language can offer a decent answer to that question. Thus, this act of reflection is seen and lived by Beckett as *an act of separation and isolation*. To say "I think" means that I assume a certain distance from the content of my thought and its immediate reference to a world that has been accepted as a reality that can be spoken of.

It is well known that for Descartes this separation is but a theatrical pretense to give one time for obtaining a better grasp on the external world and for setting out one's mathematical traps. For Beckett, the *Cogito* is an irretrievable act with no strings attached — especially no Husserlian strings of "something" or the "other." By this act I enter another world — "my" world, "my" little world. At this point Beckettian criticism has established a good precedent for a proliferation of interpretations. Here appear the schizoid or schizophrenic diagnostics. I have no objection to raise against these developments, save for one condition: that their perpretators admit that such analyses belong to psychology and psychopathology, or even to a general psychology of language and that Beckett is here taken as a typical guinea-pig.

Many critics, moreover, employ the duality macrocosm/microcosm as if it were Beckettian and connected with the *Cogito*. It is true that Beckett often refers to the little or small world; but it is always with a touch of humor. He very seldom mentions the big world. To my knowledge he employs only very rarely the specific words "macrocosm" and "microcosm." In *Murphy*, for example, I have noted two uses of the adjective "microcosmic" — but none of the noun itself. One thing is certain: even if, as in chapter VI of *Murphy*, Beckett may seem to agree with the realist philosophy according to which there exists an external world independent of my consciousness, he does not accept the traditional and hermetic meaning of the relationship between the universe and Man as microcosm. On the contrary, the old moral ideal of a harmony between these two worlds is for him inadmissible.

The vision of the universe, as shown in the frontispiece of Robert Fludd's book, *Utriusque Cosmi Historia* (see F. A. Yates, *The Rosicrucian Enlightenment* — the illustration between pages 72 and 73), with the macrocosm encircling the human microcosm (a human body with arms and legs in full extension and taking their points of support on the circle of the macrocosmic Zodiac), is impossible for the Beckettian *Cogito*. For Joyce it could have provided a useful image, like the Proustian circle (another of these tempting traps). I do not mean to imply that Beckett avoids the images of the circle or the sphere. Far from it! They serve, with him, not to effect a cosmic harmony, but to express the act of closing, which is being conscious of admitting the impossibility of any way out. In this sense, but only in this sense, Beckett is an idealist and follows Berkeley, whose "esse est percipi" is a direct consequence of the *Cogito*. "To be is to be perceived" means that one's only contact with the reality of the external world is a sensation, whatever it may be. To perceive and to be perceived are only parts of my consciousness. Beckett is no longer a realist. The outer world — the macrocosm — is the Unknowable. But Beckett has no interest in the Kantian concept of "Unknowable Noumenon." He will transfer it and himself into the *Cogito*, which will give sense to the relation speaking/spoken and make it the Unnamable.

To sum up, in philosophical terms: the Beckettian *Cogito* is the act by which Beckett gets rid of the modern duality between realism and idealism. Contrary to Descartes, this act discovers the vanity of the epistemological pretension which implies a communication between two worlds; it destroys thought as the thought of something (else). No communication is possible, and recognition of this will lead to the ultimate secret of the writer: that language communicates with itself. Beckett's *Cogito* has, finally, no philosophical bearing. To say "I am mistaken, therefore I am" is to say that philosophy is impossible and that Descartes is impossible — but inevitable. In this perspective, the act of reflection marks an awareness of language as the permanent problem of man.

The duality of mind and body. For Descartes, as is well known, this is the direct consequence of the *Cogito*. I am a thinking substance; as such I cannot be a material substance; my body belongs to the universe of space; my mind and space are foreign to, if not opposed to, each other. It is also well known that Descartes proves the existence of God in order to ascertain the existence of the material/spatial world. I am not sure that Beckett's position has been well understood by the many critics who have more or less followed Mintz's interpretation. All of them have been impressed by Murphy's problems with his body and have adopted the same viewpoint to consider the body's problem in *Watt* and the French works. Now, it seems to me first of all that Beckett has never been interested in Descartes's proofs of the existence of God in their relation to the proof of the existence of the material world. In *Whoroscope* he mentions the second proof (I who have in me the idea of the infinite cannot be my own creator), but only to show its mystic implication (I am a part of the Infinite, but I have no assurance that my body exists).

At *Murphy's* level, Murphy's body raises a practical problem concerning the neutralization of corporeal activities to permit free development of the mind (the real, rather than the symbolic, function of the rocking chair). Thus the Cartesian duality of mind and body is for Beckett an immediate "given" of one's consciousness, and it never becomes the duality of two substances with contrary qualities. Descartes betrays the *Cogito* in giving to his body a reality alien to that of his mind. Beckett persists in seeing the *Cogito* as act and an art of separation by which man is isolated once and for all in his own universe. Yet Beckett believes in the duality of mind/body. For this strange intellectual impasse there is only one possible conclusion: the duality of mind and body has a meaning within the existence of *the perceived — within the Cogito.*

Does this mean, in philosophical terms, that Beckett is an absolute phenomenalist or a radical solipsist? I do not think so, since (as I shall continue to remark) he is not a philosopher. He never dares to tell us that our body is merely our representation, or that our body exists, but independently of our mind. But he does say that our body is part of that which is perceived, so that his true problem is not how these two parts can be adjusted to each other, but *how one feels within himself the duality of mind and body.* With this question "in mind" it should be possible to interpret one of the most important aspects of Beckett's works — those physical monstrosities and deformations which recur in all his writings, with a rather timid beginning in *Murphy* and regular appearances from *Watt* to the last texts.

I do not suggest that the problem of the human body in Beckett's work can be solved by this unique reference to the *Cogito* and the clear duality of mind and body; and I plan to discuss this hereafter when we shall be confronted with the general problem of dualism. But I am convinced that the Beckettian meaning of the body should be apprehended by an act of reflection, as part of an internal duality. For example, the rocking chair and the bicycle are not symbolic objects typifying psycho-physiological relations; they are real experiences within the *Cogito* — not in the language of *as if,* but in the only possible use of language in its emblematic function. May I observe parenthetically that the usual notion of symbolic language implies the belief in realist principles so that a symbol as a linguistic sign is seen as referring to something that is real and consequently as implying the duality of language and reality.

But what happens if I think, as Beckett does, that this duality has a meaning within itself? A symbol is then no more a symbol of reality, but reality itself. In such cases, a bicycle is not the image of the human body; it is rather the bicycle that is analogous to the human body. It is a similarity of structure and experience, not a figurative transposition. We must realize that Beckett is not simply beyond realism and idealism — he is beyond symbolism as well and (as *Watts* demonstrates) beyond empirical and analytical nominalism.

The union of mind and body. This is another Cartesian problem and perhaps, for Beckett, the most significant part of Descartes's philosophy: I make an absolute separation between mind and body, and I am conscious that their duality is perfectly clear and distinct; but I cannot deny or minimize the importance of the fact — the obscure fact — of their union. Descartes confers on this union of mind/body the status of a substance. He speaks of the "substantial union of mind and body," and thus of that union's indissolubility, except where God intervenes. But Beckett does not accept this theory and holds that one feels both duality and union, that it is merely a matter of degree. Referring to the Cartesian idea that the pineal gland (the *conarium*) is the point of junction for mind and body, Beckett observes that Murphy's *conarium* is not very active, so that his experience there is more in the nature of dissociation than association. One understands, then, why Beckett calls upon Geulincx and his *Ethics* based upon the separation of mind and body as a moral principle and as a variation of the Stoic differentiation between what belongs to us and what does not. But it would be wrong to think that Beckett ignores "the union of mind and body." His heroes live that experience through anatomical and physiological deformities. They are bodies as well as minds. After *Molloy,* the duality mind/body becomes the duality of body and language, and later, within language, the duality of physical sensations and words. From this point of view, Beckett remains closer to Descartes than to Geulincx. In a first step, Geulincx helps him to enforce the duality mind/body as seen in the *Cogito*; but in a second step Beckett restores the fusion of mind and body as the basic problem of reciprocal incarnation. One can understand Beckett's reason for alluding in *Whoroscope* to Descartes's theory of transubstantiation:

> because He can jig
> as near or as far from His Jigging Self
> and as sad or lively as the chalice or the tray asks.

Is this not the ultimate experience of mind and body for Beckett — for Man (as Christ, writer, dancer)? — the indivisible relation of the Unnamable (mind) and the named (body), a relation as obscure as that of mind and body in realistic language and its aesthetic expression of the most universal of all possible relations: the duality/unity of silence and language?

Methodological doubt. This expression designates those preliminary and necessary intellectual operations which led Descartes to the discovery of the first truth — the *Cogito*. They are the successive phases of the *First Meditation*. They begin with the usual sceptical criticism of the senses and the images derived from them; and they end with the "hyperbolic doubt" — the hypothesis of an Evil Power (*Malin Génie*) which misleads man even in his development of mathematical theorems or operations. One might object that Beckett's doubt never arrives at truth. This is correct; but one should add that, for Beckett, statements in the form of a truth-proposition (i.e., true or false, affirmative or negative) are impossible. It is clear that Beckett has studied the various Greek schools and methods of Scepticism (as can be seen at the beginning of *L'Innommable*) and that he has frequently practiced the techniques of "yes and no" and of "the indifference of judgment." However, if Beckett's doubt is no creator of truth, it still does not end in the Sceptics' confession of intellectual impotence. There is a search for truth beyond truth, i.e., at a level beyond the truth-language, beyond what modern logicians would call a logic of truth-values.

The methodological doubt in Beckett's work could even be a sort of hyper-Cartesianism. At the final moment of his doubt, Descartes looks for the most impossible situation for a thinking mind: the avenues of knowledge are closed one by one until, with the threat of an Evil Power, they are all shut off; and language itself is cut off from any possible reference to reality. The Sceptics' doubt still ends in a compromise, since it accepts a practical truth. Like the temperamental Descartes of *Whoroscope*, Beckett is deadly serious when he doubts and, unlike Houdini, he chains himself in such a way that he can never escape! As in Descartes's interior monologue, one finds in Beckett's works a recurrent linguistic leap: when things are at their worst and all the literary means of egress are closed, the writer still has an obligation to continue writing. The initial questions of *L'Innommable* ("Where now? Who now? When now?") are not of Montaigne's type ("Que sais-je?"), but the conclusion of a doubt in progress.

However, the Cartesian Evil Power is an intellectual transposition of Satan, and an effort to put dualism at God's level. The *Third Meditation* tells us that the infinite Goodness of God overcomes any form of Evil. Such a Christian statement is unacceptable to Beckett.

How can one say that Good is more powerful than Evil? Then, if one accepts the status of dualism for human creatures, why not for all Creation? Why not for the Ultimate Cause? Descartes avoids answering these questions. He concedes that his intelligence is not capable of knowing the "raison d'être" of reality as it is. Beckett refuses this sort of escapism. The Cartesian Evil Power is merely a puppet made for easy liquidation. Beckett's methodological doubt is more radical than that of Descartes. There is no way out of the hypothetical statement "if each of my phrases were false...." But with continuous awareness of this sword of Damocles and the interdiction of any Houdini solution, the writer can still begin to put words in order. This hypothetical Manichaeism must remain permanent. And for Beckett it plays the role of Categorical Imperative.

Mechanism and the theory of relative movement. As noted in our analysis of *Whoroscope*, Beckett mentions the Cartesian theory of movement, as opposed to Galileo's. At first glance this allusion may seem an ironic reference to Descartes's cautious attitude toward precisely those religious powers that had condemned the theory of Galileo. But there is something more serious involved — the concept of movement and its meaning for human life. Behind the ironic veil, Beckett takes the side of Descartes against Galileo, just as in *Murphy* he supports Descartes against Newton, who is accused of being responsible for our modern industrial civilization. From Descartes's mechanism, then, Beckett will retain certain aspects which are present in all his works.

Beckett does not care whether Descartes was right or wrong in defining a universal principle of "the quantity of movement" and in refusing the principle of "the quantity of energy" (later formulated by Leibnitz and Newton). He thinks that the image of relative movement (being in motion because one is being moved) does apply to human experience. Movement itself is illusory. One feels motion, but one is moved. Thus one can feel himself in motion when he is actually motionless and consider himself in irreversible progress when he is merely behaving like a shuttle. Beckett's walk is never in a straight line, one step ahead of another. It is a slow process of contraries and thwarted alternations. Surely, such movements are not Cartesian! Descartes favors circular and rectilinear changes. The relative movement has given a pattern to Beckett's feelings and is a condition for his style of free action. According to this imagery, the *Cogito* is a movement backward in that it represents the possibility of not following the general movement of the world!

Beckett adopts Descartes's conception of the human body as a combination of mechanical devices (and he adds that they are in poor working condition). Beckett is a long way from Bergson's notion of life opposed to mechanism and his theory on the comic as "du mécanique plaqué sur du vivant." It may be that the human body and its behavior are intensely comic because they are mechanical; but their essence is not so! Consequently, laughter is not caused by the regression of life to material inertia. Life by itself is laughable. Beckett's humor has deeper roots than Bergson's spiritualist metaphysic based on artificial dualities.

Descartes's mechanism derives from his theory of analytical geometry, wherein he unites geometry and algebra (continuous and discontinuous quantities). It has its first source in the innate, clear and distinct idea of space which he finds when, in the *Second Meditation*, he makes the inventory of the *Cogito*'s domain. Similarly, Beckett experiences his body through the *Cogito*. But Cartesian intellectualism is converted into an "affectivism" (see *Proust*) — i.e., a direct and emotional experience of the body. This is why Beckett's characters have no objective views of their bodies and cannot see them through the canons of Greek or Renaissance beauty! *They feel their bodies and describe them as they feel them.* To parody the title of Eugène Minkowski's book, *Le Temps vécu (Lived Time)*, with Beckett's characters it is "le corps vécu" (the body experienced). The perfect function of the Cartesian "machine" is transposed into a fantastic operation concerning mainly the arms, legs and head. Here a significant relationship can be seen with the mechanistic experiments of Duchamp, Picabia and the early Dali. Duchamp's Great Glass could be looked at like a Beckettian dream, but with one important difference: Duchamp's machinery is supposed to work as a good motor works, and his "ready-made" (for example a bicycle wheel) has little in common with Molloy's "acatène" (chainless) structure! Beckett's bodies are almost always in a state of decomposition or putrefaction or disorganization. Another comparison could be made with the works of Bracque or Picasso in the '20s. Even if those Cubist deformations had varied sources, all of them (about the same time, and before the French phenomenologists) invite us to reconsider the relationships between mind and body and are diverse expressions of a subjective and fantastic mechanism.

Duality of intelligence and will. In the *Fourth Meditation* Descartes opposes *understanding (l'entendement)*, with a given number of clear, confused or obscure ideas (whether free gifts of God or results of the body/mind's union), to *will*, which is infinite and the source of human actions, whether purely intellectual or related to the physical world. Beckett is conscious of this distinction; but he does not draw from it its Cartesian consequences. (Beckett seems to have studied little, if at all, the theories of judgment and freedom and their developments in the *Traité des passions de l'âme* [*The Passions of the Soul*], and he tends to transpose Descartes's duality of *understanding* and *will* into its Schopenhauerian version [opposition of *consciousness* and *the will to live*].) Yet Beckett's concept of human understanding is nearer to that of Descartes than to the Kantian-Schopenhauerian machinery of forms of theoretical reason. The Beckettian consciousness is not a matter of *a priori* forms; it has intuitive meanings inspired by a direct and internal experience of the *Cogito*. In other respects, these intuitive states have nothing to do with Bergson's "metaphysical intuition" or with Husserl's intentional relation. It is the *Cogito* in its own intimacy.

From this dualistic perspective one should consider the well-known reference to Geulincx in *Murphy*. Here, for the sake of the rich allusions involved, is its preliminary phase and its first conclusion: "His vote was cast. 'I am not of the big world, I am of the little world' was an old refrain with Murphy, and a conviction, two convictions, the negative first. How should he tolerate, let alone cultivate, the occasion of fiasco, having once beheld the beatific idols of his cave? In the beautiful Belgo-Latin of Arnold Geulincx: *Ubi nihil vales, ibi nihil velis*.

"But it was not enough to want nothing where he was worth nothing, nor even to take the further step of renouncing all that lay outside the intellectual love in which alone he could love himself, because there alone he was lovable." (Pp. 178-179.) The general problem of action is raised. The will is the source of action and of breaking out from the little world into the big one. Action is motivated by values; it is a search for values, mainly for one's personal value, as connected with self-love. Will is desire for value. If action in the outer world is an inevitable failure (a fiasco), then let us live in the little world, where there is only one solution for success: to suppress desire, as advised by Schopenhauer in his ethics — in other words, to live by the understanding, after suspending indefinitely the will's power.

Geulincx's rule, based on the Cartesian duality of understanding and will, is more than a Schopenhauerian rule of non-action (the will-lessness of chapter VI of *Murphy*); it is a liberation of the *Cogito*, brought down to its essential function of intelligence which is the consciousness of one's self. I am not trying to make of Beckett a convicted intellectualist in the style of Spinoza! The deepest experiences of the *Cogito* are emotional. To take Pascal's word, they belong to *the heart* with all its personal reasons; and they are the intuitive and continuous ordeals of human destiny. But for Beckett, there is no Husserlian or Sartrian *precogito*. There is *Cogito or nothing*. Beckett knows that deep emotions are fatally linked with intelligence and for a simple reason that it took even Beckett some time to discover: the *Cogito* (limited, but with indefinite combinations among its elements) is a hive of words. Finally, the *Cogito*, made of words and silences, of emotions and thoughts, is the act by which I try desperately to denominate myself.

The rule of enumeration. The fourth and last rule of method is formulated by Descartes as follows: "... the last was in all cases to make enumerations so complete and reviews so general that I shall be certain of having omitted nothing" (Haldane and Ross's translation). It is known that, as early as his *Proust*, Beckett was consciouss of this linguistic and literary problem. Well known also is Beckett's fascination with precise and definite inventories of verbal possibilities; and we can see him in *Watt* working at those combinations of words whose tension and appeal persists thereafter, even in the latest works, where they provide a sort of periodic musical composition. It is probable that Beckett at one time or another studied logical positivism and its analytical philosophers. But he became interested in the combinatory power for words very early — at least by his college years — so that Descartes's rule of enumeration has long been for him less a guide than a justification of a very definite gift or need of his mind. As he says in *Enough*: "The art of combining is not my fault. It's a curse from above." May I venture the hypothesis that the most secret part of the *Cogito* is made of wavering intuitions on human destiny? Those intuitions seek phrases which are forced to obey grammatical rules. But how do such phrases succeed each other when they are not fragments of a long, indefinite, unique phrase (the Proustian anguishing question)? By combinations of semantic possibilities. And how can one put these combinations in order? By applying to words and phrases the rule of enumeration!

* * *

Such is Beckett's Cartesian kit. There is nothing systematic about it. It is composed of varied devices, whose proper functions are well understood. And all of them, while keeping their original roles, are more or less associated with each other, because of their direct connection with one fundamental instrument: the *Cogito*.

Now, before we leave this field, a negative question should be raised: In that panoply of Beckett's are there not some extraordinary omissions? Many aspects of Cartesianism which could easily have played their part in the Beckettian world are neglected — e.g., the famous theory of "tourbillons" (whirlwinds) and of the circularity of the cosmic movements; the psychology of the "passions" based upon "wonder" (*admiration*); the tree of knowledge and the Cartesian anticipation of a technological civilization, as described in the preface to *The Principles of Philosophy*; the theory of "generosity," which could be the true basis for Geulincx's maxim "*Ubi nihil vales, nihil velis*" or for Spinoza's "*amor intellectualis*" (see *The Passions of the Soul*, Part III, article CLVI: "Those who are generous in this way are naturally impelled to do great things and at the same time *to undertake nothing of which they do not feel themselves capable*" (italics mine).

Except for a general attitude, those omissions are not even significant as to a particular choice among Cartesian themes. Beckett tends to undervalue the practical side of Cartesianism — not only Descartes's wish to transform the material universe into a set of human instruments, but also his directing his ethics so as to give its highest efficiency to human action. It is therefore no surprise that Beckett favors Geulincx's version of generosity! The Beckett *Cogito* is not generous in the Cartesian sense of the word. I can imagine Beckett's scepticism as to Descartes's distinction between generosity and pride, or as to his definition of "virtuous humility." For Beckett, there can be only one legitimate form of humility (and that at a zero degree of value), when one realizes that "nothing" is always more valuable than "something."

The only omission that is puzzling (and for that reason all the more meaningful) is all reference, positive or negative, to "the rule of evidence," the first principle of the Cartesian method as exposed in the second part of the *Discours* and pervading all its ulterior intellectual proceedings: "The first of these [laws] was to accept nothing as true which I did not clearly recognize to be so: that is to say, carefully to avoid precipitation and prejudice in judgments, and to accept in them nothing more than what was represented to my mind so clearly and distinctly that I could have no occasion to doubt it" (Haldane and Ross's translation).

Is it not astonishing that this writer whose entire work is dominated by the duality of light and darkness consciously ignores Descartes's absolute identification of truth, self-consciousness, evidence and clarity? Here students of Beckett will recall the last paragraph of chapter VI of *Murphy* and Murphy's mind longing for a peaceful state of absolute darkness — a passage like that in *Whoroscope* on the "starless, inscrutable hour." This invitation to darkness is in a perfect contrast with the conclusion of Descartes's *Third Meditation*: "It seems to me right to pause for a while in order to *contemplate* God Himself, to ponder at leisure His marvelous attributes, *to consider, and admire, and adore the beauty of His light so resplendent,* at least as far as the strength of my mind, which is in some measure *dazzled by the sight,* will allow me to do so." (Haldane and Ross's translation; italics mine.)

What reasons can one find for this apparently strange state of affairs?

1) Beckett experiences the *Cogito* — not its clarity; and for him there is nothing less clear than that foundation of clear statements! Going a little deeper, Beckett thinks that the duality of light and darkness is not the simple consequence of a *Cogito*'s being well or badly handled. The sources of clarity and obscurity are not operations of man's consciousness. In other words, for Beckett, Descartes's theory of evidence is itself superficial and even self-contradictory; and the Descartes of *Whoroscope* finally gives it up for darkness, and Murphy, as Descartes's new incarnation, dreams of becoming "a mote in the dark of absolute freedom" (p. 112). Such a duality cannot be locked into the epistemological opposition of clear and obscure ideas, and explained away by reference to the two sources to knowledge — the innate ideas and empirical data. Descartes reduces evidence to a

problem of the psychology of reflection. For Beckett, poet and novelist, light is at the same time an existential and linguistic matter.

2) The Cartesian evidence is the immediate justification of the philosophical language, or if one prefers, the truth-language (language of truth). Beckett denies the possibility of such a language. If it had been possible, he would have become a philosopher himself! I do not mean to say that Beckett, in the late '20s and early '30s, had actually passed from a state of philosophical scepticism or impotence to a decision to use the literary language as opposed to the philosophical one with its truth-translation of reality. But one cannot deny Beckett his seriousness of purpose! His first texts (poems and criticism) show him acutely conscious of this problem. Is not evidence a false or artificial light? Is there a natural light? What is the light or obscurity of a language? The Cartesian epistemology cannot answer these problems, and *a fortiori* this deadly question arises for the young writer: *If the philosophical language is impossible as truth-language, what is the essence of the literary language?* Here again one is confronted by the problem of the nature of symbol. It is undeniable that Beckett, at the beginning of his writing career, understands the necessity of going beyond Baudelaire's "intellectual symbolism," is fascinated by Proust's and Joyce's "auto-symbolism," but is still doubtful about their techniques for making their own light! Descartes's dualism of clarity and obscurity is actually an invitation to pass from the state of intellectual confusion to the pure moment of understanding. Proust and Joyce surreptitiously restore a monism — a unique literary world under the contemplation of a writer who is transmuted into a Sun King pouring out his rays with brilliant play of lights and shadows.

3) Thus we reach the ultimate reason for this situation: the duality of light and darkness, of clarity and obscurity, should and must be taken more seriously than it has been up to the present time by philosophers (with Descartes as their proxy), or by writers (of whom Proust and Joyce offer the best possible solution for human language). In Beckett's terms, what is it that lies beyond the usual philosophical intellectualism (whether rationalist or empiricist) and the literary symbolism (whether allegory, metaphor or mimesis!)?

Before leaving Descartes and trying to answer that question, before looking for new developments in Beckett's conception of dualities, let us raise one last query: Is there a noticeable and interesting evolution in Beckett's use of Cartesian themes or tools from *Whoroscope* to *not I* or *Sans?* This problem deserves thorough investigation, and I hope this will be undertaken, because of its crucial importance, not only for interpretation of Beckett, but more generally because of its implications in the theory of literature. For the moment, we can take up only the most evident signs of an evolution. *Whoroscope,* as we have seen in section III of this study, contains, implicitly or otherwise, all the Cartesian themes that will be developed by Beckett, and insists on the duality of matter and spirit. With *Murphy,* if that duality does not disappear, it is understood through the opposition of the body and the mind as consciousness. Later, from *Watt* on, and especially in the so-called trilogy, the main duality is that of will and understanding, which is evidence of a fatal split within human mind. Then the duality of *percipere* and *percipi* plays a very decisive role as all dualities are brought up within the field of self-consciousness. But at the same time, Beckett's predominant obsession with light and darkness is more and more affirmed and elaborated, until it has no longer a Berkeleyan tone and becomes simultaneously a sign of psychological trial and of cosmic predestination. Finally, from the time of *Textes pour rien* and *Comment c'est* the early dualities fade out or play only an occasional role and give place to the eschatological tragedy of Light and Darkness, as can be seen in the last stanzas of *Sans*.

If I am right in interpreting an evolution that began probably in the early '20s at Trinity College and has not yet ended, the most important borrowings from Descartes are the *Cogito* and dualism as an ineluctable form of being and thinking. Little by little, Beckett disengages himself from well-known Cartesian implications concerning the *Cogito* and the duality of mind and body, while always adhering to the basic meanings of these "conveniences," as he says in *Film*: the *Cogito,* as the act by which I separate myself from the world (I make that world an unknown outer X of reference; I give sense to the duality of internal-external reality within myself); and *dualism,* as the inevitable shuttle of existence (the necessary come-and-go for understanding the progression from something to nothing, or from nothing to something — the deforming mirror thanks to which I can speak of me as a person).

But let us repeat it one last time: There is in Beckett's work, from the beginning, something other than the Cartesian or the anti-Cartesian — something other than the Kafkaean-Sartrean existentialo-analytic *pas-de-deux* or scenery, such as some critics describe. Beckett's poems, novels and plays have more timeless qualities than have yet been granted them. I feel even that these works are destined to stand as they are, in their uniqueness and integrity, beyond the literary fashions and trends of their day — and beyond the apparatus of Descartes. And so I come to my last question: How has this timelessness been realized?

V

> Mais cette question de lumière mérite d'être traitée à part tellement elle est curieuse, et longuement, à tête reposée, et elle le sera, à la première occasion, quand le temps ne pressera plus, quand la tête sera calmée. (*L'Innommable*, p. 140.)

> But this question of light deserves to be treated in a section apart, it is so intriguing, and at length, composedly, and so it will be, at the first opportunity, when time is not so short, and the mind more composed. (*The Unnamable*, p. 95.)

Let us take seriously Beckett's warning and plea on "this question of light" and resolve to remain on the threshold of a basic problem of language. For that preliminary purpose I suggest analysis of a short and rare text cited earlier in our study — the two pages (p. 45 and p. 47) from Beckett's manuscript notebook, published in photo-facsimile at the end of James Knowlson's *Light and Darkness in the Theater of Samuel Beckett* with the indication that they were "written for his own production of *Krapp's Last Tape*, at the Schiller Theater Werkstatt, Berlin, October 5th, 1969."

Page 45 begins with a short list of "light emblems" and "dark emblems" (i.e., for the former: "mild zephir," "cooling wind," "bright light," "quickening fire," "clear water"; for the latter: "mist," "heat," "sirocco," "darkness," "vapour"). At this point it would be inconsiderate to generalize; but one should note that these "emblems" are all taken from three elements: air, fire and water. Would it be a hasty generalization to say that light and darkness develop their contrasts and possible intermixture within those three elements (the earth, on the other hand, being for Beckett the place for roads leading into or out of a closed world of town, house, or room)?

On the same page appear four of Beckett's apparently enigmatic thoughts — the first on "separation of light and darkness," followed by a bracketed text in German evoking the act by which light is separated from dark (separation of grain from husks) and referring to a text of *Krapp* (p. 14). A second note ("Man created by Satan") has this special notation: "Cain and Abel sons not of Adam but of Satan and Eve." Then a third remark: "Ascetic ethics" Beckett specifies that this asceticism is mainly abstinence with a sexual connotation: prohibition of marriage — and he adds in parentheses the Latin expression "signaculum sinus" (emblem of the breast). Finally, Beckett writes: "Worshipper turned toward sun, or moon, or north (seat of light)," with a German quotation referring to the Baltic Sea (see *Krapp*, p. 25). One need not be an expert in the Manichaean Gnosis to realize that Beckett's statements come directly from that tradition, with no hermetic or Cathar intermediaries.

A long and a short paragraphs covering half of page 47 could be harder to decipher; but their source is undoubtedly the same Manichaean vision. In words that recall the behavior of the hero in *Film*, Beckett notes that "Krapp decrees physical (ethical) incompatibilities of light (spiritual) and dark (sensual) only when he intuits possibility of their reconciliation intellectually as rational-irrational." In other words, the risk of a mixture of darkness and light leads Krapp to insist on their dualities, with the actual double meaning of physical and spiritual experiences. Is this not the principle of Manichaean ethics? Is it not going from Geulincx's asceticism to Manichaean purity?

Then, in a sudden return to Descartes, this duality is epistemologically transposed from ethics to the theory of knowledge and becomes the modern opposition rational/irrational. Is this not the radical Cartesian distinction between clear and obscure ideas and Krapp's absolute refusal of any sort of compromise at any level? The second phrase of the first paragraph explains Krapp's decision and emphasizes the critical function of the *Cogito*. Beckett opposes two worlds but without the hermetic implication of the macrocosm/microcosm duality. This fact seems to me essential for any general interpretation of Beckett.

Krapp introduces his personal *Cogito*; and here the verb *to turn* is significant: "Krapp turns from fact of anti-mind alien to mind to thought of anti-mind constituent of mind." This is the very turn made by the *Cogito*, i.e., the awareness of a separation between matter — what Beckett prefers to express in an idealistic way as anti-mind —

and mind. And this opposition is not the same as the *thought* of the opposition: the *Cogito* changes an actual and realistic duality into a duality within the mind. Is this not Descartes enchained by the radical principles of Manichaeism? — or Manichaeism experienced at the reflective level of the human mind as the ability to be conscious of one's self?

The third sentence draws the consequences of this situation for Krapp. Beckett says that Krapp is "ethically correct" in obeying the rule of abstinence, as formulated by the *signaculum sinus*, because the *Cogito* has not (as too many philosophers after Descartes have thought) a function of unity, of comprehension, of putting things and reality together, reconciled into the same system. The basic role of "reason" (Beckett's own word) is "not to join but to separate." Reason is identified with the *Cogito* in an entirely new mission: new in the sense that it is opposed to the epistemological dreams of Western intelligence — old in this other sense that it restores the traditional office of the mind (i.e., returning to itself, to turn away from the outer world). And in a parenthesis Beckett reveals his most secret though: "deliverance of imprisoned light." Doubt, if there were any, is no more permitted. Beckett has led us to the heart of Manichaeism: liberty as liberation — liberation as the act by which light is separated from darkness. The *road* to "deliverance" begins with the *Cogito*.

Perhaps now, and only now, can we understand the strange silence of Beckett on "the first rule of evidence." Descartes is right, Beckett seems to think, when he rules that clarity is the ultimate goal of mind. But he is wrong when he believes that our mind goes from intuitive or immediately clear ideas to distinct ideas. (Descartes has never been clear about the difference between *clear* and *distinct*.) For Beckett, on the contrary, distinction as separation comes first in the *Cogito* process, and clarity is conquered later, when light and darkness are definitely isolated from each other. Thus the Cartesian "rule of evidence" should be seen as a rule of deliverance.

The last sentence of the paragraph is hard to understand, but its general intent can be guessed. Beckett writes that, "for his sin," Krapp "is punished as shown by the aeons." For what sin? The preceding sentence notes that, "through intellectual transgression," Krapp "is ethically correct." In that case, I see only one possible interpretation: this act of separation accomplished by the *Cogito* is a sort of transgression and original sin not permitted to man; guilty of it, Krapp deserves to be punished, and he knows it. (Is this the reason for the feeling of guilt that pervades all Beckett's work?)

The Beckettian hero (Descartes and his twin successors [Belacqua being free from this sin]) is guilty of the Manichaean belief and faith, for he retains the secret of light and its liberation. As Beckett remarks in *L'Innommable,* his characters are not offspring of Prometheus: they do not pretend to have liver trouble; they have not stolen fire and the mysteries of its fabrication! They are not rivals of Oedipus in crime and the impulses of incest. Their secret is the meaning of Beckett's asceticism, which originates, not in the Stoics and their distinction between things which depend upon us and those that don't, and not in the Christian ideal of pure love *(agapé)* but in the Manichaean sense of obligation to separate the light and the dark as the primordial dualities of being and nothingness.

May I confess my inability to explain with any assurance Beckett's curious allusion to the "aeons"? Perhaps there is a useful hint in Beckett's comment on Krapp (quoted from *The Times* of April 25, 1970, by Knowlson, *op. cit.,* p. 20): "The character is eaten up by dreams. But without sentimentality. There's no resignation in him. It's the end. He sees very clearly that he's through with his work, with love and with religion." The hidden forces behind dreams could be the aeons, those spiritual creatures of the Gnosis. Could not Beckett's comment pertain to any of his principal characters, and most of all to Descartes at the moment of his death, devoured by his dreams and through with everything — with work, love, religion (that trinity of human life)?

The shorter paragraph on page 47 alludes to the emblems of the black ball and the little white dog of the play: "In the end I held it out to him and he took it in his mouth, gently. A small, old, black, hard, solid rubber ball." (*Krapp,* p. 20). Beckett notes that giving the ball to the dog "*represents* [italics mine] the sacrifice of sense to spirit." The difficulty is to give the word *represents* its proper meaning and value, while keeping in mind the last ironic caution of *Watt*: "No symbols where none intended." We shall come to that later. For the moment, let us follow Beckett's lead when he adds: "The *form* [italics mine] here too is that of a mingling." A mingling of black and white, and thus of darkness and light in a grey universe. Here again the meaning of *form* raises a key problem of Beckett's aesthetics. And again I suggest turning to the *Cogito*. The separation of light and dark is not, as Descartes believed, an instantaneous act to be performed at the beginning of any intellectual enterprise, but rather the issue, the conclusion of a long, painful life — the instant of death and separation. In the meantime, man cannot escape from the condition of mingling or, as Beckett says, the *form of mingling;* and I am tempted to add, following the indicators along the continuous road of *L'Innommable,* that this intermediary form, where the contraries are mixed and mixed up, is language itself, and language representing nothing but itself!

Let me assume that Beckett, in giving James Knowlson those two pages of his notebook (and one cannot but wonder, when one realizes the richness of those two pages, what is written on pages 1 to 44 and page 46 and the pages after 47!), was making a courteous and slightly ironic gesture to his critics with the implication: here are the guidelines, let us see what you will get out of them! I do not intend to be snared in the first open trap by making Beckett a devotee of Mani and his works Manichaean experiences. But the Manichaean vocabulary and themes can hardly be denied; and the use of the Latin *signaculum sinus* might even suggest that Beckett knows Saint Augustine's writings against the Manichaeans, especially the *Confessions, De moribus Manichaeorum et de moribus Ecclesiae, De libero arbitrio,* and *Contra Faustum.*

At all events, here is the problem: there are in Beckett's works as many implicit or clear references to Manichaeism or to the Gnosis as there are to Descartes and Cartesianism. Pending a thorough study of this question, let us note here some of the most important Manichaean themes, insofar as they offer similarities to Beckett's themes or images, but with this preliminary understanding: I am not seeking to detect influences or to unmask sources (there are matters at best of secondary interest in my present research); but I do perceive similarities of themes and expressions. The actual problem, then, can only be defined in these terms: How do Manichaean views or linguistic forms occur in the coherence or refusal of coherence of Beckett's works? I do not pretend to offer a definitive answer to this question; but I should like to write *finis* to the "Cartesian discussion" and to evoke briefly some of the trends of the Manichaean mind.

Since *Whoroscope,* Beckett has set Descartes's life within the large frame of Manichaeism, which means that Descartes's dualities have been radicalized with no possible compromise. There is no "union," only "mingling." Thus the Cartesian distinctions between clear and distinct ideas and confused and obscure ideas become basic dualities between light and darkness, with a medium state of confusion, from which we can draw a simple stylistic rule: One is permitted to be clear or obscure, but never to accept confusion — the great carelessness of Descartes being that he more or less confused confusion and obscurity, grey and black, or, if one prefers, that he did not disentangle three very distinct dualities: clear and obscure, clear and confused, obscure and confused!

Now, this Manichaean transfer of Cartesian themes indicates a passage from an epistemological level to an "ethical" level (to use Beckett's wording), with the word *ethical* taken here in a very unusual, and perhaps even new, meaning, which has nothing to do with the way philosophers raise the so-called "moral" problem in their doctrine, but which should and could be understood by starting from the Manichaean ethics, with its three emblems, or seals: *mouth*,[9] *hand* and *breast* (see Saint Augustine, *Contra Man.*, chaps. X-XIX). The Cartesian *Cogito* appears in its primordial power: to free the mind, not thanks to the *will*, which, as Descartes says in the *Fourth Meditation*, "consists alone in our having the power of choosing to do a thing or not to do it (that is to affirm or deny, to pursue or shun it)" (Haldane and Ross's translation), but in an effort of liberation, not from darkness, because the fact of darkness is as absolute as the fact of light, but from confusion (the "mess"). This is definitely not Cartesian orthodoxy — it is pure Manichaeist belief.

In an excellent, although Christianly biased, entry in the *Encyclopedia Britannica* (Vol. XIV, 1964), Manichaeism is defined as a "consistent, uncompromising dualism in the form of a fantastic philosophy of nature." The Christian Fathers accused Manichaeism of being an extravagant mixture of materialism, mythology, and elated spiritual and intransigent rigorism, but noted that it had an appeal for artists. In its doctrines, there is no distinction between the physical and the ethical (Beckett accepts that identification on p. 47 of his notebook), or between the spiritual and the natural. Thus, for the Manichaeans, two distinct beings exist, originally separated from each other, in a state of perfect balance and equality: "Darkness is likewise a spiritual

---

[9] There is no need to remind students of Beckett about the significance of the mouth and the arms in the characterization of his heroes.

kingdom (more correctly it also is conceived of as a spiritual and feminine personification)." Each of these beings has typical characteristics: "As the earth of light has five tokens (the mild zephir, cooling wind, bright light, quickening fire, and clear water), so has the earth of darkness also five (mist, heat, the sirocco, darkness and vapours)." It is clear that the first lines of Beckett's notebook are identical with that text, except for one very interesting variation: the word *token* is replaced by *emblem*.

There is no need to go into details on the mythological war between Light and Darkness, or on the first defeats of Light, which were a stratagem of war. But let us keep in mind the general structure of Manichaean thought. Upon those two principles of reality (Light and Dark) there is built up a doctrine of *three moments*: before the war (the anterior moment), during the war (the middle moment or present stage of being — the moment of mixture), and the posterior moment (the moment of separation). There is an excellent commentary on this aspect of the doctrine in H.-C. Puech's *Le manichéisme, son fondateur, sa doctrine* (pp. 158-159), with this final remark: "The birds come back to the air, the quadrupeds come back to the jungle, truth comes back to differentiation, the road (*tao*) comes back to Nirvana."

The second section of the article in the *Encyclopedia Britannica* deals with the Creation of Man, and Beckett's notes coincide with that presentation: "The first Man, Adam, was engendered by Satan.... Thus Adam is a discordant being, created in the image of Satan, but carrying with him the strong spark of light. Eve is given him by Satan as his companion.... Cain and Abel indeed are not sons of Adam, but of Satan and Eve; Seth, however, who is full of light, is the offspring of Adam and Eve."

Beckett's other notes or quotations (second paragraph on page 45 and page 47) on ethics and the "*signaculum sinus*" seem to come from another source, perhaps from Saint Augustine himself. The *De moribus Manichaeorum* devotes chapters X-XIX to a discussion of Manichaean ethics and the three symbols or emblems. In chapter XVIII on the "*signaculum sinus*" Saint Augustine addresses Manichaeists in an indignant tone: "You do not forbid sexual intercourse, you forbid marriage!" And he explains: "... Is it not you who hold that begetting children, by which souls are confined in flesh, is a greater sin than cohabitation." [10] And he concludes that with such ethics, woman becomes a harlot!

It is clear that this sort of ancient birth control fits perfectly with Beckett's well-known attitudes toward sexual relations and procreation. Since I do not intend to explore all the facets of Beckett's Manichaeism, but only its connection with the Cartesian tools, I should like to add a few remarks to introduce this fundamental question: What is the ultimate function of these Manichaean principles or methods in Beckett's works?

The Manichaean mythology of *abortive beings* is for me fascinating and could have some secret relations with Beckett's monstrous beings and *lusus naturae*. An Aeon, the third Messenger of God — androgyne, naked, handsome, perfect — is attached to the two luminaries, the Sun and the Moon, toward which the liberated souls go. Then the demons fall in love with the Messenger. Such is the origin of the abortive beings from which the plants and the animals descend. Man also comes from the abortive race, begotten by the first of them — the Prince of Smoke. Adam was engendered by the Chief of the Abortives and his companion. As a mixture of light and darkness, he is the little world within the big world (see Prosper Alfaric, *L'Évolution Intellectuelle de Saint Augustin,* chapters 1 and 2).

Another Beckettian and Manichaean theme is the definition of freedom as liberation of the soul, i.e., as an act of pure separation — an exit from the second moment or the "mixture." This aspect has been well emphasized by Simone Pétrement in *Le Dualisme chez Platon, les Gnostiques et les Manichéens*. The author shows clearly that the Logos, as Wisdom, is the power of division. The evil resides in the reciprocal exchange — in the union. To divide means to establish a frontier between the two divided parts. It is the doctrine of the *limit* — the Manichaeist identification of the limit and the Cross, the great vision of a Cross of Light, with a "Jesus Patibilis," pathetic and cosmic (see Pétrement, *op. cit.,* chapter VI, or Puech, *op. cit.,* p. 82). The same idea is present with the Cathars, for whom the Spirit of Light leads men toward *Eleutheria*. Is there a link with Beckett's title for his first play? I do not know, but the thematic similarities are striking.

---

[10] See "The Works of Aurelius Augustine. A New translation." Vol. V. Writings in connection with the Manichaean heresy. 1872.

I think also that the idea of creation as abortion is typically Beckettian, and that Beckett's heroes carry on a dramatic conflict with their deformed or aborted bodies. In her study of Beckett's monstrosities,[10] Mrs. Leisure observes that, except on rare occasions, Beckettian monstrosities are limited to mankind. I can conceive of only one possible reason for this: Monstrosity is a subjective experience — a sense of the body as experienced in the state of mixture of body and mind. Plants and animals are abortive beings by their very natures.

Saint Augustine (*op. cit.*, chapter VIII) discusses Manichaeist objections to the Christian justification of Evil through the concepts of privation and non-being. For Augustine (*ibid.*, chapter II), evil is "that which falls away from essence and tends to non-existence"; but there is no absolute evil, because, if there were, it would act against itself and destroy its own being. The Manichaeist answer to this permanent problem of Evil can be summed up with a question: Is not the scorpion (or the fire, or the poison) a nature? A nature remains as it is. But Man is conscious of his abortive origin. Body-awareness is nothing more than a feeling of being abortive. The "Cartesian Centaur" is a dream of separation. The actual reality of Man, for Beckett, is experiencing his monstrosity; and this experience is merely another term for the Cartesian union of body and mind. In consequence, "Eleutheria" as the road to freedom is the progressive division which ends with the consciousness of the *limit* and the limitless fight with words. Like the scorpion, man finally cannot escape from his monstrous and abortive nature. But he can go on fighting, for the road or the ditch has no end.

One last remark: The traditional critics against Manichaeism have ultimately concentrated upon the problem of *creation* as the act by which the world, as reality out of God, comes out of and from nothingness. This Christian concept is related to the other notion of the Uniqueness of God (for, in Christian terms, it is contradictory to admit the existence of more than one God) and thus to a *monistic* vision of Reality, so that Nothingness can be only deprivation of being and never a reality in itself.[11]

---

[10] See: Maryse Leisure, "L'Esthétique de la Monstruosité dans les romans et nouvelles de Samuel Beckett," unpublished doctoral dissertation, The University of Arizona, 1974.

[11] We may recall here the early and constantly reiterated statement of Beckett on the reality, even the superiority, of nothingness.

Any student of the philosophy of the twentieth century knows that the problem of nothingness is at the heart of our epistemological perplexities. What do I mean when I say that nothingness is deprivation or negation of Being? We know well Heidegger's analysis of the priority of Nothingness over Being, and Sartre's theory of consciousness as a power of annihilation (*néantisation*). I agree with Hesla when, in his *Shape of Chaos*, he underlines the importance of the fourth part of Bergson's *L'évolution créatrice,* in which the author tries to explain the formation of the ideas of void and nothingness and the genesis of negative judgment. But I disagree with Hesla's final interpretation. I think (see my *Pensée négative,* chapters VI and VII) that Bergson is unable to transcend a monistic vision of reality and refuses to radicalize the opposition between being and non-being, yes and no, presence and absence, etc. He tries, rather, to protect the traditional metaphysical optimism of the Western philosophies, which (whether they be dogmatic or sceptic, monist, dualist or pluralist) cling to the dogma of the infinite plenitude of Being, without providing any actual place for emptiness.

If I am correct, Beckett is an anti-Bergsonian and therefore opposed to a bi-millenary tradition of preferences and prejudices in favor of the concept of Being. It is true that Heidegger and Sartre, after Hegel and Kierkegaard, have tried to fight this ontological principle and bias; but I am not at all sure that they have won their battle. On the contrary, trying to avoid the sharp consequence of a radical dualism, they have merely sidestepped this vital issue; for to reverse the traditional process and give priority to Nothingness is merely to substitute one word for another and to remain still inside a monistic pattern. The real difficulty consists in keeping Being and Nothingness on even scales as equals in reality, but as negations of each other — and not in following the easy way of saying that there is a being of nothing, an existence of nothingness, a presence of absence and the reverse, or indulging in any similar contemporary intellectual *jeu de mots.*

Reading Saint Augustine, I was struck by a very significant attack on Manichaeists, both in his *De moribus Manichaeorum* and in his *De moribus Ecclesiae Catholicae.* In chapter XVII of the latter book he accuses them of approaching divine things with minds "quite gross and sickly, from being fed with material images." He invites them to abjure their "silly legends" and their "unmeaning material imaginations." (op. cit.) Again in *De moribus Manichaeorum* (chapter XVI), developing the same criticism, he uses the same expression ("material images"); he urges the Manichaeans "to cease saying that you have in your eyes, nose and palate qualified judges of the presence of the divine part in material objects." (op. cit.) The only solution is Christian: "Sumptuous eating is to be avoided, not to escape pollution ... but to subdue the sensual appetite." (op. cit.)

In this discussion, the most important fact is the reference to "material images" and their use. It is more than an accusation of materialism. The problem of the nature of imagination and images is thus raised, as well as that of Christian symbolism and the relation between proper and figurative meaning of words. For example, when one speaks of the clarity of the soul, the image of physical cleanliness cannot be taken literally: it looks to spiritual purity, for the physical world should be the image of the spiritual world. A symbol can be but an allegory which always follows the same direction — from the physical to the spiritual. This is why, with varying degrees of talent and with more or less spontaneity and enthusiasm, Western literatures, at one moment or another, fall into allegorical constructs — i.e., into conferring a spiritual significance upon physical images.

Needless to say, such a principle gives a definite role to literature and the arts *per se* — the function of instilling into images a spiritual dimension — of making them the incarnation of a superior world — of using words as anagogical powers of transmutation — and of changing the body into a detector-solicitor of images to be reserved as food for the soul.

Then one understands why Saint Augustine has seen in Manichaeism not only a contradictory metaphysics or an impossible ethics, but also a theory of language and an aesthetics. It is clear that this struggle between Christianity and Manichaeism, as it has been pursued for centuries at the theological and moral levels, with its direct or indirect resurgences in all sorts of so-called heresies, has had a decisive importance in the theory of literature; and thus it is not a purely philosophical matter! Far from it! I contend that, behind the screen of theological discussions and moral options, the true and basic problem is: *What are the essence and function of words as images* — or of IMAGES AS WORDS?

The practice of language, when it goes beyond simple help for action or the location of signals, has immediate metaphysical and ethical consequences. A metaphysics or an ethics is a hidden theory of literature. Beckett understood this linguistic situation at the very beginning of his life as a writer. From that beginning he was aware of the complacencies of the monist theory, i.e., the theory of the image as the mirror of another world or the emblem of another meaning. Descartes's dualities are forced into Manichaeism's uncompromising dualism. Then the writer reaches a point which is not the "rock" that Descartes is looking for to stand upon and belay his language, but a point of self-imposed torture.

This interpretation of Beckett's postulates implies a more general question which has faced us from the beginning of this study: What is the relation for Beckett (who obstinately refuses to be taken for a philosopher of human destiny) between literature and any philosophical language?

VI

I shall begin this last analysis by exploring a double feeling that has grown stronger as I have become more familiar with Beckett's work: Each successive book — long or short — stands by itself as part of a work in indefinite progress, in a shy and suspicious independence, with no tendency to establish relations with its neighbors; it seeks to avoid any commitment with the immediate present and its anecdotes; in a word, it is wrapped in an atmosphere of lofty, intransigent, unyielding atemporality.

I do not mean that Beckett's works, as they are, would have been possible at any other time, in any place of this universe, or without Proust, Joyce, Kafka — without three centuries of idealistic philosophies, etc. I mean that any of Beckett's works makes us aware that a literary language can exist with an atemporal dimension of a sort that gives to languages their indefinite powers of resurrection.

Then this act of independence from history in its becoming is strengthened by a more secret certitude — a will of absolute rupture with the literary past of Western literatures and, especially, with the combination of ethics and aesthetics that inspires the present writers of our culture. Beckett has never expressed such a feeling either for himself or in his works. But, as is well known, on one unique occasion and in three "interviews," he recognized the presence of such a break in the paintings of Bram Van Velde, "the first artist whose hands have not been tied by the certitude that expression is an impossible act," and "the first to admit that to be an artist is to fail, as no other dare fail, that failure is his world and the shrinking from it desertion, art and craft, goodhousekeeping, living."

One might say: Is this not pure arrogance? Perhaps. But reading Beckett again and again, one gets the feeling that this double act of atemporal claim and total rupture is an inevitable decision for one who was born after the Bible, Saint Augustine, the *Divine Comedy*, Descartes, Newton and *Ulysses*....

Is it a Beckettian paradox or a more general human statement? The continuity of philosophical assessments from *Whoroscope* to *not I* — the recurrence of words which belong normally to the abstract vocabulary of philosophy — the constant reference to universal statements on human destiny and cosmic involvements, are sufficient evidences of the presence of philosophy, with its problems and theories, in Beckett's work; and David Hesla is amply justified in *The Shape of Chaos* when he confronts our author with the greatest philosophers, from the pre-Socratics to Heidegger and Sartre.

On the other hand, it is impossible not to take seriously Beckett's declaration of philosophical non-commitment. He is absolutely sincere when he says, "I am not a philosopher — philosophers cannot see the actual mess we are facing every day." May I suggest the following interpretation of a rather confusing situation? First, by philosophers Beckett means — and this is simply obvious — those who use the philosophical language and pretend that a proposition made in accordance with the rules of that language is capable of being false or true. Beckett does not condemn the practice of such linguistic conduct — he merely denies its claim to be true or otherwise. This could explain, along with his permanent use of philosophical formulas, his almost constant reference to the Sceptic modes of judgment (a negation counteracted immediately by an affirmation — perhaps, maybe, etc.). Then, and possibly even more important, and very often unnoticed, there is this consequence: Beckett condemns any form of literature which even implicitly accepts the possibility of a truth-language. This condemnation involves the whole tradition of Western languages which have developed within the Greco-Latino-Christian threads of our cultural warp. And so we are once again brought face to face with the problem of allegorical language.

* * *

The traditional relation between philosophy and literature is, by way of allegory, in a sort of circle or shuttle, which leads from concrete language to abstract language and the reverse, when words shuttle between their proper and their figurative meanings. The best example of that allegorical genre is to be found in Plato's use of myths in his *Dialogues;* and Platonic myths have laid the foundations and given rules for all posterior forms of Western literatures and for the cooperation between the philosopher and the writer.

In his *Dialogues,* Plato passes from dialectic and abstract discussions to mythological narrations with a general pedagogical purpose. The myth provides a pause in the dialectic process — a time for relaxation while looking at images (like the prisoner in the cavern) or for listening to stories. But it remains connected with philosophy and is intended to help those minds that cannot stay very long at an abstract level. Moreover, the myth has two essential functions as it interferes with dialectic (in its Platonic sense): 1) it plays the role of *illustration* (the most frequent aspect of allegory); and 2) it serves as a substitute, provisory or final, when the abstract process fails to reach the truth.

All our Western literatures fall within these two functions, with all their possible degrees and nuances and the different talents of their authors (literary talent being at its best in writing allegory which does not seem to be allegory or which can never be totally transposed into an abstract language; i.e., when allegory is the despair of the critics or an occasion for unending commentaries! See, for example, how Hamlet or Prometheus is manna for the critics and teachers!)

It suffices to read Beckett's first two attempts at literary criticism (his *Dante* ... and his *Proust*) to realize that, from the beginning of his career as a writer, Beckett has been deeply aware of this problem of allegory, that it is even for him the basic problem of language, when linguistic signs are more than instruments of communication at the disposal of physiological and psychological practices. This explains Beckett's interest in Vico's historical theory of language and his accusations (cited earlier) against Baudelaire and his "intellectual symbolism." It is not by pure chance that on the same page (see *Proust,* p. 60) Beckett mentions Dante: "Here allegory fails as it must always fail in the hands of a poet. Spenser's allegory collapses after a few cantos. Dante, because he was an artist and not a minor prophet, could not prevent his allegory from becoming heated and electrified into *anagogy*" (italics mine). Then, coming back to Proust, he writes: "The symbolism of Baudelaire has become the *auto-symbolism* [Beckett's italics] of Proust."

In the early '30s, Beckett is seeking an exit from the literary tradition, and he sees in Proust the example of a similar effort under the influence of a Narrator's literary *Cogito*. Then his own experience with poetry and novel persuades him that the Proustian solution is not a definite answer, since (behind the proliferation of his dualism) Proust has to concede the fundamental duality of language itself — its two sides, universal and particular, abstract and concrete, philosophy and narration, so that *A la recherche du temps perdu* is in fact the alternance of two sides of Being (sign and reality), and *Le Temps Retrouvé* their possible juxtaposition in a book.

Beckett rejects this compromise between a language of truth and a language of reality (i.e., between truth and reality); for, in spite of Proust's intent, his work is still a gigantic allegory on Time. Thus Beckett does not make things easy for himself. Scepticism is no solution, for it fails to transcend the duality true-untrue and brings together all false propositions under the true proposition of their falsity! For the same reason, pretension to a pure language of reality is another self-deception. Here we can see the actual divergence of Beckett from the New Novelists, all of whom, in their aesthetic varieties and with their separate talents, try to escape from the *philosophical mortgage* of any Western language and to uproot their images from metaphysics as they systematically shun the bad company of abstract words. But for a particular reason they cannot divest their words of their allegorical wrappings: One can refer to reality without moral overtones, but not without identification of reality and truth or without the implication that the only *true* language is the concrete-descriptive language.

Moreover, the New Novelists have not broken away directly, or even indirectly, from the "interior monologue." They hope to go beyond the duality "language-reality," proclaiming that reality *is* language as interior monologue. They reduce the substance of the romanesque hero and destroy the coherence of the narrative. But they still remain within the Platonic alternance of "dialectics-myth"; for suppression of all references to dialectics and its vocabulary and processes affords no assurance that the myth as a collection of images can stand by itself and recreate the moment of creation: *fiat personna!*

Beckett has put himself and his friend Bram Van Velde in a radical impasse — not a faked one. At the end of his third "interview," he warns us not to yield to an "acceptable conclusion" by changing this "fidelity to failure" into an "expressive act." And he concludes: "I know that my inability to do so places myself, and perhaps an innocent, in what I think is still called an unenviable situation, familiar to psychiatrists." To substitute images for ideas, to say that images are more than metaphors, to try to separate the proper meaning of a word from all its possible figurative transpositions — all that is still in the nature of trickery to deny literature her philosophical source. But such a disavowal does not free the writer from the necessity of Platonic choices. And so comes Beckett's decision to put things at their worst: to continue to use philosophical language (vocabulary and patterns), since this is inevitable, but at the same time to deny its claim of conferring any truth-value upon its affirmations or negations. This surgical severance entails an important consequence: the relation between dialectical language and myth ceases to be allegorical, since allegory implies that the ideas it clothes in metaphor are true or susceptible to the truth-test.

I concede the possibility of another solution which I call the Zola-solution (as presented in *Le roman expérimental*), in terms of which a novel (in line with Claude Bernard's experimental methodology) would be *the verification of an hypothesis*. The relation between dialectics and myth would be changed into that between hypothesis and experience. Zola himself, as is well known, was never able to follow that model. Moreover, if it were capable of use it would be the doom of literary language *per se*. Again, for Beckett, it would provide an easy way out — the novelist assuming the role of the man of science, but retaining the novel's traditional appearance.

With those difficulties in mind it should be possible to understand the ultimate *raison d'être* of Descartes, Cartesian tools, and their connection with Manichaeist principles in Beckett's works. First, the development of these works, from *Whoroscope* to such texts as *Lessness, The Lost Ones,* etc., is a process of more and more efficient control of the act of division actualized by the *Cogito*. In terms of the history of philosophy one would say that Beckett's thought tends toward absolute phenomenalist idealism and has to face the solipsist paradox. In terms of literary process, the first *Cogito*, that of *Murphy*, is an act by which the mind separates itself from the material world and, more directly, from its own body. This act of reflection is supported by Cartesian theories, such as those of relative movement, the biology of "animal-spirits," transubstantiation, and rational proofs of the existence of God.

Then, with *Watt,* the *Cogito* puts to the test its logico-mechanical linguistic power and its own nature as a pure desire, i.e., in comings and goings within a waiting room, between absence and presence. Thereafter, with the French period of *Mercier et Camier* and the trilogy, a freed *Cogito* comes to power: all those dualisms swarming in the Cartesian basket are put under the control of the *Cogito,* which in itself is no longer the separation of "I" and the world — of mind and reality — but pure experience of separation, dualities as states of a permanent "dualizing" Ego (if I may be permitted such a phrase), which is beyond sensations, at the very center of a verbal universe.

At the same time, perhaps to avoid changing an absolute subjectivity into a new form of dogmatism, Beckett takes the *Cogito* back to its origin, to the radicalism of Manichaeism as simultaneously Cosmology and Psychology, to the absolute Duality of Light and Darknes, with its derivatives, clarity and obscurity, distinction and confusion, day and night, white and black, white and grey, etc.

But Beckett's originality does not consist only in this transposition of modern idealism into old Manichaean vision. It is, rather, a sort of experiment *in vivo*. Let us admit the existence of a *Cogito* in the purity of its reflective act. Then, let us admit that Being is a mixture of Light and Darkness, with the possibility of a separation and the usual conflicts. Let us set that *Cogito* in the midst of the real confusion and that potential division. And let us see what happens, but with one important warning: Let us never accept any form of escapism, of compromise, or of unity. For example, the "I" of *L'Innommable,* when he discovers that all his problems are linguistic (ways of saying, speaking, etc.), is on the verge of a new evasion; he is beginning to play the burlesque tragedy of words. Beckett is perfectly conscious of that risk. He merely emerges from it at the last second with a feeble, meek, final reaction: "I can't go on, I'll go on." This, in fact, is ultimately to confess that the words may not be the last words.

Manichaean realism forces the *Cogito* to non-complacent behavior. There are, after all, more serious matters for human beings than brooding indefinitely within a hot cupboard with faked glimpses through plate glass! Beckett was saved from the *Cogito* and its inevitable consequences, the interior monologue and the soliloquy (see, in the present volume book, the excellent analysis by Ruby Cohn of certain important aspects of this rhetoric) by a return to the source of dualism, which was (and not by pure chance) a great but unsuccessful meeting between Eastern and Western thought. Is not this return remarkably typical of Beckett — his taking us back to the greatest failure of our culture — or, more precisely, his confronting this fellow Descartes, one of the great men responsible for our present civilization, with the cosmic confusion of dualities? Seigneur du Perron, no more jokes, no more foolish games at the mirror! With a little luck, days and nights will go on succeeding each other — as will those alternances of *alba* and *serena* which are the only possible literary genres — before and after the era of the mess.

Such is finally the justification of my hypothesis. All Beckettian characters or impersonations come from Descartes. They have Descartes's personality — all those little Descartes waiting for their starless night, but craving daylight — those jokers unable to follow Belacqua's wise, immobile squatting! Cartesian method implies that the *Cogito* can be responsible for its own light — it would call merely for good relations between the Will and the Understanding. It suffices to rid oneself of infantile prejudices and not allow one's judgment to be hurried. Internal intellectual clarity is within one's reach, for (as we are told in the first paragraph of the *Discours de la méthode*) the power of distinguishing between true and false, distinct and confused, "what is called good sense or Reason is by nature equal in all men." This famous Cartesian statement gives a universal dimension to Beckett's characters and to his choice of Descartes as a father for them all.

René Descartes, Murphy, Molloy, Moran, Malone, *et al.* are merely human beings like the rest of us. But if Beckett decides to take Descartes and his *Cogito* as the universal man and the model for his books, he still does not let himself be seduced by the prevailing optimism of the *Cogito,* which pretends to be a master of light and truth, to become master of the whole world. No! Manichaean radical principle helps shatter this pretence of the human mind. Clarity, obscurity, and confusion are facts, "given." They are not mere ways of speaking, metaphors qualifying intellectual products or modes of action, allegories. They are real — physically real, which means that

Beckett counteracts the idealistic *Cogito* by a strict realism of light and darkness. Here a philosopher would shrug his shoulders and observe contemptuously: "This is self-contradiction; one cannot put together in the same doctrine an idealistic methodology and a dualistic realism."

I imagine that Beckett could answer: First, this self-contradiction is not mine; if one looks at Descartes's works, one finds it. Second, I am ready to accept that burden of self-contradiction. To tell the truth, I arranged it on purpose. In fact, all of Beckett's heroes struggle in the midst of what the Manichaeans call the "mixture"; and they experience there all forms of confusion — physical, psychological, logical, and moral.

To sum up, I do not think that Beckett is a disappointed Cartesian. On the contrary, I have tried to demonstrate that Beckett's work depends upon the *Cogito* for unique mental guidance. But I suppose that, very early in his literary research, Beckett recognized that modern dualism should be confronted by its source; and this brought Manichaeism and Christianity once more face to face. I leave to others the problem of exploring that alley in Beckett's world. For the present I merely add this remark: The Manichaeist reference is used to give Beckett's language the anagogical quality that Dante required for any literary language and that Beckett mentions in *Proust*. Let us quote Dante's definition of it as related to the distinctions among the *literal, allegorical, moral* and *analogical* senses (*Convivio*, II.i): "The fourth sense is called anagogic, that is above the senses; and this occurs when a writing is spiritually expounded." Thus the literal sense itself becomes an "imitation of higher matters which belongs to the eternal glory."

In Beckett's perspective, anagogy cannot afford that vertical transposition. At this very point, Manichaeism intrudes to prohibit this escape upward and to keep us within a horizontal duality. In Dante's vision, allegory must be spiritually oriented to attain its full meaning. But Beckett not only shifts from Christian spirituality to cosmic and physical Manichaeism; he even confers on the adventures of the *Cogito* an anagogical power in changing a psychological and moral experience into a physical one. The reverse movement, as suggested in *Watt*, is the only justified anagogy! (See the text beginning with the proposition: "This I am happy to inform you is the reversed metamorphosis.

The Laurel into Daphne. The old thing where it was, back again...." [p. 44].)

Such is Beckett's answer to the Platonic use of myth, and his solution to the duality of "literal" and "allegorical" when the time of genuine mythologies has been irrevocably passed by. But, as I must repeat one last time, Beckett is not a philosopher — i.e., a man who believes in the possibility of any philosophical language. So this marriage of Cartesianism and Manichaeism is not a theoretical statement. If it were, it would mean that Beckett had surreptitiously decided to stay within the range of a truth-language, and his self-contradictory option would be not theoretically, but actively, self-destructive. Thus, there should be another linguistic level where Descartes can finally meet Belacqua.

I hesitate to say that this desired linguistic level is aesthetic, because of the semantic import of that adjective, which could suggest the possibility of a solution through aesthetic ethics like Schopenhauer's. It would be more correct, though still ambiguous, to call it a *moral aesthetics*. One might even say that Beckett had decided to go to a purely linguistic level with no reference to external reality, physical or spiritual. But there are different ways to enter the universe of language. I propose, then, the idea that Beckett's literary world obeys the laws of an *aesthetics of dramatic convenience*. Merely for the sake of reference, let us cite the text which suggested to me this interpretation. In *Film*, Beckett's scenario begins with the Berkeleyan emblem: *esse est percipi*. It is followed by a *Cogito* decision: "All extraneous perceptions suppressed, animal, human, divine, self-perception maintains in being." And this consequence: "Search of non-being in flight from extraneous perception breaking down in inescapability of self-perception." Beckett recognizes the inevitability of the *Cogito* in the Manichaean situation: I try to fly from external light (i.e., from Being as mixture of light and darkness); then I must confess that I cannot escape from the internal light of my consciousness as self-perception (the *Cogito* shows that extraneous perception is still a special domain of self-perception).

Does this mean that Beckett cannot go further than the *Cogito*'s after-effects? Is the above statement an Existentialist-Kafkaean-Sartrean avatar of the *Cogito*? That might be, but for the fact that it was followed by this apparently innocuous note: "No truth value attached to above, regarded as of merely *structural and dramatic convenience*" (italics mine). This phrase should be read in connection with what has been said above on the Beckettian rejection of any form of truth-language. In other words, Beckett warns us that here — and is it not true for all his works? — he is putting his own language outside the logic of truth-values. Such is my reason for proposing the phrase *structural aesthetics of dramatic convenience* for that linguistic operation.

First, let us consider the two adjectives (*structural* and *dramatic*) that qualify the word *convenience* in Beckett's remark. "Structural" designates the act of the *Cogito* — a movement of separation interpreted as a "search of non-being." This basic form is incarnated in objective structures that delineate relations between the protagonist and the eye-camera: a street along a wall, a staircase, a room with varied objects and animals. In more general terms, a structure affords the prerequisites for the dynamics of a narration, of a film, or of any artistic expression. Thus "structural" is implied in "dramatic," and Beckett speaks of the Berkeleyan Latin principle as a dramatic structure or, more specifically, as a *structuring dramatization*.

What does "dramatization" mean? It does not refer to the usual contraries — dramatic against tragic, or dramatic against comic. Beckett opposes dramatic to philosophical, or dramatic language to philosophical language — more generally, artistic statements on behavior to truth-statements on behavior. And, not to put too great a semantic burden on Beckett's shoulders, we can remain at the pure negation of the truth-language — as the pure recognition of a use of language that is not simple communication and designation of external reality.

Now, at my own risk, and with Beckett's words in mind, I can try to go a little further along that road, with this hypothesis: "*Dramatic*" *suggests an operation that changes a truth-language into a literary one*. This operation does not consist of an act of narration; i.e., it is not the production of a group of narrative sentences.[12] It is, rather, a reference to a fictive reality, so that the truth-criterion is no longer pertinent. I realize that this concept of "fictive reality" calls for a very delicate elaboration. For my present purpose it is

---

[12] Recent important studies on "narration" seem to imply an identification of literature with narration. If this point of view may be seen as freed from the idealist postulates, it is still confined within the duality of external-internal realities.

enough to see clearly its negative meaning: literature is not philosophy; but it is also not narration — it is *the dramatization of linguistic signs*.

None of Beckett's language is a variety of narrative; excluding the rare bits of criticism, it is rather (in short stories, novels, and plays) an expression of dramatized language, i.e., the narration or staging of things that happen to imaginary people. Thus the question "Is it true?" is meaningless. The varied efforts of Balzac, Flaubert, Zola, Proust, Joyce to make the novel truer than history itself are vain pretensions. The Beckettian dramatization deals with real concerns — life and death, suffering and love, struggle and failure, ignorance and anguish, compulsive restlessness, quieting silences, etc. But Beckett avoids the traditional trap — that temptation to restore the truth-criterion at a higher level, thanks to an anagogical leap. Beckett has made himself a permanent and willing prisoner of Manichaeism — a prisoner who does not seek and would not accept any sort of probation or parole.

This pride — the pride of a prisoner and of an artist who refuse to be paroled — explains the word *convenience*. It is proper to give it its full semantic charge. Let us follow Webster's definitions: agreement, harmony, congruence, aptitude, fitness for performing some action, advantageous condition, state or circumstances, opportunity, freedom from difficulty or discomfort, ease, efficiency (e.g., a chair arranged for one's own convenience, something that provides comfort, or suited to material wants, toilet, etc.).

Do not all these meanings apply to the business of literature? For Beckett "convenience" has a direct and negative significance which is refusal to compromise with the Aristotelian logic of truth, and with that *Logique de Port-Royal* Cartesian theory of the "natural order of thought," which is supposed to give French phrases their clarity, truth and beauty. One understands then the Beckettian plays of "yeses" and "nos," the shuttle of affirmative and negative propositions, and (to borrow Pascal's definition of dialectic) the "continuous reversal of the pro and the con," all of them dualities radicalized by the Manichaeist intransigence.

Let us make no mistake: with this word *convenience* Beckett is not opening a hidden door on the literary stages, or drawing a trompe-l'œil window in his closed room. He is not seeking to escape from literary dogmatism only to fall into an aesthetic pragmatism and thus restore truth under the guise of "convenience" with a final confession that "my convenience is your truth, and your convenience is my success."

Here the logician could burst into a sardonic laugh. This convenience is worse than the Epimenidian paradox,[13] where one pretends to tell the truth in confessing one's lies, and to change the *Cogito* "I fail, therefore I am" into "I lie, therefore I tell the truth." Is Beckett, then, not basing an aesthetics of convenience upon the truth of Manichaeism? The answer is no! Manichaean dualities are also conveniences.

Beckett, in his subtle, allusive, but definite way, warns us that, in this middle of the twentieth century after Christ, we are back with the Greek sophisms after two thousand years of metaphysical literatures' pretending to have overcome them. It is not by chance that Bergson, in his *Essai sur les données immédiates de la conscience* (1889) announced triumphantly that the stream of consciousness had carried along in its inescapable dynamism the wrecks of the Eleatic Zeno's paradoxes — or that Valéry, from the height of his cemetery, apostrophized a "cruel Zeno."

But Beckett's conveniences have nothing in common with the bright and sonorous Mediterranean landscape, or with the Bergsonian symbolism of fast currents. He invites us to accept with open eyes this situation: The Manichaean dualities are not universal-truth principles; they are, rather, day after day and night after night, repetitive experiences of light and darkness. Such is the recurrent lesson of the *Cogito*. It is not a matter of truth, but of reality, the only reality we can grasp — not an external reality, not an internal and spiritual reality, not a reality outside language, but a reality which is another word for language, as language is another word for reality, because words refer to words, meanings to meanings, because "I" is a pronoun that solicits the company of the adjective "real," and longs for a proper name, but is fatally divided between two nicknames: i.e. Mercier and Camier, Molloy and Moran, Macnam and Worm, Gogo and Didi, Bem and Bon, Pim and Pin, etc.

* * *

---

[13] See the penetrating study of this question in Raymond Federman's article, "The Epimenid Paradox," in the present book.

One last word or question: After all those long discussions about Beckett's language and its values, would it not be fair to confront our conclusion on Beckett's options with our own critical language and ask: What is the status of this language that we have used, to discuss Beckett? It would be too easy to follow the logicians and say: "It is a metalanguage." This concept does not answer the crucial question: Do I pretend to enunciate truth-statements on a language that denies such a possibility? I am ready to confess my embarrassment here and to admit (borrowing Beckett's word) that the critic is in an even more "unenviable" position than the artist or the poet. Perhaps, to avoid being too uncomfortable in this impasse, the solution may be to accept the possibility of a criticism of "critical convenience." Then the question "What is the meaning of *convenience*?" could be replaced by the question in reverse, "What is the convenience of *meaning*?" — with the final and clear understanding that any duality, Cartesian or Manichaean, develops its indefinite tensions and mixtures within a politics of encirclement!

WARMING UP FOR MY LAST SOLILOQUY

by Ruby Cohn

My title is borrowed from Hamm in *Endgame*. The original French reads: "J'amorce mon dernier soliloque," literally, "I'm biting at my last soliloquy." Soliloquy, to speak alone, or, by stage convention, to speak as *though* alone and unheard. The direction of Beckett's drama is soliloquo-tropic, to coin an ugly word about a beautiful subject. Over a period of twenty-five years his seven staged plays — by which I mean actions with words, performed by actors — have warmed toward a last soliloquy, as though the ideal play would be all soliloquy.

Almost every commentator has noted Beckett's progressive, or perhaps I should say retrogressive, dramatic reduction through the years — of plot, character, movement, and words. I am going to trace some of the verbal structures of that retrogression, soliloquotropically. Hamm may be warming up for his last soliloquy in his freezing shelter, but Beckett teases us with dramatic dialogue into which soliloquy takes bigger and bigger bites. The bite is single and relatively small in *Waiting for Godot*: bites multiply in *Endgame*; and Beckett's most recent play, *Not I*, is all bite, since the one speaker is a Mouth, the one speech a soliloquy.

The play that made Beckett famous, his first play to be released to the public, is of course *Waiting for Godot*, by now a classic. *Waiting for Godot* is at once traditional and new in its dialogue. It is traditional in following Western dramatic custom; Beckett individualizes the speech of his five characters. What is inventive about *Godot* is musichall cross-talk as the basic dialogue of a play so serious that some critics have described it as tragic, though Beckett himself labelled it "tragicomedy" — in English.

Sounding through inventive cross-talk and traditional individuation is *repetition* — Beckett's signature on all his plays. The invented name Godot is the most insidious repetition, usually combined with waiting. Seven times Didi and Gogo say: "We're waiting for Godot," twice "Wait for Godot," once "We are waiting for Godot to come," once each "I'm waiting for Godot," (Gogo) and "I waited for Godot," (Didi) and finally "unless Godot comes." In Didi's conversation with the Boy there are ten references to *Mr.* Godot, and Pozzo deforms the name, when he alludes to the tramps' "appointment with this... Godet... Godot... Godin" and then their "appointment with a Godin... Godet... Godot."

As telling as these repetitions of the word Godot are those of the word "nothing," which may be its synonym. "Nothing" is spoken some thirty times, and it is spoken by each of the play's five characters, usually in innocuous phrases, as opposed to King Lear's prophetic: "Nothing will come of nothing." The "nothing"s of *Godot* seem to culminate in Didi's Act II prophecy: "In an instant all will vanish and we'll be alone once more, in the midst of nothingness!" That of course is the basic action of the play — two men, alone in the midst of nothingness, wait for an improbable Godot.

While they wait, they repeat themselves. Two words that often recur in their speech are "happy" and "pity" — sentiments we come to doubt. In each act Pozzo and Lucky enter, and when *they* speak, they repeat themselves. At the end of each act a Boy arrives to announce that Mr. Godot will come not today but tomorrow, and *he* repeats himself, as in the question: "What am I to tell Mr. Godot, Sir?" All five characters repeat themselves, sometimes with variations, and they also echo one another. Both Didi and Gogo affirm that it's not certain and that there is nothing to be done. Each friend claims: "I don't know." First Gogo, then Didi exclaims angrily: "Hurts! He wants to know if it hurts!" Each friend threatens "I'm going," and each of them suggests: "Let's go." Didi's "Yes, let's go." closes Act I, but Act II ends on the same words spoken by Gogo. Thus, speaker and context confer variety on the several repetitions.

In spite of repetitions, however, *Godot*'s characters speak distinctively. Lucky recites his well-known bravura piece. Pozzo is self-consciously rhetorical in Act I. Godot's messenger speaks mainly in monosyllables — an ironic contrast to the rhetorical tirade of the classical messenger. But Didi and Gogo carry the main burden of the dialogue, and they both speak correct English with a faint Irish flavor. Only occasionally is their idiom individuated, as when Gogo lapses into baby-talk at two junctures, or Didi toward the end of the play grows reflective and Latinate: "All I know is that the hours are long, under these conditions, and constrain us to beguile them with proceedings which — how shall I say — which at first sight seem reasonable, until they become a habit."

But despite such individuation, the élan of performance of *Waiting for Godot* depends upon the rhythmic resemblance, *the duet quality*, of the Didi-Gogo exchanges. Beckett has grounded his bleak human landscape on the cross-talk of Didi and Gogo, so that the risk and intimacy of performance involve us in the situation of the friends. The music-hall scholar, MacQueen Pope, wrote: "The difference between 'work' and 'play' was one of the great distinctions between the music-hall and the theater. The music-hall performer was identical with his act."[1] And the act was often a crosstalk duologue. The duologues of Didi and Gogo are the base dialogue of *Godot*: in a series of turns, their play becomes self-imposed work. Unlike John Osborne's Entertainer or Neil Simon's Sunshine Boys, Didi and Gogo are not professionals; they live their music-hall routines. They are their act more fully than the professional performers described by MacQueen Pope. Very early in the play this pattern is indicated by Didi's plea to Gogo: "Come on, Gogo, return the ball, can't you, once in a way?" Music-hall cross-talk is built on returning the ball. As is true of many music-hall couples, one member, Didi, is more resourceful, and the other, Gogo, is more dependent. But they address each other as equals; they are not straightman and comic, so that neither steals the few punch-lines. Their speeches are short, their sentences are simple, and the phrases are carefully cadenced, as in the well-known early exchange about Godot:

> GOGO: Don't let's do anything. It's safer.
> DIDI: Let's wait and see what he says.
> GOGO: Who?
> DIDI: Godot.
> GOGO: Good idea.
> DIDI: Let's wait till we know exactly how we stand.
> GOGO: On the other hand it might be better to strike the iron before it freezes.
> DIDI: I'm curious to hear what he has to offer. Then we'll take it or leave it.

> GOGO: What exactly did we ask him for?
> DIDI: Were you not there?
> GOGO: I can't have been listening.
> DIDI: Oh... Nothing very definite.
> GOGO: A kind of prayer.
> DIDI: Precisely.
> GOGO: A vague supplication.
> DIDI: Exactly.
> GOGO: And what did he reply?

The duologue continues, and I'll quote a little more, but notice that up to this point Gogo is indefinite about Godot. Then the compelling music-hall rhythm seems to create its own Godot, below or above or beyond the memories of Didi and Gogo.

> GOGO: And what did he reply?
> DIDI: That he'd see.
> GOGO: That he couldn't promise anything.
> DIDI: That he'd have to think it over.
> GOGO: In the quiet of his home.
> DIDI: Consult his family.
> GOGO: His friends.
> DIDI: His agents.
> GOGO: His correspondents.
> DIDI: His books.
> GOGO: His bank account.
> DIDI: Before taking a decision.
> GOGO: It's the normal thing.
> DIDI: Is it not?
> GOGO: I think it is.
> DIDI: I think so too.
> *Silence.*

There is no punch-line to this exchange, but there are a few buried jokes which announce the big sad unstated joke — their joint cliché portrait of a Godot whom they can hardly recall. In the repartee Didi affirms "Precisely" for "*A kind* of prayer," and "Exactly" for "*A vague* supplication." At the end of the exchange comes silence, announcing the end of this music-hall number, and concretizing the nothingness that continuously threatens the pair.

The immediacy of the stage situation feeds the music-hall turns of Didi and Gogo, but the diet is thin by Act II, and their invention grows so self-conscious as to become a second-degree music-hall, a kind of meta-music-hall about carrying on the act. Before they are rescued by Pozzo and Lucky, the tired old performers deliver a few elegiac stanzas which are quite foreign to the comic spirit of music-hall, and which contain much of the play's haunting imagery — voices, wings, leaves, whisper, rustle, murmur, feathers, ashes. These words have an onomatopoetic quality, suggesting how voices die like leaves. After this comes a "long silence" then

    DIDI: Say something!
    GOGO: I'm trying.

and another "long silence."

Dampened but not down, the couple consciously decides to start again, to think, to utter contradictions, to pose questions, to give thanks for mercies. We have already heard them in these simple forms of rhetoric, but now we are made aware of the *artifice* of such rhetoric. Then they hit upon the device of playing at Pozzo and Lucky, which means that one curses the other, who thinks and dances. They tire of this, then unite against an invisible enemy; they offer each other excuses, call each other angry names, embrace one another, engage in physical exercises. Finally, however, this laborious second-degree music-hall winds down to zero, and, in despair, Gogo calls on God — God, not Godot — whereupon help arrives in the re-entrance of Pozzo and Lucky.

Pozzo and Lucky might be viewed as another music-hall act, but there is no cross-talk between them. Rather, the pair is a circus avatar of Hegel's Master-Slave metaphor. Pozzo's dialogue is blatant with mastership, since its main mode is command to Lucky, but he also takes a superior tone with the two friends, whose conversation he seems to need as badly as they need his. We are far from soliloquy.

In Act I Pozzo delivers an elocution piece on the arrival of night, and in Act II he explodes feelingly. The change is striking. In Act I Pozzo is all artifice and self-consciousness. To answer the simplest question — why Lucky doesn't put down his bags — he phrases five different replies with the same meaning. He has to be asked to sit down, complimented on his delivery. He can do nothing with ease or grace, so intent is he upon the impression he is making. By Act II, however, he has lost self-consciousness along with his sight, and when he is suddenly furious at Didi's question about the duration of Lucky's dumbness, he utters the deepest lines of the play. His Act I performance is studied: "But behind this veil of gentleness and peace night is charging and will burst upon us (*Snaps his fingers*) pop! like that! (*His inspiration leaves him*) just when we least expect it. (*Silence. Gloomily.*) That's how it is on this bitch of an earth." But Pozzo's Act II summation flows with feeling: "They give birth astride of a grave, the light gleams an instant, then it's night once more." The two sentences are similar in meaning, but the second alone is rending.

Godot may thus be seen as a series of counter-soliloquies. I have already dwelt upon the music-hall cross-talk and the meta-music-hall echoes. Pozzo's recitation is a solo number, which is also a staple of music-hall. So is Lucky's celebrated aria. Solo numbers but not soliloquies; Pozzo and Lucky have onstage audiences for whom they consciously perform.

Almost every serious critic has made some sense of Lucky's surface nonsense, and this is as it should be. The play's point about words is not that they mean nothing — nothing is silent — but that meaning shifts, breaks, and repeats. So Lucky, whose words are the shards of the Western cultural tradition. The unfinished speech ends on the word "unfinished." This energetic account of entropic man is charged with archaisms and neologisms, learned clichés and obscenities, catalogues and sound play. "Style is the man," wrote Buffon, but Lucky's style dehumanizes man through mechanized mockery of his rational and progressive accomplishments.

Godot's music-hall cross-talk is varied by two solos conveying different facets of Beckett's vision — Lucky's broken record of Western civilization, Pozzo's elocution-piece about the coming of night. To these may be added Didi's round song about endless repetitive cruelties. But Gogo never manages a solo, for Didi squelches his attempts to tell a joke, a dream, or a nightmare.

Only at the end of the play, while Gogo is asleep, does Beckett offer us the play's single soliloquy, by Didi. It breaks into five parts: 1) Didi summarizes the play's events and wonders whether they have actually happened. 2) Watching Gogo doze off, he predicts what his friend will remember. 3) Echoing the keywords of Pozzo's outburst — astride, grave, birth — he modifies their picture of human life: "Astride of a grave and a difficult birth. Down in the hole, lingeringly, the grave-digger puts on the forceps. We have time to grow old. The air is full of our cries. (*He listens.*) But habit is a great deadener." "Lingeringly" is the length of a life: the time to age and suffer and grow hardened to suffering. Didi's listening personalizes these moving lines about human destiny. 4) Looking at the sleeping Gogo, Didi conceives of himself as a sleeping figure in someone else's vision. 5) Didi cries out: "I can't go on!" but then retracts to "What have I said?" When the Boy arrives, Didi does go on — "Off we go again." — waiting for Godot. In traditional manner, Didi's soliloquy has exposed his inmost fears and doubts.

Climactic, Didi's soliloquy is unique in *Godot*. *Endgame*, completed eight years after *Godot*, allots more playing time to soliloquy. For *Endgame*, unlike *Godot*, is grounded on dramatic tradition, and most especially French classical dramatic tradition. Obviously, even blatantly, *Endgame* obeys the three classical unities: There is only one place of action, and indeed the only remaining action in the world seems to be played in the stage shelter. The time of play not only falls within 24 hours; it equals the actual playing time in the theater, though this is implied rather than stated. Above all, unity of action presents a single plot with only two peripeteias: 1) Hamm announces that "Our revels now are ended." and indeed they do end for Nagg and Nell make no further appearances, and Clov prepares to "wind up." 2) But through the window Clov says he sees a small boy. However, the curtain falls before the boy's arrival or Clov's departure. The asymptotic action is scarcely interrupted by the peripeteias.

The dialogue of *Godot* is rhythmed as music-hall routines, with silences separating the turns. *Endgame* also abounds in duologues, but it departs much more often from such duologues, reflecting the rhetoric of formal drama. Hamm specifically refers to the dialogue, an underplot, an aside, a soliloquy. Clov, the only one of the four characters who can ambulate, makes 15 exits from the stage, preceding the 15th with the announcement: "This is what we call making an exit."

Classical playwrights were preoccupied with probability, and within its entropic context *Endgame* coheres quite probably. But *Endgame* diverges from the classical requisite of decorum, which rests upon genre, for the genre of *Endgame* is problematical. Nagg as foolish old man and Clov as crafty servant belong to the tradition of Latin comedy, based on types. But Hamm, unmistakably tragic, is the most traditional hero in all Beckett's drama. Like the heroes of classical, Elizabethan, and French tragedy, Hamm suffers deeply and learns from his suffering, which the Greeks summarized as pathos-mathos. No one is more aware than Hamm of his own tragic potential: "Can there be misery," he yawns early in the play, "loftier than mine?" Lofty misery distinguishes the traditional tragic hero, and his eloquent suffering commands center stage. So Hamm demands to be "right in the center." Not unexpectedly, therefore, Hamm's stage speech employs certain forms associated with classical tragedy, notably the tirade, which we may define as a long speech.

In classical drama *le récit*, a report, is a favorite form of tirade, particularly the messenger's account of offstage catastrophe. Though Hamm is hero and not messenger, his four non-soliloquy tirades are forms of *récit*: he imagines a reasonable being arriving on earth; he prophesies Clov's fate in "infinite emptiness"; he recalls the madman and engraver who saw the earth's plenty as ashes; above all he narrates his story, which he also calls his chronicle. And that narration is marked by hesitation, correction, self-criticism, and final breakdown so that he cannot continue his story even while he worries: "I'll soon have finished this story." It is in quest of other characters — there are only two — that Hamm embarks on prayer, ending the chronicle-tirade.

Dramatic soliloquy might be considered a special kind of tirade, in which the words are spoken as if for oneself alone. Of all dialogue conventions, the soliloquy is the most obviously artificial; an actor plays a character who externalizes his inmost thoughts as though no one can hear them, in a theater full of auditors. Beckett's Hamm announces the artifice of his three soliloquies with the wrenched and striking phrase: "Me to play."

Hamm's first soliloquy establishes him as the wreck of a tragic hero: he refers to the loftiness of his misery, his fullness turned to emptiness, the splendor of his dreams, and the actuality of his fatigue. At the end of that first soliloquy Hamm declares: "It's time it ended and yet I hesitate to — *he yawns* — to end." Hamm hesitates as the tragic hero Hamlet delays, but the tragic flaw is not quite the same. *Endgame*'s ethic demands that Hamm exercise his heroism by annihilating life so as to spare its suffering. When Hamm hesitates, suffering takes its course.

Near the end of *Endgame* Hamm erupts into his second and longest soliloquy. Beginning with self-blame, he rails angrily at those who wished to enjoy life on earth. He reviews his own theater actions —

narrating a story, trying to move his chair, posing questions, prophesying the end, calling on father and son, peopling his fantasies, recalling the Eleatic paradox — "all life long you wait for that to mount up to a life." He opens his mouth to continue but renounces. He will wait no longer for his life to mount up to a life. He terminates his lyrical anti-life soliloquy by whistling for Clov.

In their duologue Hamm announces to Clov: "I'm warning up for my last soliloquy." After Clov claims to sight the small boy, Hamm delivers that soliloquy — his third and last — a soliloquy because he is unaware that Clov, dressed for a journey, is listening. Hamm punctuates that speech with gestures; he introduces into it a line from Baudelaire and a fragment of his chronicle. He calls his father and son. When he hears no answer, blind Hamm unfolds his handkerchief and announces silence: "speak no more." Ironically, however, he does speak more. He emerges from his last soliloquy to personify the handkerchief, calling it "Old stancher!" As at the play's beginning, Hamm addresses the object directly: "You... remain." Clov has remained throughout the play to supply dialogue, and *Endgame* ends, not in soliloquy, but in the handkerchief's inability to engage in dialogue.

In spite of the impressive quality of Hamm's tragic tirades, much of the play's dialogue consists of duets — as in *Godot*. I have analyzed the duets of *Godot* as routines of music-hall, punctuated by silence. There are a few such duets in *Endgame* — Nagg-Nell and Hamm-Clov early in the play. In the main, however, the duets of *Endgame* resemble those of traditional drama in that they are motivated by plot; but here the plot focuses on desiring and yet delaying the end. We follow that plot in the exchanges of the servant Clov commanded by an imperious Hamm. Unlike music-hall crosstalk, an exchange between equals, the duets of Hamm and Clov are almost all initiated by the hero Hamm. In the original French version Hamm replies to Clov's question as to what use he is: "A me donner la réplique." Literally, to supply me with repartee, though Beckett's English changes this to

    CLOV: What is there to keep me here?
    HAMM: The dialogue.

Clov's dialogue is mainly repartee, as one might expect of the traditional comic servant. But his often repeated "I'll leave you" is self-initiated, and unlike traditional servants of tragedy or comedy,

Clov twice questions his own obedience: "Do this, do that, and I do it. I never refuse. Why?" And: "There's one thing I'll never understand... Why I always obey you. Can you explain that to me?" Hamm suggests that it might be through compassion, and occasionally — particularly in Clov's manipulation of the toy dog — this seems to be true. Clov tries to describe the dog Hamm desires rather than the stage reality we see, and he designates himself as a dog, even as Hamm does. But the toy dog is silent whereas Clov sustains his repartee, with two noteworthy variants.

Like Hamm, Clov's first speech is soliloquy, but unlike Hamm, he shows no sense of theater. Clov speaks tonelessly, gaze fixed, and he repeats a few words — finished, grain, one, heap — to announce that an action is beginning very close to its end, as in classical tragedy. Only then does he define his role in this ending action — to be punished while he waits for the whistle. Most of his subsequent dialogue is a literal metaphoric answer to Hamm's orders, even his final tirade. Hamm commands that Clov utter "A few words... to ponder... in my heart." But then Hamm shifts the heart to Clov: "Something... from your heart." "A few words... from your heart." The few words expand to a few hundred, and Clov speaks them as he spoke the opening soliloquy, tonelessly, with fixed gaze. But his words are charged with emotional resonance, referring as they do to ideas of friendship, beauty, order, mercy, nature. Then Clov turns against words that have so obliquely related and related to his life. He describes his departure as though it is actually taking place: "It's easy going. *Pause.* When I fall I'll weep for happiness." Those are Clov's final words from his heart — a world away from the comic servant who arouses laughter by his pratfalls.

Though Beckett's own production of *Endgame* abandoned the red faces of Hamm and Clov as against the white faces of Nagg and Nell, the colors indicate basic opposition: Hamm and Clov are stretching the present, hesitating to end. Nagg and Nell try to stretch the past into the present, and for all we know, they may reach their ends in their respective ashbins. But as Hamm and Clov are sharply individuated on stage, so are Nagg and Nell. Most of Nagg's conversation involves Nell, and as Clov serves Hamm to continue the dialogue, Nell serves Nagg in her single emergence from the ashbin. Except for her reminiscence of Lake Como, she replies to questions by Nagg, in monosyllables. Three times she answers him before understanding his question, then corrects herself in a kind of verbal double-take.

As Hamm dominates Clov on stage, Nagg dominates Nell. Nagg has two tirades of his own, one the *récit* of the Englishman and the tailor, and the other a zestful curse of his son. Hamm prophesies loneliness for his putative son, Clov, and Nagg desires it for his son, Hamm; prophesy and curse reflect the present state of prophet and curser, wishing misery on the next generation.

The four characters of *Endgame* have four factorial or twenty-four possibilities of entering into dialogue, but they never participate together; nor do they in *Godot*. However, three characters often converse in *Godot*, whereas this happens only once in *Endgame* — when the prayer goes unanswered. For the most part both plays work through duologues, with more variety in *Endgame*. Nagg and Nell reminisce together; Nagg and Hamm exchange insults. But the bedrock of the dialogue of *Endgame* is the Hamm-Clov exchanges that trickle through the dwindling world within the shelter. It is against that consequential sequence that Beckett plays the tirades of his male characters, above all the triple artifice of Hamm's soliloquies.

Beckett's own post-*Endgame* plays move toward soliloquy. Krapp is the only character in his play, and like Hamm he apostrophizes objects. Winnie of *Happy Days* chirps away at the solitude that she calls her wilderness, and she tries to persuade herself that Willie hears her, but by Act II even her determined dialogue falters until it is invigorated by Willie on all fours, with his single syllable "Win." In the triangle of *Play* we hear dialogue, but the three urned speakers think they are uttering soliloquies, since each is unaware of the others, and the spotlight is prompter more than auditor. *Come and Go* is a different triangle inscribed in a circle; a Beckettian anomaly; its dialogue is communication, but the communication proves to be a lie. Finally, *Not I,* Beckett's play of 1972, appears to be the last soliloquy toward which his drama has been warming.

Not I has not been published in this country, so that I'll have to try to summarize a play whose power lies entirely outside of events, and in the most intricate verbal texture I have ever heard on the stage. I begin with what we see. Upstage on audience right, eight feet high, hovering in darkness, is a brightly lit human mouth; downstage on audience left, on an invisible four-foot pedestal is a figure entirely cloaked in black djellaba. All the stage words issue from the Mouth, and the Figure makes four gestures at designated points in the Mouth's monologue. But in spite of the omnipresence of the hooded figure, the Mouth does not acknowledge its presence, rambling on as if in soliloquy.

The Mouth's words are heard in a rush, so that the effect is sensual rather than sensible. Only on the page is Beckett's precise phrasing evident, varying between one and 13 syllables, much shorter than a breath, and breath was one of Jessica Tandy's problems in playing the Mouth. At five points in the fifteen-minute rush of words the voice interrupts itself with four identical monosyllables: "who?... what?... no!... she!" The fifth time the voice adds its most emphatic syllable: "SHE!" To each *"vehement refusal to relinquish third person"* the cloaked Figure responds with a slow shrug *"of helpless compassion."* Or, more accurately, the Figure responds four times with diminishing shrugs, and on the fifth refusal of the voice there is no movement. So much for the visual, an exercise in perception.

The audible too demands enormous concentration, and I cannot tell how much narrative thread will sound through a first hearing. But a narrative is present; a Beckettian life filtered through five scenes: 1) a loveless conception and premature birth in a single scene, 2) survival through silently presenting a list in a supermarket, 3) the presence of tears in the palm of the hand while walking in Croker's Acres, 4) silence under questioning in a courtroom, and 5) five times evoked, an April morning eruption of late spring speech for a woman "coming up to seventy." and the effort to deny that the speech is hers until she feels her mouth move. But these narrative facts are barely distinguished from the background of compulsive phrases, repetitive and varied within the repetitions.

This long non-sentence of syntactical daring and subtle cadence is interrupted not five but twenty-two times. As I have mentioned, five of these interruptions reject the first-person pronoun; seven remind the voice of a constant buzzing or omnipresent roar in the invisible skull, to which the Mouth presumably belongs: "what... the buzzing?... yes." Seven other interruptions attempt to impose accuracy on the discourse, designating the character's sex, position —twice, age — twice, tongue — twice; another three interruptions seem to quote a brain's guesses at the reason for sudden speech: "something she had to tell" and two denials "nothing she could tell... nothing she could think." Interruptions thus limn a dialogue within the monologue: the buzzing that is translated into the words pouring out of the visible Mouth and the brain's prompting to pin the words down, including admonitions to acknowledge the words as belonging to an I. We hear neither buzzing nor prompting, but through periodic interruptions both undermine the soliloquy. As does the audience-figure with his four gestures of helpless compassion.

The Mouth frames a quiet life which has occasionally, rarely, burst into winter speech; but nearing the biblical three-score-and-ten, the woman of the discourse suddenly finds herself full of April spring-speech that the stage words have evoked and do evoke, as Beckett's verbs glide imperceptibly toward the present tense: "never still a second... mouth on fire... streams of words... in her ear... practically in her ear... not catching the half... not the quarter... no idea what she's saying... imagine!... no idea what she's saying!... and can't stop... no stopping it" and the voice goes on without stopping.

Just before the last two interruptions in swift succession to announce "buzz" and "she," the dialogue opposes: "the words... the brain" and it is the latter that seems to be the subject of the following phrases: "flickering away like mad... quick grab and on... nothing there... on somewhere else... try somewhere else... all the time something begging... something in her begging... begging it all to stop... unanswered... prayer unanswered... or unheard... too faint... so on... keep on... trying... not know what... what she was trying... what to try... whole body gone... just the mouth." The Mouth does not speak out of two sides of the invisible face, but it does split into a conflict between voice and brain.

The final curtain starts down almost immediately after the fifth denial of the first person, but the Mouth keeps moving, words pouring out, the brain trying to make sense of what the mouth forms: "hit on it in the end... then back... God is love... tender mercies... new every morning... back in the field... April morning... face in the grass... nothing but the larks... pick it up." and *"voice continues behind curtain, unintelligible."*

The conflict finally shifts to us; our incorrigible minds "pick it up," seeking significance in this melody of signifiers. In *Not I* Beckett approaches closest to a single soliloquy; though the word "soliloquy" is not uttered, the Mouth bites metaphorically at soliloquy but is interrupted by a needling mind. A lone Mouth speaks — soliloquy — but its speech is musicalized outward from an egotistical self into wide resonance, forward from a specific past into actual theater presence. The instant that any words spout out of any mouth, they betray the voice that bears them. What they express is "no longer I," not the inescapable unfathomable I.

---

[1] Phyllis Hartnoll, editor, *The Oxford Companion to the Theatre* (3rd edition), p. 666.

SAMUEL BECKETT: THE LIAR'S PARADOX *

by Raymond Federman

MORE and more we have come to recognize that art cancels itself, says Ihab Hassan in a recent essay. The Tinguely machine works to destroy itself. The blank page and the white canvas pretend to deny their existence. Modern music abolishes itself into silence or discordance. Fiction writes itself into non-sense or LESSNESSness. The last few sentences, phrases, verbal disarticulations of Beckett's *Comment c'est* do not tell us HOW IT IS, but rather that the novel is about HOW IT WAS NOT. Beckett has indeed perfected the art of cancellation of art to it ultimate degree. This radical irony is implicit in the century old statement of the Cretan who affirms that all Cretans are liars thus cancelling both the truth and the lie of this perfect rhetorical statement.

* * *

The Unnamable tells us: "I cannot be silent. About myself I need know nothing. Here all is clear. No, all is not clear. But the discourse must go on. So one invents obscurities. Rhetoric." (p. 7)

* * *

The world of Samuel Beckett is full of such paradoxes — deliberate contradictions which negate every possibility of movement,

---

* Some of the material in this essay is rethought and reworked from an earlier essay published in *Samuel Beckett Now* (Edited by Melvin Frieman. Chicago University Press, 1970, pp. 103-117) under the title "Beckettian Paradox: Who Is Telling the Truth?"

knowledge, understanding, and coherence on the part of the creatures that inhabit that world. Yet, the more these creatures are immobilized, dehumanized, the more they find themselves locked into fictional and verbal impasses, the more freedom they seem to gain to extricate themselves. Quite often they counteract the paradox of fiction imposed upon them by a fictional paradox of their own. Quite often they cancel the "hypothetical imperatives" (as Molloy calls them) of their fictitious existence by a clever indicative manipulation of their own. Thus, most statements made by the voice (or the many voices speaking in Beckett's fiction — whether that of the author disguised as an ironic or unreliable narrator,[1] or else that of the narrator-hero, certainly unreliable but seemingly responsible for his own fiction) lead to flagrant contradictions: "Here all is clear. No, all is not clear."

The often quoted closing statement in *Molloy*,[2] spoken by Moran (whose fiction functions both as an affirmation and a negation of Molloy's), is another striking example:

> Then I went back into the house and wrote, It is midnight. The rain is beating on the windows. It was not midnight. It was not raining. (p. 241)

Of course, no one is to argue that whoever makes this statement is free to write: "It is midnight. The rain is beating on the windows," even if, actually, it is not midnight, and it is not raining. The paradoxical effect of this statement is, in fact, cancelled if one recognizes that it is formulated on two different levels of rhetoric. The affirmative part of the statement (in the present tense, it should be emphasized) corresponds to a fiction invented before our eyes by the narrator-hero Moran ("I went back into the house and *wrote*..." he specifies), whereas the negative part of the statement (in the past tense) merely points to a reality which may or may not be true, and therefore does not necessarily relate to what is being written by Moran in "the report" he claims he has been told to write. Fiction, in other words, need not agree with reality, with the truth of an event, par-

---

[1] The expression "unreliable narrator" is used here in the same sense which Wayne C. Booth gives it in *The Rhetoric of Fiction* (Chicago University Press, 1961); see pp. 339-374.

[2] All references to Beckett's work are to the Grove Press editions unless otherwise indicated.

ticularly when it is explicitly presented as subfiction, when it points to itself as being reported second-hand, as being an invention of the characters' imagination. However, since the author never speaks in his own name in this narration, the reader is under the impression that what is stated omnisciently (in the past tense) is the truth. Thus the statement, "It was not midnight. It was not raining," produces the effect of being factual, real, and truthful, even though it may be a fictitious illusion, a lie, and what becomes clearly questionable, clearly unreliable is the sub-fiction written by Moran: "It is midnight. The rain is beating on the windows."

We are confronted here with the specific problems of modalities in the narrative process and its ambiguous relationship with reality and imagination in regard to the various levels on which a narrator can function. Dealing with similar problems in his essay entitled "Réalité et imagination dans *Le Grand Meaulnes* et *Le Voyeur*," [3] Maurice Lecuyer writes of the narrator: "If he describes conditions and actions in the present, whereas in reality he is sitting in front of a sheet of paper, pen in hand, in the process of composing that description, is this not the sign of a non-reality? Described in the past, the scene reveals itself under its true identity: one knows it to be only a representation of a souvenir; described in the present, it does not appear, however, reconstituted or relived, but truly experienced in an interior manner. It is no longer a representation which rises from the memory, but a phantasm born of the imagination." This is apparently the situation in *Molloy*, or for that matter in most of Beckett's fiction. The paradoxical interplay between reality and imagination, between recalled events and invented events results from the fact that there is a confusion, a deliberate confusion between representation (events told in the past tense) and invention (events told in the present tense).

As all good readers of Beckett's fiction know, his creatures have a prodigious talent for forgetting, even their own names, and therefore often substitute a fiction invented on the spot for memories of their past existence. The Unnamable says: "My inability to absord, my genius for forgetting, are more than they reckoned with. Dear incomprehension, it's thanks to you I'll be myself, in the end." (p. 51).

---

[3] Rice University Studies #51 (Spring 1965), p. 9 (my translation of Mr. Lecuyer's French).

Therefore, since fiction (traditionally) is based on remembered experiences and realities (transformed of course by the process of imagination), every statement made by the Beckettian voice is likely to be invented rather than remembered.

When Molloy is forced, by public authority — a policeman who wants to arrest him — to name himself, he cries out with deliberate effrontery:

> And suddenly I remembered my name, Molloy. My name is Molloy, I cried, all of a sudden, now I remember. Nothing compelled me to give this information, but I gave it, hoping to please I suppose. (p. 29)

Molloy is quite obviously inventing a name for himself, making of himself a phantasm of his own imagination rather than giving to himself a nomination which rises from the memory.

Moran's report, similarly, is (or will be) fraudulent — just as Molloy's self nomination is fraudulent — because it is postulated against the background of a narration which purports to pass for reality, but which actually is invented, and therefore unreliable. What creates the paradox here is that this narration (the whole second part of the novel — Moran's oral description of his search for Molloy) opens (in the present tense) with the same statement Moran uses when, at the end of the novel, he begins to write his report:

> It is midnight. The rain is beating on the windows. I am calm. All is sleeping. Nevertheless I get up and go to my desk... My report will be long. Perhaps I shall not finish it. My name is Moran, Jacques... I remember the day I received the order to see about Molloy. It was a Sunday in summer. (p. 125)

Moran then relates (in the past tense) his adventures and misadventures as he SET out in search of Molloy until the day he WENT back into the house to write his report. He gives us only the first two sentences of his report (in the present tense) which, supposedly, will relate what he experienced (in the past) from the moment he received "the order to see about Molloy" to the day he sits down to write his report. But what happened in the course of his narration is that the affirmative statement about the night and the rain beating on the windows (which opened part two of the novel) has passed from one level of fiction to another — from the level of representation or pseudo-reality (remembered events) to the level of invention or sub-fiction (invented events). Consequently, the negative part of the statement that closes the novel ("It was not midnight. It was not raining") is not only in direct contradiction with what Moran has just written and what he told us at the beginning of his narration, but also with the whole second part of the novel. Moreover, by extension, since the second part of the novel is postulated against the background of Molloy's own unreliable fiction, the entire narrative becomes a paradox, a liar's paradox which cancels both its truth and its lie.[4] In other words, Moran cancels his own fiction with his closing statement, just as Molloy kept cancelling his own fiction with his repeated contradictory declarations, for instance when he tell us:

> And when I say I said, etc. all I mean is that I knew confusedly things were so, without knowing exactly what it was all about. And every time I say, I said this, or I said that, or speak of a voice saying, far away inside me, Molloy, and then a fine phrase more or less clear and simple, or find myself compelled to attribute to others intelligible words, or hear my own voice uttering to others more or less articulate sounds, I am merely complying with the convention that demands you either lie or hold your peace. For what really happened was quite different. (pp. 118-119)

Molloy is evidently speaking here of the confusion which exists between actuality (the present) and pseudoreality (the past) created by the conscious writer, the story-teller. It would be preferable indeed for Molloy (and similarly for Moran) not to try to relate what he thinks happened, for as he well knows "what really happened was quite different." But since Molloy, like all the other Beckettian creatures that are given the delusory power to talk for themselves, cannot

---

[4] Some critics have argued that the second part of the novel should have preceded Molloy's fiction, and that Beckett's reversing of the order of the narration is purely gratuitous. If that were so, the paradoxical effect, essential to Beckett's fiction, or for that matter to all fiction, would be destroyed. Edith Kern in her essay, "Moran-Molloy: The Hero as Author," *Perspective* 11 (Autumn 1959), points out, quite correctly, that "a reversal of the order in which the novel's parts are presented reveals, indeed, that the work would lose in artistic appeal what it would gain in clarity through such reorganization. If Moran's account of his adventures were to precede that of Molloy, the reader would be deprived of the element of suspense..." (p. 189).

"hold his peace" and must go on talking, we can assume that what he is telling us is a lie — pure invention. Or as he explains himself: "I speak in the present tense, it is so easy to speak in the present tense, when speaking of the past. It is the mythological present, don't mind it." (p. 34) Consequently, when Molloy says: "I say, I said," speaking of the past in the present, he is obviously inventing a fiction, even though he claims repeatedly "I quote from memory." In fact, earlier in his narrative, Molloy makes it quite clear that his predicament as narrator-hero (narrator/narrated) forces him to deal in paradoxes:

> Not to want to say, not to know what you want to say, not to be able to say what you think you want to say, and never to stop saying, or hardly ever, that is the thing to keep in mind, even in the heat of composition. (p. 36)

The meaning here, of course, is clear in spite of the contradictory aspect of this declaration, or to paraphrase Beckett himself on the creative act of Bram van Velde:[5] The situation is that of him who is helpless, cannot act, in the event cannot *speak (or write)*, since he is obliged to *speak (or write)*. The act is of him who, helpless, unable to act, acts, in the event *speaks (or writes)*, since he is obliged to *speak (or write)* — "that is the thing to keep in mind, even in the heat of composition."

The whole fiction of *The Unnamable* is based on the same helplessness and obligation to speak, to go on speaking ("you must go on, I can't go on, I'll go on" [p. 179]), even if it means inventing, getting more and more caught up in the liar's paradox. Early in the novel The Unnamable states: "Past happiness in any case has clean gone from my memory, assuming it was ever there." Therefore, since he "cannot be silent," he too invents "obscurities. Rhetoric." But The Unnamable, whose "genius for forgetting" is explicitly noted, is much more of a deliberate inventor, much more of a liar than his predecessors. As such he is able to create for himself not only a hypothetical beginning, but he even attributes to himself a memory:

---

[5] I am taking the liberty of substituting the words "speak (or write)" for the word "paint" in the original dialogue with Georges Duthuit on the work of Bram van Velde, but as it has so often been suggested, Beckett may have as well been speaking of his own creative act.

I remember the first sound heard in this place, I have often heard it since. For I am obliged to assign a beginning to my residence here, if only for the sake of clarity. Hell itself, although eternal, dates from the revolt of Lucifer. It is therefore permissible, in the light of this distant analogy, to think of myself as being here forever, but not as having been here forever. This will greatly help me in my relation. Memory notably, which I did not think myself entitled to draw upon, will have its word to say, if necessary. [6] (pp. 9-10)

On this fraudulent basis, The Unnamable can now invent a past for himself, and even an origin, but he can also negate his own self, his own fiction anytime he wishes by simply speaking about nothing: "Would it not be better if I were simply to keep on saying babababa, for example." (p. 28)

The muttering creature of *How It Is* goes even further in cancelling his own inventions. Though he insists throughout the narrative that he is quoting from memory "past moments old dreams back again or fresh like those that pass or things things always and memories," the opening statement of the novel (set on the dual level of the past and the present) reveals the ambiguity of his fiction: "*How it was* I quote before Pim with Pim after Pim *How it is* three parts I say it as I hear it" (p. 7; my italics). Once again we are confronted with the paradoxical relationship between remembered events and invented events — the "how it was" and "how it is" that cancel one another as they go along. But in this case, the negation of fiction is even more deliberate, even more flagrant. The narrator ends his verbal contortions in utter confusion as to the possibility of deciding whether or not he has told us anything reliable in what he calls the "last version" of his life. His only certainty is about HOW IT WAS NOT rather than HOW IT IS or HOW IT WAS — his only certainty is that he is totally submerged in darkness, and that he is lying face down in the mud of his own discourse, of his own "quaqua." That is the actuality of his predicament — fiction on the first level. But he cannot understand how he has managed to give us the record of his verbal

---

[6] The French text (Paris: Editions de Minuit, 1953) is even more explicit in revealing that the narrator-hero is inventing his own fiction: "Car je dois supposer un commencement à mon séjour ici, ne serait-ce que pour *la commodité du récit*... Voilà qui va singulièrement *faciliter mon exposé*." (pp. 16-17; my italics)

progression — fiction on the second level. His last resort, therefore, is to cancel the hypothesis on which his babblings ("this unqualifiable murmur") was postulated:

> all these calculations yes explanations yes the whole story from beginning to end yes completely false yes
>
> *that wasn't how it was* no not at all no how then no answer how was it then no answer HOW WAS IT screams good
>
> there was something yes but nothing of all that no all balls from start to finish yes this voice quaqua yes all balls yes only one voice here yes mine yes when the panting stops yes (pp. 144-145)

One could quote endlessly passages from the novels and plays of Beckett which cancel one another as they are brought together — statements which end into verbal impasses from which the speaker extricate himself by formulating yet another statement that negates what has just been said.

* * *

Most readers of fiction object to see taken away with one hand that which they have been given with the other, but unless they can accept this cancelling aspect of Beckett's fiction they will continue to deal with it as a paradox. Undoubtedly, it is this kind of uncertainty, this backtracking ambiguity which gives Beckett's fiction its paradoxical aspect, as though it were constantly on the brink of crumbling into nonsense, into self-negation. Only if one accepts the interplay between the two levels of rhetoric upon which Beckett's fiction functions can one gain an understanding of the Beckettian discourse. In other words, when reading Beckett, one must constantly guard against imposing on the fiction one's own notions of order, truth, plausibility, and reality.

Beckett, of course, did not invent fictional ambiguity. He merely exploits it to its utmost degree of confusion, and, as he himself said:

> The confusion is not my invention. We cannot listen to a conversation for five minutes without being acutely aware of the confusion. It is all around us and our only chance now

is to let it in. The only chance of renovation is to open our eyes and see the mess.[7]

This much quoted admonition reveals to what extent Beckett is willing to allow confusion to enter into his work, and at the same time it warms us that we should be ready to accept confusion in whatever form it may take: contradictions, negations, cancellations, paradoxes. It is only when we attempt to reconcile the contradictory aspects of the Beckettian dialectic on the basis of our preconceived notions of fiction (that is to say of truth and of reality) that we encounter the paradox. Too often, we are guilty of reading paradoxes into Beckett's fiction because we cannot accept that which cancels itself as it creates itself — that which is contrary to common sense, or that which points to itself (even though ironically) as paradoxical. And yet, as defined by the most basic dictionary, the primary meaning of a paradox is: "A tenet contrary to received opinion; an assertion or sentiment seemingly contradictory, or opposed to common sense, *but that yet may be true in fact.*"[8] This definition can certainly apply to the whole Beckett canon, and more specifically to the narrator-hero's ambivalent role as a recipient of fiction and a dispatcher of fiction, as a creature that is both, as The Unnamable calls himself, "the teller and the told." And certainly, the first person narrator of Beckett's fiction is a perfect example of the double I, the divided I, who speaks both the truth and the lie of fiction at the same time, who contains in himself both the enunciation and the denunciation of what he says.

Moran, for instance, experiences on the one hand his quest for Molloy, and, on the other, writes (or will write) a report about it. Supposedly, these two versions should coincide. But as pointed out earlier, they contradict one another, cancel one another. Moreover, even though Moran is launched on the traces of Molloy (who remains untraceable), and in a sense substitutes himself to Molloy, the two narratives (part one and part two of the novel) never become a perfect correspondence, a perfect superimposition because of the many contradictions one can read in the two parts of the novel, and eventually both parts cancel one another.

---

[7] As quoted by Tom F. Driver in "Beckett by the Madeleine," *Columbia University Forum*, #4 (Summer 1961), p. 22.

[8] *Webster's New Collegiate Dictionary* (6th ed.), s.v. "Paradox"; my italics.

This paradoxical aspect of the narrative discourse can be explained by the fact that in *Molloy*, where everything appears to be duplication and repetition, the essential of the monolog/dialog (monolog/dialog of the double I) lies in the commerce that Molloy entertains with himself (writing himself, telling himself, commenting himself) just as Moran, the other pole, the other voice of the fiction writes himself, tells himself, comments himself. Moran is the Moran-of-Molloy (and vice versa) just as consciousness is always consciousness-of-something, but in this case a curious consciousness which destroys the object it seeks to apprehend, or as Moran says:

> Between the Molloy I stalked within me thus and the true Molloy, after whom I was so soon to be in cry, over hill and dale, the resemblance cannot have been great. (p. 157)

But there is a further complication, a further confusion in the Beckettian paradox (particularly as exploited in *Molloy*) which prevents us from accepting it readily on the terms of our own preconceived opinion. The paradox, like the metaphor, brings together two normally remote, and even exclusive elements; but whereas the metaphor reconciles what may be two incongruous objects or two incompatible concepts by placing them on the same level of comprehension, on the same level of rhetoric, the paradox, on the contrary, creates a split between the two elements it brings together, whereby one negates the other. Very often, in Beckett's fiction, this split occurs (as exemplified by the closing statement in *Molloy*) on two different levels of rhetoric within the same verbal articulation, and as such even the paradox itself is undermined, negated, not only within a single statement, but in the entire fictitious discourse. Thus while there is a seemingly perfect duplication of events between the two parts of *Molloy*, and it appears that Moran becomes Molloy in the end, or his alter ego, there is also a perfect negation of one part by the other, just as there is also a total substitution of Moran for Molloy and vice versa.

Molloy's fiction negates Moran's report because it is unreliable, unconfirmed as it were (Moran never finds Molloy), and Moran's fiction negates Molloy's adventures because it is invented and without fundations. Therefore, when Moran reveals at the end of his failed quest that he "had not been able to go to him, and grow to be a friend, and like a father to me," and he adds that, consequently, Molloy has not been able to "help me do what I had to do..." (p. 222), he is flagrantly admitting the failure of his quest, and the fraudulence of his fiction. But in fact what is denounced here is not fiction itself, nor the idea that fiction can no longer match the reality of a past experience. What is denounced here is an obstinate and obsolete (traditional) concept of fiction: the concept of story-telling, the concept that fiction must tell a coherent and logical story. Neither Moran, nor Molloy, nor The Unnamable, nor any of the other narrator-heroes, has been able to tell a coherent story about himself or about his invented playmates. This is undoubtedly the most crucial, if not the most original aspect of Beckett's creative process: his fiction no longer tells a story (past realities reshaped into a plausible aesthetic form by the process of imagination), but it simply reflects upon itself, upon its own chaotic verbal progress, upon its own deficiencies — that is to say upon its own defective substance: language.

When the anonymous narrator-hero of "The Calmative" states: "All I say cancels out, I'll have said nothing," (p. 28 in *Stories and Texts for Nothing*), or when The Unnamable affirms: "To tell the truth, let us be honest at least, it is some considerable time now since I last knew what I was talking about," (p. 49) they, like all the other Beckettian derelicts, are merely reflecting on the language of their fiction, merely admitting the failure of their language as an instrument of story-telling, and not simply reflecting on fiction. The *Texts for Nothing*, as ambiguous as the title may be, are not stories about nothing, they are reflections, meditations on language, on the nothingness of their language. They are stories without stories whose only substance is the "flow of words" which makes them, or, as the voice in "Text VIII" says: "It's an unbroken flow of words and tears. With no pause for reflection... it's for ever the same murmur, flowing unbroken, like a single endless word and therefore meaningless, for it's the end gives the meaning to words." (p. 111)

In this respect, Beckett's fiction separates itself from the traditional narrative, and even from such a bold experiment in "antifiction" as *The Counterfeiters* of André Gide which is primarily a reflection on fiction by fiction, rather than a reflection on fiction by its own language. Or, as it was said of Gide's novel: it is "le roman du romanesque,"[9] now it can be said of Beckett's fiction: it is "le roman du language."

---

[9] Claude-Edmonde Magny, *Histoire du roman français depuis 1918* (Paris: Editions du Seuil, 1950), p. 251.

André Gide based his whole concept of fictional counterfeitness on the premise that fiction cannot pass for reality, and in *The Counterfeiters* (undoubtedly one of the great paradoxes of the French novel), he deliberately toys with his narration to force the reader to distinguish fictitious events from what may appear to be real events. He does so not only in *The Journal of the Counterfeiters* which functions as a critical mirror for the novel, not only by his interventions in the novel itself, but also by introducing in the narrative a writer-in-residence, a writer-protagonist, Edouard, who seemingly assumes responsibility for shaping the various elements of the fiction. Gide can then pretend to give away his authorial control in order to criticize and even contradict the course which his novel is taking: "Events fell out badly," he tells us. And elsewhere, referring to his characters as though they had a life of their own, independently of his creative authority, Gide deplores:

> Such people are cut out of a cloth which has no thickness... No past weighs upon them — no constraint. They have neither laws, nor masters, nor scruples; by their freedom and spontaneity, they make the novelist's despair. He can get nothing from them but worthless reactions. [10]

The same could be said of Beckett's creatures — free and spontaneous, they are the despair of the novelist. In that sense, Beckett's fiction seems to function in a way similar to that of Gide. His narrator-heroes create themselves and their fictional environment, "without any scruples," and with total disregard for their creator's responsibility towards the narrative. However, the essential difference is that Gide makes of authorial interventions the subject of his novel, whereas Beckett tends to disappear behind his creations thereby making of them free agents of "speechlessness." Gide's attitude is that of the self-conscious author who injects a functionless reflexivity into his work to undermine the traditional concept of story-telling, but no one is fooled by his disabused attitude, even when he says: "Passavant, Lady Griffith, all these people bore me; what are they doing here?" (*Idem*). Beckett, on the contrary, is subtly hidden in the voice of his

---

[10] *The Counterfeiters*, translation by Dorothy Bussy (New York: The Modern Library, 1927), p. 204; the French can be found in *Romans* (Paris: Gallimard, Editions de la Pléiade, 1958), p. 1110.

protagonists to the extent that they are capable of speaking against their "irresponsible" creator, accusing him of trying to impose on them not only a story, when there is no story to tell, but also words, when words are meaningless:

> He thinks words fail him, he think because words fail him he's on his way to my speechlessness, to being speechless with my speechlessness, he would like it to be my fault that words fail him, of course words fail him. He tells his story every five minutes, saying it is not his, there's cleverness for you. He would like it to be my fault that he has no story, of course he has no story, that's no reason for trying to foist one on me. (*Stories and Texts for Nothing*, pp. 91-92)

This curious reversal of roles, whereby the voice of fiction speaks against itself, is possible, in Beckett's fiction, because having no longer a story to tell ("of course he has no story") through his characters, the author simply allows his storyless creations to define themselves on the basis of their own rhetorical substance — words: empty words — until they have nothing more to say, for "even words desert you, it's as bad as that," says the voice in the *Texts for Nothing* (p. 70).

It is through this act of cancelling the story out of language that Beckett's fiction becomes a denunciation of the illusory aspect of fiction — a denunciation of the falsness of stories which pretend to pass for reality. For the truth is that fiction is not reality, it is simply a language which tells its own story, its own TRUE story. Beckett's SPEAKING WORDS are in fact telling the truth about themselves: they are telling us that they are words: "Words, mine was never more than that, than this pell-mell babel of silence and words." (*Ibid.*, p. 104) This shift from a language that tells *a* story to a language that tells *its* own story ("I say it as I hear it," Beckett's fiction says, and that's "how it is") reveals how the Beckettian discourse has passed from one level of rhetoric to another, and as a result, how the Beckettian paradox — a paradox created by the dual level of story-telling — is also negated by this subtle shift.

Olga Bernal, in a recent essay, opens an entirely new vista into Beckett's creative process when she states: "For Beckett's Molloy, the condition of the object was to be without a name, and inversely. If the literature of the past described reality (or believed it did), that of today realizes that what it describes is not reality, but the very language of which it is captive as soon as it begins to speak. And no doubt, this is the first time in the history of literature that language no longer situates itself opposite the world but opposite itself." [11] This realization emphasizes the revolutionary stance which Beckett's fiction is taking in relation to traditional fiction, and even in relation to more recent experiments in "anti-fiction" of *The Counterfeiters*' type.

However, if Olga Bernal's claim is true, it applies only to a certain portion of Beckett's creation — those major works which follow the contradictory closing statement in *Molloy*. Everything that precedes this statement (*More Pricks Than Kicks*, *Murphy*, *Watt*, the first French novel, *Mercier et Camier*, as well as the *Stories* written around 1945-1946) led inevitably to this moment of flagrant contradiction, to this confrontation of fiction by its own language. All the fiction that precedes the moment when Moran goes back into the house to write his report is set on a dual level of story-telling. In all these works, a narrator, more or less self-conscious, more or less present and active in the narrative, reveals by his interventions (as Gide does in *The Counterfeiters*) the lie of fiction on the basis of a split between two levels of narration.

In *Watt* and in *Molloy*, the narrator almost succeeds in becoming a counterpart for the protagonist of the novel (Sam and Watt — Moran and Molloy). But it is because they cannot substitute themselves completely for the other that the Beckettian paradox is created. In the other early novels and stories, the narrator is merely a distant witness of the fiction, but not an active participant. Therefore, even though the narrator of *More Pricks Than Kicks* tells us of his relationship with the protagonist, Belacqua: "We were Pylade and Orestes, for a period, flattened down to something very genteel," [12] and the narrator in *Murphy* tells us on several occasions that what we are reading is an "expurgated, accelerated, improved and reduced account" [13] of what happened, and the narrator in *Mercier et Camier* claims: "Le voyage de Mercier et Camier, je peux le raconter, si je veux, car j'étais avec

---

[11] "L'Oubli des noms," *Le Monde*, 17 January 1968, p. v (my translation of Miss Bernal's French).

[12] *More Pricks Than Kicks* (London: Chatto & Windus, 1934), pp. 44-45.

[13] *Murphy* (New York: Grove Press, 1957), *passim*.

eux, tout le temps," [14] in fact these stories are not told by narrators, but are omnisciently controlled by the self-conscious author.

In other words, in all the fiction that led to the final statement in *Molloy*, a paradox exists because there is a split between two levels of narration — between the truth of fiction, and the lie of fiction. Starting with *Malone Dies* however, pseudoreality and subfiction unify into a single level of rhetoric as author, narrator, and narrator-hero converge into one voice, or what can be called "the voice within the voice." From a narrative that described experiences as though they had been lived in the past, the fiction beyond *Molloy* relates experiences lived in the present, or, rather, in a kind of present-future condition. This shift from a present-past narrative to a present-future narrative becomes evident in *Malone Dies* if one compares this novel with the preceding one, *Molloy*.

Ludovic Janvier explains this shift from present-past to present-future in those terms: "Moran and Molloy, from the perspective of their oral present looked toward the days of wandering they lived until then. The narration was that present-past indicating what had been. Moran and Molloy told their beginnings. Malone, on the contrary, wants to indicate that which he has not yet lived. He looks toward that near future in which his present allows itself to be drawn: Malone dies. The present of his narration nourishes itself on the coming future of this moribund who speaks. It is turned entirely toward what will be. Malone tells his end." [15] In other words, Malone has reached that condition to which all his predecessors were aspiring: he has become the true scribe of his own fiction, the writer locked in a room, sitting in front of a sheet of paper, pencil in hand, describing, not the fiction of his past, not the memories of his past, but the present of his future condition, describing, at last, the language of his fiction. However, it is true that Malone would like to be able to tell stories like his predecessors — "one about a man, another about a woman, a third about a thing and finally one about an animal, a bird probably," (p. 3) — for he cannot resign himself to the "possibility of dying without leaving an inventory behind." (*Idem*) He even proposes to himself to write his memoirs: "When I have completed my inventory,

---

[14] *Mercier et Camier* (Paris: Editions de Minuit, 1970), p. 7.
[15] *Pour Samuel Beckett* (Paris: Editions de Minuit, 1966), p. 64 (my translation of Janvier's French).

if my death is not ready for me then, I shall write my memoirs. That's funny, I have made a joke." (p. 6) Indeed, it is a joke, for he knows that in his "Present state" (as he says himself), every time he begins a story "disaster threatens." Therefore, unable to tell a story any more, "... abandoned, in the dark, without anything to play with," (p. 3) all that is left to him is the empty act of pretending to tell stories, to go on playing the game of telling stories, of writing stories, even though there are no more stories to be told: "This time I know where I am going, it is no longer the ancient night, the recent night. Now it is a game, I am going to play." (p. 2) But the game Malone plays now is no longer the one of trying to invent a life for himself out of the pseudoreality of the past, but of simply writing himself into death. By the time Malone reaches the end of his storyless fiction he is able to cancel his own self, his own voice, his own I:

> All is ready. Except me. I am being given, if I may venture the expression, birth to into death, such is my impression. The feet are clear already, of the great cunt of existence. Favorable presentation I trust. My head will be the last to die. Haul in your hands. I can't. The render rent. My story ended I'll be living yet. Promising lag. That is the end of me. I shall say I no more. (pp. 114-115)

This curious image of birth into death, backward, into the "great cunt of existence," where the voice of fiction shall no longer say I, sums up the condition of Malone progressing (regressing?) towards his own cancellation. Malone has finally succeeded in writing himself into death without the support of a story, of an author, or of a narrator. Malone is the first to tell us the truth about the lie of fiction — that fiction is but an "innumerable babble," and that his life has been but the scribbling on the pages: "With my distant hand I count the pages that remain. They will do. This exercise-book is my life, this big child's exercise-book, it has taken me a long time to resign myself to that." (p. 105)

Though Moran claims to be a writer, the scribe of Molloy's fiction which he writes (or will write) according to the instruction he has received, he only gives us the first two sentences of his report. Moran, therefore, is only on the threshold of the true condition of fiction — he is neither the teller nor the told. He remains controlled by the "hypothetical imperatives" which govern all of Beckett's fiction prior to *Malone Dies*. Moran does not fulfill his mission. And if he fails, it because he and Molloy, like all the others who preceded them, are still physically, socially, and somewhat realistically in movement in the landscape of story-telling, still turned towards memories of the past, even though they gradually suffer disintegration both of the mind and the body. Neither Molloy, nor Moran can achieve the solipsist condition of Malone, of the Unnamable, and of all the other derelicts who will follow them, up to the faceless, voiceless grey figure of *Lessness* who can only perpetuate his fiction, or rather whose fiction can only perpetuate itself, among its own grey ruins, by turning to the future tense.

Nevertheless, the question remains as to the credibility of their fiction. Who is telling the truth? Is Moran telling the truth about the lie of his and of Molloy's fiction? Or is Malone lying about his fictional truth? Once again we are caught in the vicious circles of the liar's paradox. For if Molloy, Moran, and their predecessors are telling the truth, it is about a lie (the lie of fiction), and if Malone, The Unnamable, and their successors are lying, it is about the truth of their condition (verbal authenticity). The only hope, therefore, is that beyond the game of fiction, beyond the cancellation of fiction by its own language, another story will be told, another true story will be told. One can only hope, as does the voice in the *Texts for Nothing*:

> And yet I have high hopes, I give you my word, high hopes, that one day I may tell a story, hear a story, yet another, with men, kinds of men as in the days when I played all regardless or nearly, worked and played. (in *Stories and Texts for Nothing*, p. 105)

But before Beckett can tell another story (a kind of story) with men (kinds of men), as, in fact, he does in *The Lost Ones*,[16] he must ultimately get rid of the voice within the voice which took shape in the fiction beyond *Molloy*. He must create now a voiceless fiction: a fiction which frees itself of the paradox that exists, and will always exist between the truth of fiction and the lie of reality, even when

---

[16] *The Lost Ones* (New York: Grove Press, 1972) is the English translation, by Beckett as usual, of *Le Dépeupleur* (Paris: Editions de Minuit, 1970). Written around 1966-1967 (with the last sections written around 1970), it is, in my opinion, to be considered as one of Beckett's major works even though 55 pages long in the original version.

the voice of fiction manages to contain in itself both the teller and the told.

* * *

The Lost Ones is the kind of text which sets out to be that perfect voiceless fiction, which sets out to free itself of all connections with creator, narrator, voice, teller, and thereby transcend its own paradox. Even though *The Lost Ones* is not Beckett's most recent text in the chronology of composition, in my opinion, it is the kind of fiction that goes beyond all possibilities of fiction in abolishing its own sustaining paradox. *The Lost Ones* is almost that perfect fiction which Flaubert dreamt of writing.

To achieve this perfection means abolishing for ever the space, the essential space (present-past or present-future) into which all fiction is scribbled. It means, in other words, taking the risk of never again being able to write fiction, for the perfect text transcends the teller, thereby negating all plausibility, all connections with reality. The perfect text has no referential elements outside of itself — in the past or in the real world.

The careful reader of Beckett's fiction — a fiction which has evolved over the past forty years or so — knows that this fiction establishes its own rules of order and chaos as it goes along; that it establishes also its own system of reading. Beckett's discourse always contains means, expedients, stratagems which draw the reader's attention to the fact that language is in the process of being used, that language is in the process of becoming fiction, or what one of the voices calls: "cette horreur chosesque." (*Nouvelles et Textes pour rien,* p. 58) That careful reader also knows that Beckett's fiction undercuts (denounces) all mimetic pretensions of fiction. And finally, that Beckett's fiction presents forms which (freed of their mimetic functions) are free to create new meanings.

The Lost Ones goes further than any other Beckett text in exploiting these axioms. In this "Abode where lost bodies roam each searching for its lost one. Vast enough for search to be in vain. Narrow enough for flight to be in vain," (opening lines, p. 7) in this perfect geometrical figure — the cylinder of fiction — there is no way out, no way to cheat. The cylinder calls the reader's attention only to itself; it refuses to be a representation of something else, and it creates its own arbitrary meaning (or meaninglessness). The place, the setting, the "abode" is closed from all sides. No exit, therefore! The bodies, the people, the characters (if one may still use this term) are anonymous, naked, speechless, almost inhuman. As for the action, it is totally useless; it is performed in vain, for, as we are told: "Whatever it is they are searching for it is not that." (p. 36) Ans so the text constantly repeats: "All is for the best."

The Lost Ones is dividied into 15 sections which form two categories: Sections 1, 3, 5, 6, 7, 11, 14 deal with the cylinder (the space of fiction) — its volume, its surface, dimensions, light, heat, ladders, tunnels, etc.; Sections 2, 8, 9, 10, 13, 15 deal with the human reality — the bodies, their nomination, division into groups, classification, action, conditions of life, etc. Only one section does not belong specifically to these two categories. It is a kind of digression, a rupture in the perfection of the text. It is Section 4 which deals with the myth of the exit. This section talks about an ELSEWHERE of the cylinder. It is a sign of the arbitrary nature of this strange topology where form is content and content form.

The cylinder/fiction then appears as a historical continuity (a linguistic continuity) readable and irreducible in its self-contained perfection, and at the same time it reveals its mechanism of repetitions and duplications which justify the summary one can give of this text. Inside a giant cylinder, a vast closed space, fifty meters in circumference and eighteen meters in height, "for the sake of harmony" we are told, whose walls and ground are made of solid rubber or a "suchlike substance," some two hundred "bodies," each occupying one square meter, are involved in a frantic and futile activity which consists of climbing up and down a set of ladders ("the only objects" we are told), about fifteen in all (the smaller one being not less than six meters tall) to reach little niches ("or alcoves") half-way up the walls (above "some imaginary line"), "disposed in irregular quincunxes roughly ten meters in diameter and cunningly out of line," some of which are connected by tunnels, where the climbing bodies rest for a while. These creatures, all of them naked, of both sexes (some young, some old, some still children or infants), are divided into various groups: the climbers, the searchers, the carriers (of ladders), the watchers, and the vanquished who no longer attempt to climb the ladders. Indeed, we are here in the presence of a perfect and meticulously arranged model in miniature of the human condition and the mechanism of fiction reduced to their most basic and primordial elements. In fact, the only way one can speak of the cylinder is to quote it in its entirely as it repeats itself, as it rectifies itself from different angles and perspectives, for the cylinder/fiction only represents itself. The cylinder of fiction does not represent anything exterior to itself; it has no outside references to past, to reality, to memory, or even to creator. This is why repetitions and duplications in this text do not serve the purpose of screening the paradox of fiction, as was the case in all other Beckett fiction. Repetition here reveals only a useless self-contained divergence: the fiction no longer allows the distinction between the "teller and the told." The imaginary line of writing turns around its own axis, but an axis which is also imaginary. This forces the linearity of the discourse to undermine the circularity of the cylinder. The cylinder of fiction is really a system of recuperation by loss. In order for the space (the "abode" — "Séjour" in the French text) to be created, the discourse has to take the risk of being written.

What is said, seen, measured, calculated, formulated, within the cylinder, also corresponds to what is said again, seen again, calculated again, measured again, and so on; in other words, what is constantly repeated in the text with slight variations. For to say something new is possible against a background of something already said, already seen. However, since there is nothing exterior or anterior to the cylinder (not even a prior fiction upon which to repeat the present fiction, as was the case in Beckett's other fiction), the text can only proliferate from itself, from its own linguistic substance. To write, therefore, as it is exemplified by the cylinder of fiction, becomes a work of weaving on an old canvas. To build, to come back upon, to retrace on the same lines already traced, already inscribed, that is the course of action in *The Lost Ones*. This is the only truth of writing — the only certitude of writing and of fiction, for, as we are told quite explicitly: "in the cylinder alone are certitudes to be found, and without nothing but mystery." (p. 42) The exit — "the issue" — out of this fiction is a myth, a lie. Writing, in other words, is a form of *clôture,* to use the French term.

If Moran's report, even though fraudulent, was postulated against the background of Molloy's fiction, if Malone's fiction grew out of the stories he told himself, as is the case with most Beckettian narrator-hero, if The Unnamable was able to perpetuate himself in spite of his helplessness to go on, it was because their discourses relied on the material of an elsewhere. In the cylinder/fiction of *The Lost Ones* there is no elsewhere, no past memories to reshape. Therefore, if there is an elsewhere of the cylinder, it can only be a defect in the cylinder itself. And in fact, there is such a defect — deliberately instilled into the text, since we are told that "the use of the ladders in the cylinder is regulated by conventions of *obscure origin.*" (p. 21; my italics) The obscurity of this origin is veiled by the text, but nonetheless it suggests an activity, a beginning, elsewhere which violates the perfection of the text, which violates the voice that wants to speak in this text but cannot speak. By this allusion, this reintroduction of the notion of origin, the text no longer leads us to its own emptiness, to its own meaninglessness and functionlessness, particularly since we are told: "All has not been told, and never shall be" about this place. (p. 51)

The question then remains: who speaks here? To whom does this neutral voice belong which masks, like a speaking-subject, the questioning subject from whom the narration comes and towards whom it sometimes seems to go? What is this threat of another paradox? But this is a false threat, a false voice. The speaking-subject is absent — *in absentia* — since the text continues without answers, without reconnecting itself with the past or with reality. What there is instead is a threat of a possible staging, of a possible mise-en-scène, for, from the "unthinkable beginning to the unthinkable end" (referred to several times in the text), there is only a set of conditionals — a set of IF's — "If the notion is maintained," we are told repeatedly. And it is as a result of these conditionals (and no longer present-past or present-future quasi-certitudes) that the text desituates itself constantly from the original certitudes it pretends to offer. The cylinder of fiction which wanted to be perfect has faults, holes in it. The metaphors miss their targets. This tale, this anonymous tale says less than it wanted to say (or perhaps, says too much). The holes, the faults, the defects announce from time to time an effort of narration, a return to storytelling. But who wants to narrate here? And from where? From which elsewhere? "It is curious to note," it says. "To be noted finally," it repeats. And it is as though a voice in an off-limit situation, off-stage, off-fiction, was attempting to comment from afar. "It is curious." "It is indeed curious." "Picturesque detail." "In short." "So much roughly." These are the remarks formulated, indirectly, by the absent voice. Thus, one can assume that an authority, a subjectivity is trying to assert itself into the text. There is then a form of staging in this fiction, as there was in all other Beckett text, but in this case the staging is a weakness, a void, rather than a force, or a source, or a "hypothetical imperative" that controls the narrative, because, in fact, better was expected. What was expected here was perfection, that is to say a fiction that would function without staging, a fiction that would remove itself completely from the authority of its teller, from the unreliability of its creator. Therefore, it becomes clear now that the perfect text of fiction which Beckett undertook to write cannot, must not be perfect. It would be perfect if the cylinder was, as we are told: "suitably lit from above," or "if an intelligence were tempted to see better," or if "it were possible to follow...", and so on. Numerous such phrases suggest that the situation could be improved, that the cylinder/fiction could be perfected. And it is because that someone cannot hear better, cannot see better, that there is an admission of failure in the cylinder, a trace of the paradox of fiction.

The cylinder, like a personnage, needs to be seen, perceived, apprehended. Therefore, the text-cylinder designates the one who sees him, who reads him, or else it is condamned to non-existence. Hence the connivance with the reader: "an intelligence would be tempted to see..." the text says to the reader. But unable to say it all, the voice from elsewhere, which came to see, and perhaps to tell again, can only conclude by saying: "suffices to affirm," or "so much roughly speaking...", thereby admitting its false presence — false presence since the subject which is (or should be) at work here is not really present. It is delegated (after the writing) to the process of reading.

The cylinder of fiction is an anonymous machine which is set in motion by the questions, affirmations, negations, speculations of the text: by the texture of the text. Unlike most fiction, therefore, nothing takes place outside the text — HORS-TEXTE. No escape, no contact with exterior reality or fiction, with the past, or with the physical world, except for the allusions to Dante (in section 4), and to a place beyond the exit (if that exit were to be found) where "the sun and other stars would still be shining." (p. 18) But these allusions to another space, to an elsewhere in culture and in nature, are parts of the deliberate imperfections of the cylinder. These allusions to another place and another fiction are not to be read as sources for the text, or as infrastructures. Consequently, *The Lost Ones* functions neither as a symbol nor as a metaphor, nor as a microcosm of reality. It is, to use Ludovic

Janvier's term, "un mythocosme" similar to that of Dante's *Divine Comedy*. It is a gigantic edifice of words integrating in its figures the space between which it takes place. It is the most perfect rhetorical statement that cancels itself as it is spoken or written.

* * *

This then is the ultimate situation, the ultimate goal towards which Beckett's fiction was progressing: the ultimate cancellation of human, fictional, and linguistic possibilities. The paradox of fiction has been transcended, and fiction has reached that impossible region of LESSNESS where nothing is even less than nothing, but where, nonetheless, the language of fiction continues to perpetuate itself, to repeat itself in the vacuum of its own ruins — or of its own perfection.

In a sense, what we have reached here is the only form of UTOPIA Beckett could conceive for humanity and for fiction. Along the ambiguous line of a future-past, which transcends the present-future of *Malone Dies*, Beckett's fiction has come full cycle back to a prehistoric condition of man and of fiction. Locked in a last refuge, the cylinder of words, the "issueless space" of writing, Beckett's creatures no longer speak, no longer relate their own story, no longer seem to have a memory and words to give themselves the illusion of existing. And so, Beckett's own words have, once again, mocked the paradox of fiction, mocked silence and oblivion both for humanity and literature, for he has succeeded in creating yet another possibility for fiction out of the impossibility of fiction. And this he was able to do because, as he himself said some years ago in *Molloy*: "It seems to me that all language is an excess of language." (p. 159) Or, better yet, as he said, more recently in *How It is*, in a typical Beckettian paradox, still about language: "a rumor transmissible *ad infinitum* in either direction." (p. 120)

* * *

INTRODUCTORY NOTES TO BECKETT'S POETRY

by Melvin J. Friedman

WE are reminded again and again by his critics that Beckett has never stopped writing poetry, even though the last verse to appear were the two poems placed in the Addenda to *Watt* (1953). Martin Esslin, for example, remarked in his contribution to *Beckett at 60: A Festschrift*: "And indeed, all of Beckett's writing is ultimately poetry...."[1] Francis Doherty in his 1971 book on Beckett accounted for the recent text, like *Lessness* and *Imagination Dead Imagine,* as being "a complexly working poem."[2] Ten years ago Josephine Jacobsen and William Mueller entitled a chapter of their *Testament of Samuel Beckett* "The Dimension of Poetry" — a chapter which has nothing whatever to do with Beckett's poems, indeed does not quote a single line from any of them. The chapter has this characteristic beginning: "Since Beckett is primarily a poet, there is no aspect of his work which is not poetically relevant."[3]

All this agreement about the poetical nature of Beckett's art seems to be accompanied by a curious reticence to discuss in detail the verse written in the 1930s and 1940s. Some of Beckett's most talented critics, like Hugh Kenner, Ruby Cohn, Martin Esslin, and John Fletcher, have seriously confronted the early poems, like "Whoroscope" and

---

[1] Martin Esslin, "Samuel Beckett's Poems" in *Beckett at 60: A Festschrift* (London: Calder and Boyars, 1967), p. 60. All subsequent references will be to this edition.

[2] Francis Doherty, *Samuel Beckett* (London: Hutchinson University Library, 1971), p. 21.

[3] Josephine Jacobsen and William R. Mueller, *The Testament of Samuel Beckett* (New York: Hill and Wang, 1964), p. 35.

some of the lyrics in *Echo's Bones,* but usually with the sense that they are looking at apprenticeship writing.

John Fletcher, in his skillful overview of the poetry in *Samuel Beckett's Art,* for example, has this to say about the first poetic soundings: "At its origins, we have seen that Beckett's verse is the frivolous pastime of an exceptionally gifted and intelligent young man."[4] Esslin is more eloquent and encouraging but still not quite positive: "... we cannot but treasure Beckett's poems for the glimpses they give us of the rare, ascetic and saintly personality from which those voices issued forth." (p. 60) The suggestion is that we need the poetry for the light it casts on the writer even if it is not precisely first-rate. (The New Critics, especially, would have difficulty with this reasoning!)

Even a very recent study, A. Alvarez's *Beckett* (1973), dismisses the poetry in less than a page. After classifying "Whoroscope" as a "jeu d'esprit" and commenting on its derivativeness, Alvarez remarks: "With the best will and the most piercing hindsight in the world, it would have been impossible to guess that the author was a genius in the making."[5] Hugh Kenner quite brilliantly goes about the task of glossing certain of the poems — even finding satisfaction in some of them like "The Vulture" — in a chapter of his 1973 study, *A Reader's Guide to Samuel Beckett.* Yet he cleverly maintains: "Unlike his mature writing, which speaks to numerous readers though Beckett himself is apt to be blank about it, the poems are apt to leave a reader blank...."[6] Kenner insists, as Esslin did before him, that the poetry, more than any other part of Beckett's work, is tied to his biography. And the suggestion is still present that that is its chief virtue and source of illumination.

Lawrence Harvey's *Samuel Beckett Poet and Critic* (1970) is the only full-scale treatment of the poetry we have. It is longer than any other book I know of on Beckett, longer even — by some seventy pages — than that inspired work of scholarship, Federman and Fletcher's *Samuel Beckett: His Works and His Critics, An Essay in Bibliography.* One's first reaction almost has to be that 450 pages is too

---

[4] John Fletcher, "The Art of the Poet" in his *Samuel Beckett's Art* (London: Chatto & Windus, 1967), p. 39.

[5] A. Alvarez, *Beckett* (London: Fontana/Collins, 1973), p. 24.

[6] Hugh Kenner, *A Reader's Guide to Samuel Beckett* (London: Thames and Hudson, 1973), p. 43. All subsequent references will be to this edition.

much to give over to such a minor part of the Beckett canon. (Actually only somewhat more than two-thirds of the book is directly concerned with the poetry while the rest moves through the early fiction, *Watt*, and the literary and art criticism.) Several reviewers came down rather hard on Harvey — mainly those, I noticed, who work under the crippling pressure of deadlines for weeklies like *The New Republic* and *The New York Times Book Review* and who do not have the time or patience to bear with Harvey's thoroughness and his New Critical way of dissecting a poem. Fortunately, we have now had time for second and third reactions to *Samuel Beckett Poet and Critic* and can appreciate the extent to which Harvey is tuned into Beckett's poetic soundings. Before Harvey came along there had been too much restructuring of Beckett's house of fiction from the roof down. Now we have some sense of the foundation stones.

Harvey seems to write out of a sense of mission. He is himself convinced that the verse does more than shed light on the biography and illumine dark crevices of the later work. He puts it this way in his preface: "I am principally interested in what the French call a 'critique des beautés.' While I cannot claim that the poetry, with its more limited purpose and scope, is comparable to the major achievement represented by the later novels and plays, it has many values that make it important per se."[7] These values do indeed come out as Harvey makes his way, with seemingly endless tact and patience, through all the poetry from "Whoroscope" through the French poems of 1946-48 ("the culmination of a poetic evolution toward the pure lyric" [p. 223]) and the two poems in the Addenda to *Watt*. Few references and echoes escape his notice as he summons up an incredible number of writers, ancient and modern, to help explain the turns of Beckett's allusive sensibility. Perhaps only Joyce does not quite get his due. Beckett wrote the English poems of the 1930s under the shadow of *Finnegans Wake* and reverberations of Joyce's last book are certainly heard with frequency in the background of the early verse. David Hesla, in his *The Shape of Chaos: An Interpretation of the Art of Samuel Beckett,* explains something of this when he says: "They [the words] belong supremely to Beckett's landsman James

---

[7] Lawrence Harvey, *Samuel Beckett Poet and Critic* (Princeton: Princeton University Press, 1970), p. xii. All subsequent references will be to this edition.

Joyce, master of those who can, who made the world's words his own, whose art is the art of opulence."[8]

The title "Whoroscope," for example, may not be unrelated to these words from *Finnegans Wake:* "*How to Pull a Good Horuscoup even when Oldsire is Dead to the World.*"[9] The two Enueg poems of *Echo's Bones* seem especially close to Joyce. A starting point might be the stanza from "Enueg I":

> Next:
> on the hill down from the Fox and Geese into
>   Chapelizod
> a small malevolent goat, exiled on the road,
> remotely pucking the gate of his field;
> the Isolde Stores a great perturbation of sweaty
>   heroes,
> in their Sunday best,
> come hastening down for a pint of nepenthe or
>   moly or half and half
> from watching the hurlers above in Kilmainham.

Lawrence Harvey has already convincingly explicated these lines without any help from Joyce (see *Samuel Beckett Poet and Critic,* pp. 134-35). Still one is very tempted to go back to *Finnegans Wake* for "Fox and Geese," "Chapelizod," and "Isolde Stores." There are several references to Fox and Geese in Joyce's last book: "And fox and geese still kept the peace around *L'Auberge du Père Adam.*" (p. 124); "...wildflier's fox into my own greengeese again...." (p. 446); "...goodmen twelve and true at fox and geese in their numbered habitations...." (p. 557) The Earwickers, who control the narrative focus of *Finnegans Wake,* live in Chapelizod (which means Chapel of Isolde), a suburb of Dublin. There are constant references in the book to the Tristan and Isolde legend, one of the recurring mythical

---

[8] David Hesla, *The Shape of Chaos: An Interpretation of the Art of Samuel Beckett* (Minneapolis: University of Minnesota Press, 1971), pp. 28-29. See also David Hayman's "A Meeting in the Park and a Meeting on the Bridge: Joyce and Beckett" and Ruby Cohn's "Joyce and Beckett, Irish Cosmopolitans," both found in the special Beckett issue of *James Joyce Quarterly,* VIII (Summer 1971), pp. 372-384; 385-391.

[9] James Joyce, *Finnegans Wake* (New York: Viking, 1947), p. 105. All subsequent references will be to this edition.

patterns which help to shape the novel.[10] In the next stanza of "Enueg I" is a reference to the Liffey, the river which figures so prominently in *Finnegans Wake* and helps shape the crucial name Anna Livia Plurabelle.

"Enueg II" seems also to have its Joycean elements. The "Guinness's barges" may have something to do with the Guinness barrel in which Shaun the Postman floats down the Liffey in chapters 13 and 14 of *Finnegans Wake*. Shaun's identification with Christ and his passing through the 14 Stations of the Cross, as William York Tindall has told us, are central to these chapters.[11] At Station 6, Veronica wipes the face of Jesus, and this is represented in *Finnegans Wake* as "And this, Joke, a sprig of blue speedwell just a spell of floralora so you'll mind your veronique." (p. 458) The relevant lines from "Enueg II" are:

> veronica mundi
> veronica munda
> give us a wipe for the love of Jesus

When we see "Guinness's barges" following four lines after "O'Connell Bridge" in this same "Enueg II," we should probably not forget these sentences from the "Lestrygonians" section of *Ulysses*: "As he [Leopold Bloom] set foot on O'Connell bridge a puffball of smoke plumed up from the parapet. Brewery barge with export stout."[12] The first person of this poem, by the way, displays emotions not entirely unlike those of Bloom.

These are merely a sample of possible Joycean rapprochements. They are offered very tentatively to suggest the startling range of this poetry. It would probably not be wrong to use Anthony Burgess' coinage "palimpcestuous" (which is intended to describe *Finnegans Wake*) when we speak of the early poems, especially those 13 contained in *Echo's Bones*.

---

[10] See David Hayman, "Tristan and Isolde in *Finnegans Wake*," *Comparative Literature Studies*, I (1964), pp. 93-112.

[11] James Joyce commented on this matter in a letter to Harriet Shaw Weaver dated May 24, 1924: "It is written in the form of a *via crucis* of 14 stations but in reality it is only a barrel rolling down the river Liffey." See *Letters of James Joyce*, ed. Stuart Gilbert (New York: Viking, 1957), p. 214.

[12] James Joyce, *Ulysses* (New York: Vintage/Random House, 1961), p. 152.

To speak now in more general terms, we should notice a pattern in Beckett's career which is not uncommon. His beginnings as a poet are in certain ways comparable to the early soundings of two other major twentieth-century novelists, Joyce and Faulkner. We have long been familiar with Beckett's proximity to Joyce and the shaping influence the older writer had on the apprenticeship years of the younger one. Beckett began his career with a contribution — the lead one as it turned out — to the volume honoring and studying what was then known as *Work in Progress, Our Exagmination Round His Factification for Incamination of Work in Progress* (Shakespeare and Company, 1929). He was also involved in the translation of the "Anna Livia Plurabelle" into French which was published in the May 1931 issue of the *Nouvelle Revue Française*. A third literary connection was the 1934 acrostic, "Home Olga," written for James Joyce (with his name spelled out by the first letters of the ten lines of the poem). Lawrence Harvey thinks of this poem as "the young poet's farewell to Joycean virtuosity" (p. 273) and as "an admirer's farewell to the master." (p. 296) (It should be noted here that "Home Olga" was first published in the third volume of *Contempo*, a magazine published in Chapel Hill, North Carolina.)

When we liken, then, the literary beginnings of Beckett to those of Joyce we are not noticing anything very startling. Still we should mention that both seemed to offer promising careers as poet and critic before they turned to fiction. Indeed each started with an admiring essay about an older writer whom he held in high esteem: Beckett with his "Dante... Bruno. Vico... Joyce" and Joyce with his appreciation of Ibsen's *When We Dead Awaken*. It would be more difficult to parallel "Whoroscope" and the poems in *Echo's Bones* with Joyce's early lyrics contained in *Chamber Music*. The preoccupation with love in *Chamber Music*, for example, seems very much at odds with the concern of a collection like *Echo's Bones*, which starts off with a poem called "The Vulture," ends with a poem called "Echo's Bones," and has two poems in between called "Sanies." Hugh Kenner revealingly tells us: "... they [the poems in *Echo's Bones*] preserve complex hermetic miseries. They are strangely frozen poems...." (p. 42) The suggestion is that there is something Mallarméan about them, that they share a Symbolist inheritance. Joyce's early poems look back to an earlier, less sealed-in, less cloistered tradition; they are far less allusive. In fact, one can conclude from this that the careers of the two writers proceed in opposite directions: Joyce moves from the relative verbal spareness and restraint of *Chamber Music* to the unprecedented intricacies of *Finnegans Wake* while Beckett moves from verbal opulence in the early poetry to the near-silences of the recent texts.

Ruby Cohn, in her *Samuel Beckett: The Comic Gamut*, mentions Verlaine when she discusses "the over-all tone" of the poems in *Echo's Bones*. Interestingly enough, one of Faulkner's earliest literary gestures was to translate four of Verlaine's poems into English.[13] Like Beckett and Joyce, Faulkner turned to poetry before he wrote fiction. By the time of his *Paris Review* interview in early 1956 he was able to look back on these early soundings with some amusement and detachment and speak of himself as "a failed poet." What he said following this sums up his own career as it does, with some qualification, both that of Joyce and Beckett: "Maybe every novelist wants to write poetry first, finds he can't, and then tries the short story, which is the most demanding form after poetry. And, failing at that, only then does he take up novel writing."[14] The pattern is there for all three writers even if the word "failure" does not always apply. Though all three may possibly be "failed poets" in their early verse, they are certainly among the most accomplished poets we have in their mature fiction (and in Beckett's case, drama).

---

[13] These translations, together with the rest of Faulkner's early verse, appear in *William Faulkner: Early Prose and Poetry*, ed. Carvel Collins (Boston and Toronto: Atlantic-Little, Brown, 1962). See also Richard P. Adams, "The Apprenticeship of William Faulkner," *Tulane Studies in English*, XII (1962), pp. 113-156.

[14] *Writers at Work: The "Paris Review" Interviews*, ed. Malcolm Cowley (New York: Viking, 1960), p. 123.

* I should like to thank Charles Caramello for help with *Finnegans Wake*; he is a sensitive reader of Joyce.

THE BAWDS OF EUPHONY: IMAGES OF WOMEN IN BECKETT'S EARLY POEMS

by *Lori Hall Burghardt*

IN "Thirteen Ways of Looking at a Blackbird," Wallace Stevens says:

> At the sight of blackbirds
> Flying in a green light
> Even the bawds of euphony
> Would cry out sharply.[1]

The clash in this stanza betwen illusion and reality, between the Other and the Self, between art and experience, plus the sense of pain that contact engenders and the use of green and black, calls to mind the depictions of and the emotional responses to women in Beckett's poetry.[2] Their relationship to his more mature works has been underestimated. These women provide the careful reader with nascent images, they reflect Beckett's evolving philosophical concerns, and they undergo a parallel diminution of aim and representation through concentration and distillation that is so apparent in his plays and

---

[1] Samuel French Morse, *Poems by Wallace Stevens*. (New York: Vintage-Knopf, 1961), p. 13.

[2] The texts used for this paper were: *Poems in English* (New York: Grove Press, 1961); *Les Temps Modernes*, No. 14 (November, 1946), pp. 288-293; *Cahiers des saisons*, No. 2 (October, 1955), pp. 115-116; *Transition Forty-Eight*, No. 2 (June, 1948), pp. 96-97. All references will be to these.

No critic can write about Beckett's poetry without giving recognition to the Herculean labor of Lawrence Harvey in *Samuel Beckett: Poet and Critic* (Princeton: Princeton University Press, 1970). His careful scrutiny of the poems provides a wealth of information for the careful reader. Further, the thesis of his study runs counter to the notion, asserted by so many scribes, that the poems are an inferior portion of the Beckett canon.

novels. Here, quite literally, this compression is carried to its logical conclusion. Beckett has not published any poems since the early 1950's.[3]

His first women are strong symbols, named images, to whom he responds vehemently. He portrays them with tenderness in "Alba" and with sympathetic understanding in "From the Only Poet to a Shining Whore." Conversely, he wrenchingly rejects them in spite of his own need in "Sanies 1." He bitterly mocks and castigates them in *Whoroscope*. And, on occasion, he views the entire ritual of coupling with a Swiftian obscenity that slips into a painful crying out, as in "Sanies 2." These are the women of the first stage, present in these poems written during the early thirties. She is a catalyst intruding upon the world of man, causing upheavals as he seeks stasis. These females are vivid, lyrically or realistically described, and, frequently, they are modern parallels of Biblical or literary figures.

As Beckett becomes convinced of the impossibilities of the poetic craft, and as he moves from the concerns of the macrocosm to the hermetic world of the microcosm, from the self that suffers to the self that watches, these vivid women will become "les elles," broken images at the edge of male consciousness, impressionistically recorded by a mind bored with the conflict and seeking self containment. Poems from the 1937-39 period depict this transitionary stage in Beckett's development. Only four of the twelve poems deal centrally with women and their impact. Thus, a poem such as "elles viennent / autres et pareilles" records the utter sameness of women essentially. They no longer have a name nor are they embodiments of figures of the past. The focus is on the small personal acts the women perform as the poet watches them. The basic techniques are compression and repetition, which symbolically underscore the increasing meaninglessness of even contemplating such issues.

The last poems of 1946-48 contain no important allusions to women. Instead the emphasis is on the conceptual level; love, self, friends, and the abstraction itself are considered. As the poet cherishes his isolation, his solitude, his aloneness, he pushes women beyond the realm of his poems. Beckett's poetic women, then, provide ongoing and underscoring images and symbols for his concern with Cartesian

---

[3] The revelation that Beckett is still writing poetry was made by Ruby Cohn at the Beckett Symposium, Chapel Hill, Spring 1974.

dualism. Further, they are a link to the religious irony which is coordinated as the background of this dualism. Since time is limited, the remainder of this discussion will focus on the early poems.

These women are variations of two models: Beatrice and Rahab, the "good" and the harlot of Jericho. Fletcher says in *Samuel Beckett's Art* that "underlying the Beckettian Man's nihilism is a frustrated hunger for the good and the pure." [4] This would appear to be substantiated in the early poems, although this hunger is tinged by disappointment and the sense of it being "too late." Man is no longer open to redemptionary relationships. The most explicit delineation of the whore and the good, and Beckett's opinion of them, occurs in what Harvey calls a "jettisoned" poem, "From the Only Poet to a Shining Whore." [5] Here Dante contrasts Rahab, the "bright patient / pearl-brow dawn-dusk lover of the sun" with Beatrice, "mother, sister, / daughter, beloved / fierce pale flame / of doubt," "radiant" and "angry." Her doubt, contrasting with Rahab's act of faith, becomes "God's sorrow, / and my sorrow." Beatrice fails men with her lack of understanding and forgiveness. The whore, with her emphasis on bodily love, disturbs in another way. She breeds desire out of a dead land and her failure is in the trap of procreation. [6] The use of these two models provides an interesting corollary reference to religion. The entire Christian dualistic view of woman is implied; Beatrice the saintly, the virgin, leads man to religious salvation; Rahab, the fallen, seduces God's chosen. Beckett, in reworking these allusions, calls into play an irony which weaves through many of his works.

The philosophical dualism of *Whoroscope* is reinforced by the title and by the Descartes persona's seemingly rambling references to specific women, who are both Beatrices and Rahabs. The introductory epithet of "Porca Madonna" climaxes with "Christina the ripper, the Rahab of the snows, the murdering matinal pope-confessed amazon" who, in the name of religion, mind, and salvation, quite literally

---

[4] Samuel Fletcher, *Samuel Beckett's Art* (London: Chatto and Windus, 1967), p. 14.
[5] *Henry-Music* (Paris: The Hours Press, 1930). Text reprinted in Harvey, pp. 306-307.
[6] The effect of the whore calls to mind the opening lines of Eliot's *The Wasteland* (New York: Harcourt, Brace & Company, 1958), p. 29: "April is the cruelest month, breeding / Lilacs out of the dead land, mixing / Memory and desire."

disposed of bodies. (p. 15) There are two innocents in the poem and they too are the object and the cause of suffering. Francine, Descartes' daughter, and the "slim pale double-breasted" foetus in the egg are both "abortions of fledglings," violently removed before they fulfill their roles. Yet these roles, cynically enough, are hardly joyous. They can die now or they can die later. The reference to Anna Maria reinforces the corruption of yet another Beatrice: "She reads Moses and her love is crucified"; "she bloomed and withered, a pale abusive parakeet in a mainstreet window." (p. 14) Thus, a failed Beatrice confronts a Rahab of the snows in Descartes' recollective mind and philosophical system. The women symbolize various stages of development in the poem and they concretize difficulties of that philosophy.

In *Echo's Bones,* the emphasis shifts; the whore and the good are no longer two tensions of the same personality. Rather their impact on the poet is recorded separately, and the bawd becomes increasingly important. Further, the conceptual impact of the title, of an Echo loving a Narcissus, is reinforced by the two models.

The Beatrice-type figure appears in three of the poems. As the "veronica mundi / veronica munda" of "Eneug 2," she is a universal figure of compassion who takes pity on man making his painful way through the Calvary of his existence. Through this brief allusion, the spectre of Christianity is called forth and negated. For while Veronica was able to comfort Christ, she is unable to help Beckett for she is "too late to brighten the sky." (p. 27) Man must endure of himself. Although Beatrice is not mentioned explicitly in "Alba," she is the prototype and the point of reference. In a wonderfully lyrical and poignant verse, Beckett recognizes the salvation that Dante experienced, but concludes that Beatrice's "beauty shall be a sheet before me / a statement of itself drawn across the tempest of emblems / ... only I and then the sheet / and bulk dead" (p. 28).

Here as the Beckettian world condenses, Beatrice in "Sanies 2" becomes "the blissful," pre-*Vita Nuova*. She is frozen in a picture hung in a house of prostitution and she surveys the perversions of that life. Such is the end of the Beatrician ideal for Beckett.

The bawds, in keeping with the theme of "bleeding meat," are a sharper focus for this collection.[7] They seduce, provoke, and yield either respite, suffering, or both. In "Dortmunder," the bawd is queenly and beautiful: "royal hulk... the eyes the eyes black." She offers the poet escape through darkness, music, and quiescence after sex. The religious theme is once more part of the context. The poet goes past the "red spires of the sanctuary," the church. There is a transposition of the values of the church to those of the house of prostitution. While the passivity is emphasized, the quiet is transient and gives way to the "plagal east": "Schopenhauer is dead" and "the bawd puts away her lute" (p. 29).

The bawds of the two "Sanies" poems intrude upon the world of the poet in a more active way, and there is a conscious rejection of them by Beckett. This rebuff extends to and includes the supposed harbor of religion. In "Sanies 1," the woman is the "dauntless nautch-girl," a "daughter of desires in the old black and flamingo." (p. 32). Although the poet's need for her is apparent, the horror of creation, of birth and suffering, impinges and he tells her "to get along." "Sanies 2" depicts the sexual orgies of a brothel in a rollicking tone which slowly gives way to horror. All the bawds are united into Becky, from whom Beckett painfully begs a respite from all this begetting and becoming: "spare me damn thee / spare me good Becky." (p. 34). In Eliot fashion, the persona then calls upon God's mercy. The laceration of sex becomes synonymous with the agonies of existence. The inference is that the avoidance of the one will mollify, will deaden, the other.

"Serena 2" utilizes the metaphor of the mother-slut, the clonic earth, who, as the smothering parent, keeps man a prisoner because he takes his nature from her. The agony of childbirth and the life of man is symbolized through the fear of the bitch; birth and death are two sides of the coin in her mind and "she is ashamed." Beckett's increasing fluidity of reference is apparent; "She" refers to earth,

---

[7] Many critics have taken the closing lines of "Enueg I" as emblematic of the series of poems.

>   Ah the banner
>   the banner of meat bleeding
>   on the silk of the seas
>   and the arctic flowers
>   that do not exist. (p. 25)

dog, the harbour, his mother, the light randy slut. The reactions tumble over each other until the poet says: "all these phantoms shuddering out of focus / ... all the chords of the earth broken like a woman pianist's" (p. 39). Death is the only release from this cycle, for which woman seems to be responsible.

"Serena 3" reflects both the sense of loss the poet experiences and the increasing commitment he feels to reject the woman-sex-religion triad. The main section of the poem is a frank evocation of the separation of the lovers, replete with phallic symbols and vaginal images. Yet again the temptation is resisted and he must "hide not in the Rock / must keep on the move / keep on the move" (p. 42). The only specific named reference is to the "something heart of Mary," a rather clever obfuscation of religious overtones and physical longing.

Beckett's poetic depictions of images of woman, then, provide a key to understanding some of the concerns of his poetry and of his later work. He must ultimately reject them for they catalyse feelings and needs which draw him away from self-contemplation and containment. Perhaps one of the best ways to conclude is to quote a rather sensitive and lovely poem, in which Beckett summarizes these tensions between body and spirit, love and religion, and a "lonely freedom" [8] that is only partially wanted.

YOKE OF LIBERTY

The lips of her desire are grey
and parted like a silk loop
threatening
a slight wanton wound
She preys wearily
on sensitive wild things
proud to be torn
by the grave crouch of her beauty.
But she will die and her snare
tendered so patiently
to my tamed watchful sorrow
will break and hang
in a pitiful crescent. [9]

---

[8] Harvey, p. 313.
[9] *The European Caravan* (New York: Brewer, Warren, and Putnam, 1931), p. 480.

FROM POETICS TO ANTI-POETICS

by Stephani Pofahl Smith

A central concern of Beckett's poetics, one which persisted throughout his career, is his preoccupation with dualities. These extend in endless paradigms of binary opposition: microcosm and macrocosm, mind and body, subjective and objective knowledge, intellect and emotion, life and death. An esthetic focused on these oppositions is already evident in Beckett's poetry, as Laurence Harvey has shown,[1] and they remain in later works.

Beckett's esthetics did, however, undergo a fundamental change. This alteration must be situated in a changed attitude towards the relationship between art and the unrelieved tensions of existence. In his early career, while he was writing primarily poetry, Beckett's view of art was an essentially poetic one. Art, like Proust's involuntary memory, recaptured the conflicts of experience in a transcendent fusion. It lifted man temporarily out of time and space and provided him with an asylum from the confusion of being. Art could unify the dualities of existence in the magic of poetry, replacing the tensions of a divided experience with the verbal tensions generated by fusing conceptual opposites.

In the later essays, as Laurence Harvey has noted, Beckett begins to emphasize a different role for art: "to shed light on the issueless predicament of existence."[2] It is from this attitude that his mature works and his later statements on esthetics have grown. An emphasis on dilemma rather than symbolic synthesis is an essentially anti-poetic

---

[1] *Samuel Beckett, Poet and Critic* (Princeton, New Jersey: Princeton University Press, 1970), pp. 1-247.
[2] P. 419.

stance. The later Beckett refuses the magical unity of metaphor as he refuses every other transcendental escape. At the same time he becomes increasingly conscious of the limits of language, especially of the problems generated by binary opposition where opposites are inseparable in mutual dependence yet logically irreconcilable. Beckett leaves behind an esthetic of poetry for an art of insoluble contradictions.

As Beckett evolved from a poetic to an anti-poetic view of art, from unity to dilemma, he turned from poetry to verbal humor. Beckett employed verbal humor from the beginning of his career, but only as he was abandoning poetry for the theater and the novel did he become aware of the unique potential of humor for realizing his new esthetic aims. Humor is by nature an expression of insoluble contradictions where conceptual contraries are related but not combined. While verbal humor and metaphor involve the same linguistic mechanisms, they function in opposite ways. Where metaphor unifies, humor divides.

In explaining the psychic mechanism of humor, Freud emphasized its dual nature. Both an inhibition and a means to avoid it must be active for the joke to succeed. In Beckett's verbal humor the inhibition is found in language itself, in the conceptual habits which automatically place our perceptions in one category or another and exclude all that is confusing and contradictory. Beckett uses humor to interrupt and contest these habits and to provide a new perspective on the artificial limits they impose.

Let us briefly consider an example of Beckett's poetic treatment of duality in the opening section of "Serena II," an early poem:

> this clonic earth
>
> see-saw she is blurred in sleep
> she is fat half dead the rest is free-wheeling
> part the black shag the pelt
> is ashen woad
> snarl and howl in the wood wake all the birds
> hound the harlots out of the ferns
> this damfool twilight threshing in the brake
> bleating to be bloodied
> this crapulent hush
> tear its heart out
>
> in her dreams she trembles again
> way back in the dark old days panting

> in the claws of the Pins in the stress of her hour
> the bag writhes she thinks she is dying
> the light fails it is time to lie down
> ....
> in a hag she drops her young
> the whales in Blacksod Bay are dancing
> the asphodels come running the flags after
> she thinks she is dying she is ashamed [3]

Birth and death are fused in the opening words, "this clonic earth." Earth, so often associated with the adjective "mother," suggests generation, while "clonic" suggests the spasms which announce death. The first line thus identifies the convulsions which precede creation and procreation with those which precede destruction. Transformed into the animal sphere, this identification becomes a pregnant Kerry Blue, half dead in sleep but vibrantly alive as she dreams of a chase which is to result in death for her victim. The twilight, "bleating to be bloodied," calls out, not for the mother's succor, but for the blood of death which is also its birth in red light. The dog's real pain excites dreams of giving birth, and this section closes on the words, "she thinks she is dying she is ashamed." The animal's habit of going off to hide both to die and to whelp is translated as shame in the human perspective. We are thus reminded of the human fear of death in childbirth, at once a real fear and a superstitious association of birth and death.

As Beckett turned away from poetry such as that exemplified by "Serena II," he abandoned above all the principle of symbolic unity, the verbal fusion of disparate or opposed elements which takes place in the metaphor. He continued to employ his poetic gifts in a theatrical production which is at once poetic and anti-poetic: poetic in that it rejects a structure based on conventions of spacial and temporal relationships, action and character, in favor of a structure based on verbal relationships, allusion and symbolism; anti-poetic in that its minimal unit of structure is humorous contradiction which is reenforced rather than resolved on the symbolic level.

All That Fall provides a good illustration of Beckett's unique combination of poetry and humor. Within the text, which is predominantly humorous, form and content are unified in a symbolic rejection

---

[3] *Poems In English* (New York: Grove, 1961), pp. 38-39.

of the symbolic fusion of metaphor. It is this metaphoric unification of matter and spirit which is the essence of Judeo-Christian religion. The title of the play is juxtaposed in ironic contradiction with the verse from Psalms from which it is taken: "The Lord upholdeth all that fall and raiseth up all those that be bowed down." This poetic passage attempts to unite the spiritual and material domains. The words, "fall" and "be bowed down," belong exclusively to a material world of gravity while the words, "raiseth" and "upholdeth" (with its suggestion of suspension) are designated by the word "Lord" for the spiritual domain. The passage is a paradox or, one might say, a ruse. It poetically suggests a victory over gravity and death, but it is actually applicable only in the spiritual system. Man is not rescued from a material fall but from a spiritual fall which is given a material form. Because man is both matter and spirit, he can "fall" in two ways, but he can be uplifted by a spirit only spiritually.

The Rooneys' laughter at the mention of the passage is a clear rejection of its metaphoric significance. Humorous contradiction arises only when one imagines the material fall of a material being, such as man, arrested by an immaterial being such as God. The passage becomes humorous when the two descriptive systems are conceptually separated rather than metaphorically fused. By detaching that part of the passage associated with materiality ("all that fall") from its metaphoric context Beckett emphasizes that the salvation of the metaphor is only a metaphoric one. The union of the material and the spiritual can be achieved only in poetry.

We should note here that the verse from Psalms which includes the title of the play arises in conjunction with another title of a Sunday sermon: "How to be Happy though Married." This amusingly incongruous title recalls, of course, that the Rooney's are an incompatible couple whose association is not likely to be improved by a Sunday sermon. The sermon title again emphasizes and rejects the purely metaphoric role of religion in unifying the spiritual and the material. The Rooneys' unhappy marriage is a necessarily contradictory association of matter and spirit, body and mind. Maddy Rooney represents the needs of the body in her longing for sexual pleasure and children. Dan Rooney, her husband and opposed counterpart, represents the needs of the mind. He hates children, refuses sexual love, and enjoys the abstract precision of mathematics, though he lives in a world where the number of steps never seems to remain the same.

The opposed positions of the Rooneys on the "life-versus-death" question are embodied in their attitudes towards children. Dan wants to kill a child and Maddy wants to call one back to life, but both express themselves with humorous contradiction. Dan wonders, "Did you ever wish to kill a child? — Nip some young doom in the bud." With the riming substitution of "doom" for "bloom" the absent cliche and its present variant are polarized in direct opposition. On the side of the cliche we have a cultural habit which assumes that the death of a child is a purely negative event which cuts off a life about to "bloom." Such an assumption must presuppose that existence is a positive state. Dan's parasytic, humorous statement assumes that existence is a negative state and that the death of a child is a positive event which cuts off fated misery. Neither position can be absolutely maintained because it is contradicted by the other. Existence is both positive and negative. It must include both good and bad because each is defined relative to the other. If there can be no absolute evaluation of existence, there can be no uncontradictory evaluation of death.

Dan Rooney suggests throwing out the baby with the dirty water, eliminating misery by eliminating life. The humorous form which his speculation takes includes its own contradiction. This contradiction is then reflected in his behavior, for he is deeply upset by the death of a child under the train and tries to avoid talking about it.

Maddy's attitude towards children is equally subjective and untenable though precisely opposed to that of her husband. She assumes that reproducing life is a positive activity although she well knows that to be is to suffer. She too expresses herself with humorous contradiction as she wishes her daughter Minnie had lived: "In her forties now she'd be, I don't know, fifty, girding up her lovely little loins, getting ready for the change..." In a fond evocation of this sort, the wish for life is logically associated with a positive state, as in the cliche, "He'd be a man now, with children of his own." Beckett inverts the cliche to read, "She'd be an old woman now, losing her reproductive powers." Maddy's humorous realism contests the conventional coherence of the cultural habit. She simultaneously desires life, a positive, and the decay which precedes death, a negative, for her beloved child. Since one cannot have life without decay and death, one cannot decide if it is to Minnie's advantage to be dead or to be alive and dying. One cannot decide absolutely in favor of reproduction or against it, as one cannot choose between conscious, suffering being and senseless non-being.

As body and mind Maddy and Dan are married in an impossible contradiction. Dan aptly characterizes their relationship when he compares them to Dante's damned walking "arsy-versy," irreconcilable and inseparable. Like the binary opposition they represent, they are mutually dependent and mutually exclusive. The body longs to reproduce itself as the only kind of regeneration possible. The mind refuses procreation as the only way to end the misery of existence. Taken separately, the approach of each is apparently rational, but together each refutes the other as each disputes himself in humorous contradiction. The combination of body and mind makes every choice a false one.

Maddy grieves for her lost daughter while she muses to herself, but she never mentions Minnie to others. Minnie is the child who died because she had never been really born, and her name is derived from the German word for love, "Minne,"[4] as in "Minnesinger." The ideal satisfaction of love would unify the body and the mind, fulfilling the mind's need for esthetic pleasure and the body's need for sexual pleasure. Like Godot, the love which would reconcile Maddy and Dan is present only by its absence.

The harmonious unification of matter and spirit, body and mind, is found in two domains, both associated with poetry. These are religion and love. Both of these are rejected as means to transcend the dualities of existence. In two different ways Beckett refuses the gratuitous choices made by Proust. Proust succeeds in unifying the self only by suppressing one half of it. He chooses art over love, the mind over the body. Swann's story is one of inverted sublimation, an abortive attempt to satisfy the esthetic needs of the mind by pursuing a physical love object, just as the narrator, fascinated by the poetry of a name, pursues an esthetic experience through social contacts with the real Guermantes. Swann and the narrator both fail because both seek the union of the material and the spiritual in the material domain rather than in the domain of art. There is a solution, and Proust chose again with his poetic prose. The esthetic joy of involuntary memory gives

---

[4] Cf. "Minnie! Little Minnie! (Pause.) Love, that is all I asked, a little love, daily, twice daily, fifty years of twice daily love like a Paris horse-butcher's regular, what normal woman wants affection?"

birth to an art which provides an escape from the conflicts of existence in time. The body is transfigured and preserved in esthetic experience. Sensation coupled with esthetic distance, emotion coupled with intellect, metaphorically satisfy both body and mind, metaphorically unify the self in the spiritual domain of art. The painful failure of love and its analogue, social climbing, are transformed into esthetic pleasure.

For Beckett there is no escape. Poetry can be no more than a metaphysical fusion which in fact ignores the reality of the body by transferring it only symbolically into a paradoxical system. The self of Beckett's concerns is divided among couples who are joined in humorous contradiction. The needs of the mind and the body are equally valid, eternally linked and eternally opposed. The body is matter and can never be extracted from time. It can never be regenerated by esthetic pleasure or artistic recreation. As spirit the mind can never be regenerated by sexual pleasure or reproduction. The mind can no more accept the poetic ruse of love than the body can accept the poetic ruse of religion, be it a religion of gods or of art. Beckett rejects the metaphoric unity of poetry in favor of the irreducible contradictions of humor, as he refuses every necessarily gratuitous choice which would produce coherence by effectively excluding one half of the mutually dependent opposites which compose human existence. Though the concerns of Beckett and Proust are similarly focused on duality, Beckett moves away from Proust and poetry when he realizes that his own esthetic is centered in dilemma rather than in apotheosis and transcendence.

ECHO'S BONES:
STARTING POINTS FOR BECKETT

by Dougald McMillan III

MOST of us have approached Beckett first through "Waiting for Godot." Some scholars out of deference to chronology of publication dates have begun with "Whoroscope." Beckett himself has suggested that if we want to know the source of "Godot" we should begin with *Murphy*. From there he has sent at least one scholar to Geulincx for an understanding of *Murphy*. I would like to suggest another starting point. The experience recorded however obliquely in the 13 poem sequence *Echo's Bones* underlies nearly all that follows in Beckett. In that first book of poems we have the primary presentation of material that persists in transmuted form as an important element throughout Beckett's later works.

The problem of beginning with *Echo's Bones* is that even after extensive explication by careful and informed critics like Lawrence Harvey[1] and John Fletcher,[2] the series remains at best enigmatic even for Beckett scholars. The problems are twofold: first, the poems are written from a set of aesthetic assumptions quite different from those that have determined the expectations of most readers of 20th Century English poetry. And secondly, the poems depend upon a detailed knowledge of place that very few readers possess.

If our literary experience is in the English tradition, our expectations for 20th Century poets are likely to be so conditioned by imagism that consciously or unconsciously we will base our attempts

---
[1] Lawrence Harvey, *Samuel Beckett: Poet and Critic,* Princeton, 1970.
[2] John Fletcher, "The Private Pain and the Whey of Words," in *Samuel Beckett* ed. Martin Esslin, Englewood Cliffe, N.J. 1965. pp. 23-32.

to find coherence in complex works on a search for single unifying images. Failing to find them, we are likely to conclude that we are dealing with a surrealist tradition. With Beckett this seems justified by his own statements that poetry "does not make clear" and should be made with a "minimum of rational interference." [3] It is easy to decide that in reading these poems we need respond only to an inexplicable order of the unmeditated mind of the poet, but that is not the case.

Beckett is quite consciously outside the imagist tradition. He showed his bemused disregard for Ezra Pound's dicta by ironically entitling his 1934 review of *Make it New*, "Ex Cathezra." Elsewhere his own statements and metaphors define a kind of literature in direct opposition to that advocated by Pound and practiced by such figures as Eliot, Yeats, and Wallace Stevens. Pound's famous metaphor of the image as a great vortex suggests that in poetry experience is concentrated centripitally into visual presentation. And Pound compares poems to chiseled cameos. Similar suggestions of small, non-verbal, concentrated, carefully-wrought works are contained in Eliot's symbol of art, the Chinese jar in "Four Quartets." The implication of these metaphors is that the poem is a moment of magical stasis. Beckett envisions an art that is not dedicated to stasis. He praises Proust because "he chisels no Bellenisque pommels." [4] In his unpublished novel "A Dream of Fair to Middling Women," Beckett's characters discuss art as the "inward decrystalization of experience." [5] He criticizes the art that presents character "artificially immobilized in a backwash of composure so that a precise value can be assigned." [6] Instead of extolling the ability of art to capture and hold experience in stasis, Beckett describes a scene in which experience orders itself into an image with particularized significance and says "alas, cang of emblem." [7] To reduce the world to ordered images is perhaps inevitable, but it is like confining the head in the yoke of a Chinese torture implement. In the poem "Alba" he celebrates the ability of music to bring relief from the "tempest of emblems."

---

[3] Samuel Beckett, "Denis Devlin," in *transition* 27 (May, 1935), p. 293.
[4] Samuel Beckett, *Proust*, N.Y., Grove Press N.D., p. 61 (original edition 1931).
[5] Quoted in Harvey, p. 261.
[6] Harvey, p. 341.
[7] Harvey, p. 261.

In contrast to an art which strives towards stasis, Beckett describes a dynamic art, the record of experience that is protean and irreducable.

> The inviolable criterion of poetry is figured in the night sky. The ecstatic mind ... rises to the shaft heads of its statement, its recondite relations of emergal, from a labour and a weariness of deep castings that brook no schema. The mind suddenly entombed, then active in an anger and a rhapsody of energy in a scurrying and plunging toward exitus. [8]

The elements of his art are like sea wrack "refractory constituents" reluctant to bind together into a synthesis.

> Their movement is based on a principle of repulsion, their property not to combine but, like heavenly bodies, to scatter and stampede, astral straws on a time strom, grit in the mistral... Their centres are wasting, the strain away from the center is not to be gainsaid, a little more and they explode. Then, to complicate things further, they have odd periods of recueillement, a kind of centrepedal back wash that checks the rot." [9]

In metaphors from music and mathematics Beckett's character Belacqua describes his own autobiographical work as a form requiring awareness of what is present only by implication and suggestion. "The experience of my reader shall be in between the phrases, in the silence communicated by the intervals not the terms of the statement... his experience shall the menace, the miracle, the memory of an unspeakable trajectory." [10] This trajectory is traced in varying ways in "Dream" itself, the stories of *More Pricks than Kicks,* and *Echo's Bones,* but the menace, the miracle, and the unspeakableness of the original experience are presented more directly in the poems of *Echo's Bones* than in the stories or the available fragments of the unpublished novel. To follow the trajectory, however, we must be attuned to what is communicated in the silences and to do that we must lay aside our expectations that some single image or set of images will fix the experience for us in a simple way. We must be willing to accept an experience as dynamic as that of the poet.

---

[8] Harvey, p. 342.
[9] Harvey, p. 340.
[10] Harvey, p. 342.

But even when we have adjusted our aesthetic expectations, there remains the practical problem of a detailed knowledge of place necessary to understanding. At one level at least the trajectory is a real one situated in geographical locations not necessarily familiar to Beckett's readers. His use of locations is, moreover, more specific than we are likely to realize at first. In the latter part of "Serena I," for example, it is insufficient to be vaguely aware of a watershed in the Wicklow mountains with whatever connotations that may evoke; we must be able to situate the action of the poem at that specific vantage point from which county Meath will be prominent to the north with Dublin and its suburb, Foxrock, site of Beckett's birth, in between. Otherwise we will miss the suggestions that the "fairy tale" experience of Meath is separated from the poet by the realities of birth and death associated with Foxrock and Dublin.

Beyond particularity there is the problem that arises from the fact that Beckett feels no obligation to make his poems self-contained. Not only particular knowledge but knowledge of a geographical context larger than that given in the poem is frequently required of us. The most direct example of this is in "Serena III" where we need to know that the action described in the poem stops just short of Dun Leary, the harbor from which one would depart from Ireland. Awareness of a larger context plays a similar role in poems like "Sanies II" and "Serena II." And indeed, part of an understanding of the whole series depends upon our being aware of the map of Europe and the pattern of a great spiral outward from Dublin and then back to it that the movements and places described in the poems chart upon that background. In one sense our starting point must be a set of maps.

Finally, Beckett's use of place involves a familiarity with local monuments and connotations not always provided in the poem either. In "Serena III," for example, he writes "Hide yourself not in the rock." In the context of the movement down the Dublin coastline it is not difficult to associate this with the town of Blackrock, but only a more intimate knowledge or help from a source like Weston St. John Joyce's *The Neighborhood of Dublin* can make the reader aware that the rock for which the little town is named had long since disappeared when the poem was written and the rock referred to is Blackrock's most famous landmark, a curious stone cross with a carved face at its center. And yet this cross connects this poem with "Enueg II" and plays an important part in unifying the series.

That is the nature of the difficulties. They are not minor, but once we are aware of them we have a chance at least of coming to understand something of the experience recorded in the poems. If the series is not reducable to a single image, it nevertheless begins with one which suggests the nature of the trajectory — a hungry vulture circles above its prey. It descends but is unable to consume its prey because though its victim is dying it still has life. (The sense of an unfulfilled desire and an incompleted form here and the fact that the series begins with an emblematic presentation soon dissipated into more narrative and discursive forms invites direct contrast with Wallace Steven's "Sunday Morning." There in an almost archetypal pattern of imagist poems the image of pigeons making "ambiguous undulations as they sink down to darkness on extended wings" is used as a culmination point condensing and bringing into stasis and a sense of completion all that has gone before.)

This uncompleted action of "The Vulture" implies the first of several metamorphoses that must be achieved in the series. The bird is "mocked by a tissue" that "cannot serve" until it has become "offal." As in Shakespeare's "Tempest," to which there are several subtle references in the series, there must be a miraculous change through death or fictional death. In Beckett, though, death is not only the agent of change. It is death itself that must be changed — its victims must be altered from dying creatures to lifeless carrion.

From the emblematic six lines of "The Vulture" the series moves in "Enueg I" from sky to earth and to a narrative presentation of the poet's own direct experience with 'mocking tissue.'

> Exeo in a spasm
> tired of my darling's red sputum
> from the Portobello Private Nursing Home
> its secret things

Here for the first time the center of dying flesh — a young girl dying from tuberculosis — about which the series turns is present as a "term." Hereafter this central experience will be present more often by implication in the "intervals." Even here it is presented so briefly and undramatically that it is possible to miss its importance.

The nursing home at Portobello Place on the Grand Canal south of Trinity College and its "secret things" are the geographical and emotional starting point which defines the trajectory of the series. Again and again the poet's wanderings bring him back to this neighborhood and into contact with its painful memories. The presence of the girl absent in reality from the poet's life permeates the series and forms a part of each of the poems. She is the Echo of the title and the series traces a metamorphosis like that in Ovid from a living girl to a disembodied phantom, to bones and offal and finally to a memory attested to only by a rock cairn. The poet, too, undergoes a metamorphosis from a real person in a real Dublin to the purely fictional character Belacqua. Until these changes can be effected, the poet is menaced by the presence of the girl and moves in panic from one extremity to another in attempts to elude her memory. As Beckett wrote in "A Dream of Fair to Middling Women" "His truest self was Belacqua, his second truest self was Narcissus fleeing Echo." [11]

The movements traced in "Enueg I" suggest the pattern of the whole series. Leaving the hospital he crosses the canal, turns about one "banner," follows the canal westward, and recrosses the canal amid suggestions that he is passing again into the world of the dead. He comes at last to the pit of the river Liffey where "vigilant gulls" circle above "the grey spew of the sewer." (In a similar passage in "Dream" he uses the term "meatus of the sewer" and the same word "offal" used in "The Vulture" to describe this scene.) [12] His exit and subsequent journey has taken him away from the consideration of dying humanity embodied in red expectorations so wearying to him because they are associated with individual suffering to a contemplation of humanity's discharges as mere refuse. (The complex associations of predation, meat, and excretion seen here are treated more explicitly in another early poem, "Casket of Pralines for a Mandarin's Daughter," where he refers to the beauty of art as gastro-intestinal purgation.

> Beauty, oh thou predatory evacuation,
> from the bowels of my regret —
> readily effected
> by the assimilation of a purging gobbet
> from my memory's involuntary vomit)

---

[11] Harvey, p. 267.
[12] Harvey, p. 254.

The journey does not bring a longed-for consummation. Even as the poet looks northward where relief might lie, reminders of his darling's bleeding flesh remain. The suggestions of a quest for consolation in an ideal symbolized by mythical flowers is seen as futile.[13]

> Ah the banner
> the banner of meat bleeding
> on the silk of the seas and the arctic flowers
> that do not exist.

The Provencal Enueg is a complaint. In "Enueg I" Beckett defined the first of the two main complaints that animate the series — as humans we are flesh that dies. In "Enueg II" he defines the second — images of the dead and dying persist. The poet lies on O'Connell bridge between the world to the north of the Liffey with its associations with the ideal and the world to the south which contains the reality of Portobello. As he gazes into the sky, the face of his beloved appears and disappears. It is like the image left by the sweat of Christ on Veronica's napkin. In its appearance it is "veronica mundi" — true image of the world with its suffering. Its disappearance "veronica munda" — a true image of purgation. In the end it is the image of suffering that prevails, the face returns as an "overtone." Like an echo, the memory returns involuntarily as a reminder of her physical suffering and also of his own mental suffering which it causes. While there is no real movement in the poem, the allusions to the legend of Veronica and the reference to his sweating suggest that he is traversing a kind of Via Dolorosa.

In the two Enuegs it is clear that efforts to elude the experience of Portobello in Dublin fail. The next two poems of the series, "Alba" and "Dortmunder," comprise a pair in which release is sought in foreign travel and music. "Alba" is an aubade. — traditionally a song lamenting the parting of lovers at dawn. In Beckett's use the form is at once a song of parting from his earthly love and a song of celebration

---

[13] Beckett frequently associates the quest for the ideal with Novalis' "blue flower." The tone is almost always one of ironic disparagement. Cf. "Assumption," "Sedendo and Quiesciendo," "Dream of Fair to Middling Women" (quoted in Harvey, p. 274), "A Wet Night," p. 60. The lines quoted here are from Baudelaire but the "arctic flowers" have much the same significance of a distant ideal, with the important difference that for Novalis the blue flower does exist.

of his union with the ideal of music which will mercifully erase the images that trouble his memory. Praising Schopenhauer, whom he mentions specifically in "Dortmunder," Beckett had written in his essay on Proust of the ability of music to efface images. In that essay published the same year as "Alba," he wrote:

> Music is the idea itself unaware of the world of phenomena existing ideally outside the universe apprehended not in space but in time only ... The essential quality of music is distorted by the listener who, being an impure subject, insists on giving a figure to that which is ideal and invisible ... Music damns the life of the body on earth as a pensum and reveals the meaning of the word defunctus. [14]

In "Alba" he expresses the hope that the ideal will stoop to him and establish a "white plane of music."

> a statement of itself drawn across the
> tempest of emblems
> so that there is no sun and no unveiling
> and no host
> only I and then the sheet
> and bulk dead.

The imageless ideal will free him from the particulars of existence and reduce death to a painless, generalized experience.

The title and reference to strata, mysteries and white sheets above bulk dead suggest that the location of the poem is Alba Longa in Italy, a famous archaeological site, the seat of sacred mysteries associated with the druidic rites of Ireland and a great marble-covered mass grave. As in the case of the alternation between sky and earth in the previous four poems, the series also moves between extremes in these two poems. In "Dortmunder" the scene changes from southern Europe to Kassel in the north of Germany according to information Beckett furnished Lawrence Harvey. [15] From contact with the disembodied ideal at dawn in "Alba," it moves to a prostitute at evening in "Dortmunder" and from pure music to the famous north German beer that provides the title. And from white purity it moves to a scene infused with the entire range of the spectrum (red spires, green

---

[14] Beckett, *Proust*, p. 71.
[15] Harvey, p. 77.

jade earrings, purple lamps). Like "Alba," "Dortmunder" is a lute song, but in it the lute is associated with sensual pleasures. The prostitute seems for a while to provide a moment's release by disolving the memory of the lost girl, but the poem ends on a renewed note of complaint. In the awaited moment of ecstasy which effaces all others the solace is seen to be temporary,

> Then as a scroll, folded,
> and the glory of her dissolution enlarged
> in me, Habbakuk, mard of all sinners.
> Schopenhauer is dead, the bawd
> puts her lute away.

Flight to Europe, the ideal, the pleasures of the flesh have all taken the poet outward away from the center of his experience. The form of his trajectory is not, however, a widening gyre, he is drawn back to Dublin in "Sanies I" and at the climax of the poem he comes to the point where he must cross the Liffey to enter again the neighborhood of Portobello.

In an unpublished short story also entitled "Echo's Bones," Beckett wrote "Sometimes he feels as though this old wound of his life had no intention of healing... he had tried everything from fresh air and early hours to irony and great art." [16] A "Sanie" is the draining of a wound. In the story "Yellow," in *More Pricks than Kicks*, as Belacqua moves toward release through death, he watches the movement of the sun in his hospital room. "On the grand old yeller wall, crowding in upon his left hand, a pillar of higher tone representing the sun was spinning out its placid deaiseal. This dribble of time thought Belacqua, like sanies in a bucket." [17] "Enueg I" illustrated that simple westward movement is insufficient remedy for the pain of life. The passage of time is not enough to drain the wound of life. The movement of "Sanies I" is a great counterclockwise spiral in a ritual attempt to undo time by traveling back to the womb. "Backward the shadows lengthen" and he longs to be "back in the caul" free of "spoilt love." (Hence the emphasis in the poem on encounters with others moving in the opposite direction.)

---

[16] Harvey, p. 323.
[17] Samuel Beckett, *More Pricks than Kicks*, N.Y., 1972, p. 167. (original publication, 1938).

The physical movement in the poem begins at Portrane on the coast north and east of Dublin. The poet bicycles counterclockwise west through the suburb of Donabate, past the old Barnwell estate at Turvey with its crest of "sad swans" bearing the motto "moriendo cano" (dying we sing), down through the village of Swords then turns eastward through Dublin "bound for home," his larch-shaded birthplace in Foxrock, southeast of the city.

"Sanies I" is in effect Beckett's anti-deasil with negative correspondence to all the suggestions of that ancient Celtic ritual form. For the Celts, to imitate the motion of the sun was a charm for good luck. In their religious rituals they moved in deasils, clockwise processions about rock cairns. In light of the myth of Echo and Narcissus, the whole series of *Echo's Bones* is a deasil about a cairn. And "Sanies I" begins in the area of County Meath north of Dublin disclosed in "Serena II" and the short story "Fingal" as the site of events which when they have become memory are, like the cairn of rock in Ovid, the final remnants of Beckett's Echo. (It is also significant that a cairn figures prominently in "Serena II" at just the point when the poet deals with his earlier memories of the girl.) But the movement of Beckett's series partakes of none of the mood of celebration normally associated with the deasil.

In Celtic folk customs the auspicious movements of the religious rituals were carried over to celebrate the important events of secular life. Clockwise processions called deasils marked weddings and births to bring good fortune to those involved in these new beginnings. "Sanies I" is a movement in disparagement of marriage and birth. It seeks an end to life. In *Ulysses* Joyce had begun his celebration of the birth of young Andrew Purefoy in the lying-in hospital in Holles Street with the words "Deshil. Hollis Eamus. Deshil" and traced the growth of the fetus until the moment of vagitus into the world. Beckett disassociates himself from the place of birth, "get along with you to the hob of your web in Holles Street," and traces a movement back to the womb and caul treating the celebration of his own birth ironically on the way.

The marriage disparaged is not his own but his parents' which he describes as having taken place on "Spy Wednesday," the day of Judas' betrayal of Christ, playing on the fact that he was born on Good Friday the thirteenth. That Beckett was aware of the ritualized movement of the deasil at weddings and associated it with the clockwise movement of time is evident from his description of the marriage procession in his story "What a Misfortune": "There was something so bright and meaty about the assembly, something so whorled in its disposition with the procession loosely coiled in the midst waiting to move off that Walter was slowly but surely put in mind of a Benozzo fresco." Later he refers to the same procession as a "mainspring" that will "tick off merrily to its stand up lunch." [18]

The disparagement of his birth is accomplished with another aspect of the deasil in mind. The word "deasil" itself was also uttered as a charm to those choking on food, to start the food moving in the proper direction. Beckett's delight in this early period in allusions that are both obscure and scatological, his concern with the "vomit" of involuntary memory, and the fact that in the story "Yellow" the cause of Belacqua's death is a failure to ausculate him (i.e., to clear his throat and lungs before administering anesthesia) also suggest that "Sanies I" as a form counter to the deasil even takes into account this folk custom of saying "deasil" to people choking on their food. The poem refers sarcastically to the ingestion of the first food (beestings) after birth: "Sparkling beestings for me," "for the proud parent he washes down a gob of gladness."

His attempt to undo life by executing his anti-deasil is not, however, successful. Before he can complete his journey out of the world back into the womb, the poet must face another encounter with "spoilt love." Like Narcissus, who even in Hell peers into the Styx, he is troubled by a reflection in the water as he crosses the Liffey. At first this appears to be a consummation at the end of his ride like the awaited verb at the end of a German sentence.

> I see main verb at last
> her whom alone in the accusative
> I have dismounted to love
> gliding towards me dauntless nautch-girl on the
> face of the waters
> dauntless daughter of desires in the old black
> and flamingo.

This vision proves only an enticement and not a consummation. He is soon urging her to "get along" but she cannot be dismissed so easily.

---

[18] Beckett, *More Pricks*, p. 142.

From the Liffey where the poet's path has brought him, their ways should now part. If he continues his unnatural path back to the womb he will head east at this point. If she should follow the natural path for a person of her age toward home and hearth and ultimately to Holles Street to give birth, she will have to head south at this point. That does not happen. His dismounting to love her is like that of the lady from Niger who smiled as she rode on a tiger. In her case

> they returned from the ride
> the lady inside
> and the smile on the face of the tiger

In his case too, but in a less comic sense, the lady is inside him and their ways home are fused together.

> Let the tiger go on smiling
> in our hearts that funds ways home.

The attempt to execute a spiral that will counter the effect of time ends not at Foxrock or "back in the caul" but in the neighborhood from which he began in "Enueg I." Visually the Holles Street hospital is the center of the web-shaped configuration of the neighborhood of Trinity College and Portobello Place south of the Liffey, north of the Grand Canal, and west of the shore. It is a web in the metaphorical sense, too. Home, hearth, and family have been denied by the death of his love, but he is still emotionally entangled. In "Enueg I" the poet appeared as a fly with his feet in marmalade. In "Serena I" he will refer to "My brother the fly, the common housefly" and in "Echo's Bones" he will be included among the maggots (the larval stage of the fly), which throng the bones of the dead beloved. If the lady would accept his offer of a free ride home, "be off," as he says, the figure of the smilling tiger might be more than bravado, but since she is inside him, he remains in her web. She is not his victim, he is hers.

The trajectory has led from earth to sky, from east to west, from Dublin to Europe, Europe to Dublin, now it leads back to Europe. Finding no refuge in the small, familiar world of home and family, he attempts next to lose himself in exotic experience. "Sanies II" takes us again to a foreign brothel, giving a sense of repetition. The addition of the elements of many nationalities and sexual perversion further indicate the growing desperation of the series, and the ever wider extremities to which the poet is being pushed in his flight. The scene in "Sanies II" is the bordellos of rue Mouffetard in Paris with their international clientel and atmosphere of varied activity and superficial gaiety. No longer embarked merely on a homeward spiral back toward birth, the poet moves in this poem simultaneously toward birth and death. He is "slouching, sailing the gauntlet of tulips" up to Puvis: he is moving "frescoward" as he says later. The frescoes of Puvis de Chavanes in the Pantheon at the top of the steep hill depict the life of St. Genvieve in a tryptich portraying her infancy, a scene of her looking out over Paris menaced by the plague, and a scene of her arrival by ship to bring aid to the fever-stricken inhabitants. Together the verbs "sailing and slouching" with the strong Yeatsian overtone of "Sailing to Byzantium" and "slouching toward Bethlehem to be born" suggest both ageing and return to innocence, birth. Despite the superficial gaiety and the relief from desires promised in the frescoes of Puvis, the rue Mouffetard remains a steep gauntlet and the goal of relief distant. It is typical of Beckett's ironic use of unstated geographical details that the street got its name from the ill-smelling canal befouled by a tannery nearby and so in spite of the vivacity associated with it, it is pervaded by the smell of death. This fact is further underscored by the presence of a bas-relief of bulls on the butcher's shop at the head of the street which likely prompted the Latin

vivas puellas mortui incursant boves

(the dead bulls assault the live girls). In running the steep and narrow "gauntlet" of the rue Mouffetard, he must pass the rue du Pot de Fer to his left and rue de l'Epée de Bois to his right. Then to reach the Puvis frescoes in the Pantheon he must go through rue Descartes and rue de l'Estrapade. His path is a torturous one through the perils of human duality.

The Latin line adapted from Platus' "Assinaria" alludes to flagelation and links it with the power of the dead to inflict pain on the living. As rawhide whips, "dead bulls" can still attack. At one level the line merely refers to flagelation as a part of the wide-ranging sexual fare of the bordellos, but at another it is directly related to the major theme of the series. In a less physical way the dead can also torture the living. Like the central character in Platus' play, the poet is found by his jealous lover even in the midst of the gaiety with which he would replace her. The power of the kind of silent presence with which the series deals is evident when inexplicably the loud laughter of the bar ceases and the jovial French madam previously only playfully sadistic becomes a true torturer associated with Dublin's most famous prostitute, Becky Cooper, celebrated in a popular Dublin quatrain as having greater attractions than foreign girls:

> Italy's girls are pretty
> and France's girls are willing
> But dearer far to me
> Is Becky's for a shilling.

Obviously something has brought to his mind the image of what he wants to forget. In a line recalling the cang of "Enueg I" — his head fixed upon the girl in the hospital — he cries out for other torture implements:

> Oh subito subito ere she recover the cang

and pleads first to her, "Becky, spare me," and then to God in terms of the Kyrie from the mass: "Lord have mercy on us," acknowledging his own guilt in trying to escape from her.

The sense of desperation and extremes increases in "Serena I." There, in contrast to the weary but free-flying vulture of the opening poem, the poet is at first passive and indifferent to prey, like the caged vultures he sees in Regent's Park zoo. But he is even more like 'his brother the fly' who alternates between moments of quiet and frantic flight. Traced on the map of London, the path followed by the poet in "Serena I" appears as a motiveless series of spirals about monuments and towers. He leaves the quiet of the British Museum, heads west through Regent's Park, crosses a small canal, enters the "Inner Circle" of the Botanical gardens, traverses the zoo, and comes to the "Outer Circle" of Regent's Park. His thoughts continue to move westward to Ireland briefly, but he turns abruptly to the southeast and the twin towered Crystal Palace. From there he heads north through the towers of Tower Bridge, turns west again passing the Bloody Towers and Married Men's Quarters of the Tower of London, and finally "screws" himself up the spiral staircase of St. Paul's Cathedral.

Like a creature confined by invisible boundaries, he has moved from one extreme of London to the other. As in Dublin, rivers and canals delineate his progress. The Outer Circle of Regent's Park marks the western edge of old London while the moats of the Tower of London with St. Catharine's Basin just across the road define the eastern limit of "The City." Nor are the extremities confined to latitude and longitude. The Crystal Palace to the south of the Thames is a tawdry amusement center, a kind of mockery of the blessed isles. St. Paul's to the north "Wrens great bully" is the supposed center of English spiritual life (cf. similar associations of the north side of the Liffey with the ideal, and the south side with earthly reality in "Enueg I"). He also alternates with seemingly little purpose between the surface of the earth, subterranean passages (the underground, the pedestrian underpass at the zoo, the moats of the Tower of London), and elevated observation points (Primrose Hill, Tower Bridge, and St. Paul's).

As the title, "Serena," (a song calling for the night to come so that the poet can join his beloved) suggests, the poem implies a longing for death. It is a form of release that still eludes him. In the underground a boy with "cerened eyes" demands if he is "done with the mirror" and he stomps off in a rage. He is not yet through with the superfice recorded in the daily press; he still has breath to show he is alive; and he is still troubled by reflected images. As the trajectory becomes more harried, the silence grows. In this poem no familiar place recalls his darling, no female figure is present to bring her to mind, she exists only in the repeated rhetorical question: "In Ken Wood, who shall find me." Ken Wood, outside the configurations of the city and the park with their canals and rivers, would seem to offer refuge. It would take a special effort of will on his part to seek out things that would stimulate memory. There "only the most quarried lovers" would confront his mind. His desperate flight is ample testimony that this hope is vain, that he is himself a most quarried lover, and that his love will be present everywhere, even in Ken Wood.

Predictably from the pattern of alteration now established, "Serena II" returns the poet to Ireland. The movement in the poem repeats the pattern of rapid movement from one boundary to another. The scene of action moves across the whole map of Ireland from the western islands to the eastern shore at Blacksod Bay, and from the Bens in the North to the Wicklow mountains in the South. That Crough Patrick, the site of the well-known annual pilgrimage to "the West," should be to the east of the starting point is an indication that once again the boundary he has reached is ultimate. At this point even the earth itself strains westward in reefs of tresses "out from the doomed land."

This time, however, we are no longer dealing with actual physical journeys on foot, bicycle, or public transportation. The movements here are visual and mental. The sense of place is determined not by where the poet goes, but by where he looks and what he remembers. We are concerned with the external and internal movements of his head. The poem begins with lines that emphasize repetitive motion and visual perception:

> this clonic earth
> see-saw she is buried in sleep

It continues with a pattern of alternation of perceptions of a dog and the landscape. His thoughts move first up then down, west then east, north then south, far then near. The accompanying head movements reveal the subdued panic of a confined animal. In his nervousness he must cast his head from side to side like those creatures which so trouble Murphy — Petrouchka the trained bear and the owls in the grotto of Battersea Park. In larger perspective these alternations of place in a poem in which the dream of the dog confuses and intermingles the experiences of birth and death trace a large circle around the poet's birth-place and the scene of the girl's death. From his final point of perspective, a rock cairn on a watershed in the Wicklow mountains, the city has remained an unattended background in the first part of the poem, but as night falls and the landscape fades, the city threatens to emerge as a figure dominating the field of perception which also includes the larches of his birthplace as foreground. He hopes to avoid that:

> so say your prayers now and go to bed
> your prayers before the lamps start to sing
> behind the larches

The vision that the realities of birth and death threaten to efface is that of Meath, a fairy tale land shining in the distance, a place associated with past outings with his love (cf. "Fingal" in *More Pricks than Kicks*). In Ovid's account the final stage of Echo's metamorphosis is a cairn of stones which keep the memory of her alive after all physical traces of her body have disappeared. In the metamorphosis traced by Beckett the cairn and the associated memories of an earlier time are the penultimate stage. The poet's confrontation with "all these phantoms shuddering out of focus" is an experience still subject to further reduction. So long as his Echo is a living memory, she is not yet mere bones. He may say his prayers at her cairn and hope like a child for untroubled sleep, but his trajectory cannot really be complete until she is reduced in his mind to offal.

The quiet valedictory tone that stilled the movements of panic briefly at the end of "Serena II" is absent in "Serena III," but still there is a sense of valediction in the poem as it describes a decision to depart. Two forms of movement are juxtaposed in the poem. One alternative is to continue the nervous zig-zag of panic displayed in earlier poems, the other is to abandon his love and follow the gentle curve of the Dublin coastline away from her.

If he does not "leave her," he will find himself again in a middle state between two extremes casting his eyes back and forth. He will find himself on Butt Bridge. He will be like a child between two great breasts looking first from sky to earth and from Misery Hill to the south where the red gas tanks are symbols of "carnation" to the north where the church of The Immaculate Heart of Mary is a purple reminder of spiritual immaculation. This will be a position permanently irreconcilable like the two lighthouses on either side of the Liffey "the Bull And Pool Beg that will never meet, not in this world."

To "leave her" as he admonishes himself and follow the gently curving coastline south from Irishtown to Dun Leary is to fix the "pot hook of beauty" on the palate of his experience. That is, to trace the form of the sigmoid line extolled by William Hogarth in his *Analysis of Beauty*.[19] There is a chance at least that this form will sum up experience and bring it to a final state. As in "Alba" where "fingers of compassion" stoop to "endorse the dust" this form is associated with Christ's act of writing in the dust to signify forgiveness for the

---

[19] Hogarth, William, *The Analysis of Beauty*, ed. Joseph Burise, Oxford, 1955.

woman taken in adultery. "Jesus Christ Son of God Saviour His Finger," he says when he sees Merrion flats scored with a "thrillion sigmas." Before he can get from Butt Bridge to the shoreline, though, he must first pass through the web in which he was caught in "Sanies I." As long as he is in the neighborhood of Portobello he must move fearfully and guiltily. He "buckets" over Victoria Bridge where he must cross the Grand Canal leading to Portobello Place. And he "slinks" down Ringsend Road away from Portobello Place until he reaches the shore at Irishtown. Then for awhile the path seems easy. As he passes the ruins of the old "Hell Fire Club," a well-known Dublin landmark, he jokes, "puzzle find the Hell fire." He has renounced the upward struggle toward Paradise associated with his love, yet experiences no torment. Soon enough, though, it is apparent that he is approaching the inferno as he sees "the tide making the dun gulls in a panic" and feels "the sand quicken in his hot heart." It seems for a moment that he will stop at Blackrock, since ancient times the southeastern frontier point of the municipal jurisdiction of Dublin, but he goads himself on

> Hide yourself not in the rock
> keep on the move, keep on the move.

The stone cross of Blackrock with the carved face at its center marks the southern boundary of Dublin. Its associations with the city, fleshly suffering, and persistent memory symbolized by the face make it an emblem of all the poet has sought to escape in the series. Though this town is not mentioned in the poem or even alluded to directly, it is clear that his goal must be the next town down the coastline, Dun Leary, the harbor from which he can leave Ireland forever to begin a life of wandering.

In turning away from ascent to paradise and in entertaining the idea of refuge in a rock, the poet began to assume some of the characteristics of Dante's Belacqua, the indolent lute player condemned to spend the span of his life in antepurgatory. In "Malacoda" he has entirely assumed the role of the unrealistically fictionalized Belacqua figure. We have left the world of real cities and real streets for a fictional limbo. The perspective is no longer in the first person. "Lay this Huysum on the box mind the imago it is he," says Malacoda, the undertaker who superintends the death rites of Belacqua, indicating that the final stage of metamorphosis has been reached. But even fictional death is denied by a "nay" prohibiting passage across Charon. Belacqua's final stage is not after all a corpse but a butterfly (a completed "imago" in entomological terms). Like the butterflies that are the hallmark of the paintings of Jan van Huysum, he hovers about the flowers that surround death. In light of the non-existence of the arctic flowers in "Enueg I," the hovering is no doubt only the beginnings of more flights of futility.

"Da Tagte Es" is a final aubade. It acknowledges that real death is the only consummation. All the other attemps are like the fictional death of the previous poem, "surrogate goodbyes." Only when breath is gone will there be freedom from images and "the glass unmisted above your eyes." All the previous motion is fruitless, no course of action short of setting out on the final journey of real death can bring relief.

In the final poem the poet reemerges clearly as a realistic persona, no longer the fictional Belacqua. His trajectory is complete; it has brought him in his own person to the grave of his love. She is there beneath his feet. His movement toward her is finished, "the gantelope of sense and non-sense run." Her metamorphosis to offal is also complete. Ostensibly, the death once so painful is now transformed, the "miracle" of "the unspeakable trajectory" complete and its "menace" overcome: the bones have found "asylum" under his tread and they are "taken by the maggots for what they are." He can even make crude puns; her flesh will fall "breaking without fear or favor wind." But again the air of bravado is unconvincing. If the bones are really nothing to him, why has he been "all this day" at her grave? In a series of poems dealing so much with metamorphosis we might well remember that maggots become flies.

There is no reason to suspect that the transformation to offal is final, that the phantoms "worse than dreams" will not once again "shudder into focus" and the panic-stricken flight about this center recommence. Even bones are not so easily forgotten. As Beckett wrote in "Cascando" published a year after *Echo's Bones*

> they always start dragging too soon
> the grapples clawing blindly the bed of want
> bring up the bones the old loves
> sockets filled once with eyes like yours.

An understanding of the coherence of *Echo's Bones* casts light both forward and backward on Beckett's other works. It helps us to see the pattern of "Whoroscope" as Descarte's own desperate trajectory of alternation between philosophical and geographical extremes with his illegitimate daughter's death by scarlet fever as its center. It helps us to see that Beckett's description of himself in *Quatre Poems* (1948) as "treading these long shifting thresholds" and "wandering ... in a convulsive space among the voices voiceless that throng my hiddenness" has reference to an external reality as well as an internal one. It lends a special note of poignance to Estragon's question to Pozzo "you don't need the ... er ... bones, Sir?" It suggests why the word "viduity" and "the viuda bird" should hold the attention of Krapp who has also held vigil across the canal from a hospital. And it makes even more relevant Beckett's acknowledgement of Lamartine's *"un seul être vous manque et tout est depeuplé"* as the source of the title of *Le Dépeupleur (The Lost Ones)*.

And starting from these poems and comparing the experience presented there with the ironic presentation in *More Pricks than Kicks* we can see what the narrator of the story "Echo's Bones" meant by saying that he had tried irony to heal the wound of his life. We can see in Belacqua Shua's recoil from women and his attachment to the austere "Alba" the transmutation of a more serious flight from spoilt love. And in his comic wandering back and forth in "Ding Dong," parodied by comparing his movements with those of an elaborate moving neon sign, we can see a comic reduction of the pathetic wanderings of the poet in *Echo's Bones*. Or recalling "Alba" and "Dortmunder" we can recognize the portrait at the end of *Watt* of a nude piano player covering his genitals with white sheet music as Beckett's ironic self-portrait as a man seeking refuge in the absolute of music. We can also see why it is *Songs by the Way* with which Watt scrapes off the slops with which he is covered, and we can understand the significance of the Galls' declaration that the piano, the tuner, and the piano player all are doomed.

In other works we can see the material of this experience subjected to abstraction. Malone creates his vision of MacMann on a bench with his back to the river (*i.e.*, looking toward the canal). The river nevertheless "appears to him" in the

> cries of the gulls that evening assembles in paroxysms of hunger round the outflow of the sewers opposite the Bellevue

> hotel. Yes, they too, in a last frenzy before night and its high crags, swoop ravening about the offal.[20]

We can, of course, respond to this as only a piece of decription evoking a general feeling of frenzied need, but by associating it with the specific pathos of *Echo's Bones* and the attempt to excape it in "Enueg I" we achieve a deeper understanding of Malone's process of being "born into death."

And we can also see why the Unnameable, who has 'spent his life in spirals round the earth,' should be so concerned with expunging images from his consciousness. His path is like that traced in *Echo's Bones*.

> I've never left the island, God help me. I was under the impression I spent my life in spirals round the earth. Wrong, it's on the island I wind my endless ways. The island, that's all the earth I know. I don't know it either, never having had the stomach to look at it. When I come to the coast I turn back inland. And my course is not helicoidal, I got that wrong too, but a succession of irregular loops, not sharp and short as in the waltz, now of a parabolic sweep that embraces entire boglands, now between the two, somewhere or other, and invariably unpredictable in direction, that is to say determined by the panic of the moment. But at the period I refer to now this active life is at an end.[21]

In two works of the late sixties we can see the resurfacing of pieces of the material from *Echo's Bones* in more direct references with new elements of pregnancy and suicide added — perhaps in an effort by Beckett to alter the experience for assimilation by fictional elaboration as he had altered it with irony in *More Pricks than Kicks*. In *How It Is*, one of the recurrent memories is of Pam Prim, Pim's "wife above." She is remembered as a pale creature dying in a white hospital room. The repetition of the phrase "I assure you" and the idea of cleansing the world link her with the girl of "Enueg II";

> A moment of the tender years the lamb black with the world's sins the world cleansed the three persons yes I assure you and that belief the feeling since then... the feeling since

---

[20] Beckett, Samuel, *Three Novels*, N.Y., 1965, p. 229.
[21] Beckett, *Three Novels*, p. 326.

then the vast stretch of time that I'd find it again the blue cloak the pigeon the miracles he understood. [22]

The hospital is not Portobello, the information in another passage that she jumped or fell from a window is new, an incident in which she asks for greenery and he brings only pale white Margurietes is added, but the essence of an experience with death that has by now the stature of a personal myth in the works of Beckett is evident.

Perhaps the clearest indication of this experience as a residual core in Beckett's work is in "Eh Joe," the television play Beckett wrote for the BBC in 1966. There we are again presented with a girl who "went young" as the voice of Joe's interior phantom tells him. She is linked to Pam Prim of *How It Is* by references to the shaving of her body hair alluded to in both works. She will be the last to go the voice tells him, "when you're done with yourself... All your dead dead... silence of the grave without maggots" she will remain. "The green one... the narrow one... Always pale... the pale eyes... there was love for you." [23] Again the details are much altered and the account of three attempts at suicide, the last successful one with an overdose of pills, do not coincide with *Echo's Bones* or *How It Is*, but the larger contours of the experience do coincide and certain details like the reference to the silence of the grave without maggots do lead directly back to *Echo's Bones*. The voice describes how after attempting to cut her wrists the girl binds the wound in a scrap of silk. "Slip clinging the way wet silk will... This all new to you, Joe?... Eh Joe?" [24] All new? Here is the old emblem of Beckett's first series from "Enueg I." "The banner, the banner of meat bleeding on the silk of the seas." And as the voice relating the details of the suicide grows slowly less audible we hear the words "imagine" "stone," "Joe," "imagine," "stones," "solitaire," "stones," "Breasts," "hands," "Imagine stones," "There's love for you Eh Joe?" The details of her death fade into a nearly inaudible background and it appears almost that she is turned to stone. However much she may have been altered by the process of fiction, Beckett's Echo remains, if only in the stones that call her to memory. She has never been reduced once and for all to offal.

---

[22] Samuel Beckett, *How It Is*, N.Y., 1964, p. 70. Also see p. 77.
[23] Samuel Beckett, *Eh Joe and Other Writings*, London 1967, p. 19.
[24] *Eh Joe*, p. 21.

We see in *Echo's Bones,* then, the beginnings of a personal myth central in Beckett's writing. It was Beckett's starting point and it might well be the starting point of readers who want to understand the coherence of Beckett's work as a whole.

MURPHY, OR THE BEGINNING OF AN ESTHETIC OF MONSTROSITY

by Maryse J. Leisure

BECKETTIAN criticism is divided into two main currents of thought. Some critics find the unity of the work in a moral philosophy or a vision of life. Others consider Samuel Beckett as an artist and an artisan of writing. Perhaps the best way to view Beckett is through a fusion of those two currents of thought in a vision of man as well as an esthetic ideal.

Accent has often been placed on the Beckettian bums and clowns without the consideration that they represent human nature in its monstrosity. In fact, the esthetics of monstrosity seems to encompass the entire novelistic work of Beckett from *Murphy* to *How It Is*.

Medically the word "monstrosity" means that which is abnormal or which differs from our usual vision of man. My approach does not intend to transform Beckett into a "médecin malgré lui" but rather to see him as an artist who uses the language of medicine to describe "the pathetic aspect of life." [1] A certain "esthetics of pathology" [2] emerges from Beckett's novels as early as *Murphy,* where Beckett uses physical, physiological, and psychopathological anomalies to describe his characters, his "patients." Beckett, like Murphy, displays a "surgical" quality.

The different categories which I have used imposed themselves in the reading and correspond to the natural classification found in

---

[1] Eugene Minkowski, *Traité de Psychopathologie* (Paris: Presses Universitaires, 1966).

[2] Gabriel Deshaies, *L'Esthétique du Pathologique* (Paris: Presses Universitaires de France, 1947).

medical books; however I did adapt them to the monstrosities which become Beckettian constants. I added a category for the objects because they are an integral part of the monstrous Beckettian universe. After *Murphy* the movements and nature will complete the list of categories used, all of them undergoing a progressive deformation.

Anatomical Anomalies

The anatomical anomalies in *Murphy* are not as severe as they become later starting with *Watt* and particularly in the trilogy. No one suffers the amputation of a limb, except a "Chelsea pensioner" who in the French text becomes a one-armed invalid.

Mr. Kelly is particularly handicapped by his legs, but the most deformed character is Miss Dew, who suffers from duck's disease. Beckett explains the illness: "Duck's disease is a distressing pathological condition in which the thighs are suppressed and the buttocks spring directly from behind the knees, aptly described in Steiss's nosomony as Panpygoptosis." [3] Panpygoptosis etymologically means all rump falling! She looks like a "stunted penguin."

Miss Counihan possesses extremely thick lips and an anthropoid character to match. In contrast to Clinch, a giant male orderly, Wylie and Cooper have minuscule heads. In fact, "Cooper's only visible human characteristic was a morbid craving for alcoholic depressant" (54). Concerning Murphy's appearance, a chandler in the street remarks, "E don't look rightly human to me" (77).

For Beckett, the body is an object to be described, and any deformity or a least irregularity is always emphasized, thereby rendering each character unique. To the corporal shortcomings are added numerous sensory ones, especially those concerning the eyes and the skin. The one-eye Cooper has a glass eye which is "blood injected." Mr. Kelly has eyes of a "phytonic glaze." Murphy's eyes are as "cold and unwavering as a gull's" (2). Celia has eyes which roll "everted like an aborting goat's" (137). But the longest and most monstruous description is the one of Mr. Endon's eyes:

> In shape they were remarkable, being both deep-set and protuberant, one of Nature's jokes involving sockets so widely

---

[3] Samuel Beckett, *Murphy* (New York: Grove Press, Inc.), p. 97. All further quotations taken from this source will be identified by page number in the text following the citation.

splayed that Mr. Endon's brows and cheekbones seemed to have subsided. And in colour scarcely less so, having almost none, For the whites, of which a sliver appeared below the upper lid, were very large indeed and the pupils prodigiously dilated, as though by permanent excess of light. The iris was reduced to a thin glaucous rim of spawnlike consistency, so like a ballrace between the black and white that these could have started to rotate in opposite directions, or better still the same direction, without causing Murphy the least surprise. All four lids were everted in an ectropion of great expressiveness, a mixture of cunning, depravity and rapt attention. Approaching his eyes still nearer Murphy could see the red frills of mucus, a large point of suppuration at the root of an upper lash, the filigree of veins like the Lord's Prayer on a toenail and in the cornea, horribly reduced, obscured and distorted, his own image. (248-249)

This long quotation reveals Beckett's detailed examination of deformities. He scrutinizes carefully the abnormal condition of ectropion, which is a turning outward of the eyelids. The expression "one of Nature's joke," translated "lusus naturae" in the French text, can actually describe all monstrosities.

The skin also shows some problems. While Cooper is grey-faced, Murphy is of a yellow color and has "an extensive capillary angioma of most unusual situation" (266). Neary is covered with bedsores. The young man in the park is covered with eczema.

Sexuality adds to the anatomical difficulties: the Lord of Wormwood "seeks testamentary pentimenti from the *au-delà*" (99), and cannot even have a little girl. Cooper suffers from a monstrosity "per abundans"; he is "triorchous."

In conclusion, the deformities are concentrated on the limbs, the head, and the eyes; and Beckett is careful to use precise medical terminology in his descriptions: triorchous, angioma, acathisy, ectropion. The head is very important in the ratio of brain to body. Beckett contrasts this physical relation in Mr. Kelly: "Yet a little while and his brain-body ratio would have sunk to that of a small bird" (11). In *Murphy* the anatomical monstrosities are relatively few, but they exist in men, women, and animals. Celia is an exception in the Beckettian world. Her measurements show a very attractive woman; she is not anatomically deformed.

Physiological Deformities

The heroes in *Murphy* have difficulties with bodily functions. Cooper cannot sit. Murphy is not satisfied sitting down; he must lie down as soon as he is away from his rocking-chair. Mr. Kelly cannot stand up and has to use a paralytic chair. While he lay in bed, "his body seemed spread over a vast area, parts would wander away and would get lost if he did not keep a sharp look-out, he felt them fidgeting to be off" (115). Celia is plagued with irrepressible trembling, and her Hindu friend cannot stand up. He feels that his feet have become minuscule. The legs, columns of support, cannot function in maintaining in position the "Doric pelvis" of Miss Carridge, who looks like an ostrich. Ticklepenny cannot control his legs either; his legs are like those of "a chicken after ablation."

Murphy suffers from asthma; his feet and neck hurt like those of the hero in his "Belacqua fantasy." A spasmophile, his bodily agitation contrasts with his bouts of temporary paralysis. Murphy needs no support in order to walk, but he prefers supination to any other position when he cannot be in his rocking chair. The fetal position is an ever present quest. Murphy rolls on the floor with convulsions; he cannot subdue his movements. Once, he tilts over his rocking-chair and falls. Celia will have to put him back in it and then to "empty" him on his bed. The human architecture collapses.

Eyes's physiology also captures Beckett's attention; they do not usually function well. Murphy is near-sighted. Mr. Kelly does not see very well; his eyes are like doll's eyes. Mr. Endon, an hypermetrop whose eyes Beckett has so clinically described at length, suffers from ectropion, and Cooper has a bloody glass eye. The visual scope is reduced and poses the general problem of perception. Murphy sleeps with open eyes, thereby cutting out perception. He is retiring to his "little world."

The sense of hearing is defective in Beckett's characters. A friend of Murphy's (although Celia claims that Murphy has no friends) is a deaf mute. Since he cannot hear, he is particularly isolated. He, like Mr. Endon, is a chess player. In fact, he could be Mr. Endon, or at least prefigure him. No precise details are given concerning Mr. Endon's hearing, but we know that he never speaks.

The skin, a point of contact with the world, suffers a transformation and seems to reflect the human regression. Skin plays an essential role for Murphy. His yellow complexion becomes "ashen." He suffers from "pruritus ani" and feels "incandescent," finally succumbing to a "thermic traumatism." Neary's bedsores reveal the long Nearian supinations, anticipating Malone's *locus ameni*: his bed.

The head also poses functioning problems. Murphy complains about his bad memory and feels his head is "full of gelatin." His face has a painful "tic mental." Neary declares that he would not be surprised if Murphy's "conarium has shrunk to nothing" (6). "Conarium" is a key word in Descarte's *Traité du foetus*.[4] Descartes believed the soul to be in contact with the body through the conarium, which is the pineal gland.

Beckett, as we have seen, reduces Mr. Kelly anthropologically, his brain being compared to that of a small bird. Such a reduction will be found for the brain in general. Furthermore, Beckett often places the heads of his characters in the pillory of the shoulders. He describes Cooper's scarf as a "cangue." These are the heads of condemned men.

Still other deformities occur within the cardio-vascular system. The cardiac system is unique in Neary; he can control it. When Murphy learns how to do the same, he provokes false cardiac arrests although his heart is congenitally perfect. The pale blood which comes out of Murphy's mouth is a sign of anemia. Here also Beckett applies his "principle of reduction": blood, the symbol of life, is itself weakened.

Two secondary characters are alcoholics. An illness brought on by drinking produces the image of man's continual search for a life source although the source might kill him. Ticklepenny, a tavern poet, works at Magdalen Mental Mercyseat where he takes a "mild course of dipsopathic discipline" (88). The relationship between poetry and drinking is humorously established: the "breakdown had been due less to the pints than to the pentameters" (88).

Sexual malfunctioning and deviations are numerous. Ticklepenny is a homosexual, and Neary wants to show his lack of virility by shaving off his mustache. Celia exceeds in sexuality since she is a prostitute; and Murphy reproaches her by saying, "a decayed valet severs the connexion and you set up a niobaloo as though he were your fourteen children" (138-139). Murphy gives up his sexual appetite

---

[4] René Descartes, *La description du corps humain: Traité du fœtus*, Œuvres philosophiques, Tome III, 1643-1650 (Paris: Editions Garnier Frères, 1973), p. 824.

and chooses the asylum. All the couples are childless; the family does not exist. The only family whose genealogy is detailed is that of Bim, who has quite a family working under him. "Bim Clinch had no fewer than seven male relations, linear and collateral, serving under him, of whom the greatest was Bom and perhaps the least an aged uncle ("Bum") in the bandage winding department, as well as an elder sister, two nieces and a by-blow on the female side" (166). The French text adds three aunts and four bastards, two of whom are blind. Unlike the Lynch family in *Watt* (102-114), the Clinch family does not suffer severe deformities.

The inter-relation between mind and body is difficult, even painful. Miss Counihan declares in one passage, "Everywhere I find defiled... in the crass and unharmonious unison, the mind at the cart-tail of the body, the body at the charlot-wheels of the mind. I name no names" (218). She adds that Murphy is the only one who does not suffer from this "psychosomatic fistula."

Psychological monstrosities

The psychological reactions of the characters result sometimes from the physiological handicaps; on the other hand, the physiological handicaps can be psychosomatic. The pathological monstrosities are in the majority of cases related to perception. It is the reaction of the individual choked by outside reality, or rather, at the asylum by the non-contact with reality. Here we enter our inner world. Beckett's heroes are not all certified as insane, only about fifteen percent (160); however, all are possible cases.

At the asylum-sanatorium the patients are described as "cut off from reality" (177). Murphy sees in them a mirror of himself, particularly in the "limpid psychosis" of Mr. Endon. All suffer from a "life syndrome," but they respond to it in the best possible way.

Beckett gives a detailed enumeration of the clinical cases. One patient suffers from a catatonic stupor, which is a form of schizophrenia characterized by negative actions, stupor, and excitement phases.[5] To Ticklepenny's fright, Murphy sometimes plunges himself into a catatonic stupor.

---

[5] W. A. Newman Dorland, *Medical Dictionary* (Philadelphia: W. B. Saunders Company, 1941).

All types of mental cases are gathered at the asylum; each one is isolated in his cell. One finds hebephrenics, retifs, maniacs, melancholics, psychastenics, paranoids, schizoids, and schizophrenics. The medical categories are very well defined by Beckett, and he wonders if gas could "turn a neurotic into a psychotic" (175). The hebephrenic has a clinical form of "dementia praecox" occuring after puberty. He is a victim of hallucinations and laughs without reason. In the Beckettian universe laughter exists only in the asylum.

The retif is characterized by his refusal to advance. The manic suffers from hyper-irritation and cannot stop talking. The melancholic is marked by state of depression and inhibition. The psychastenic cannot come to grips with reality. He goes through stages of anxiety, obsession, self-accusation, and depersonalization. The paranoid is a victim of a progressive mental disorder characterized by the development of distrust systematized in a logically constructed delirium.

The use of technical terminology such as "neurotic," "psychotic," "schizoid," and "schizophrenic" demonstrates the precise pathological categories used by Beckett. The word "schizoid" is used for the closed-in, or anti-social. Such people have a sort of introspective personality. The schizoid is at an early stage but could reach the accute terminal level of schizophrenia. The schizophrenic suffers from dementia praecox, which represents a cleavage or a splitting of the personality.

The asylum is protected from becoming pitiable by Beckett's black humor, which comes through in such descriptions as "a hypomanic teaching slosh to a Korsakov's syndrome" (168). The reader who is not attentive to the medical terminology associates the piano mentioned in the preceeding sentence to the composer Korsakow. Actually, Korsakow's syndrome is a chronic sickness caused by alcoholism and characterized by hallucinations and lack of orientation. What qualifications to play slosh! Another example of Beckett's black humor is his description of a hypomanic who "bounced off walls like a bluebottle in a jar" (247).

Murphy does not find the asylum to be full of the "monsters" Ticklepenny has described to him. Instead, he finds himself among those of his own race. He would like to be admitted to their private world: "They caused Murphy no horror. The most easily identifiable of his immediate feelings were respect and unworthiness. Except for the manic... the impression he received was of that self-immersed indifference to the contingencies of the contingent world which he has chosen as the only felicity and achieved so seldom" (168).

The basic problem is the internal separation the individual feels in front of his "self, unredeemed split self" (188). This of course is a clearcut definition of schizophrenia, a cracking of the mental function.

Murphy must master his bodily unrest, an unrest which corresponds to the Pascalian "divertissement." [6] Once the body is controlled, the brain is permitted to function. In Beckett, the hero suffers an outside world which acts as an obstacle, a "colossal fiasco."

The reactions of the individual patients are judged by textbook psychiatrists, but the books have not presented a true picture. Beckett's feelings echo those of the surrealists, who in a letter to the chief of staff of the Paris hospital, accuse the doctors of seeing nothing more than a scramble of words in the dream images of dementia praecox. [7]

Beckett has translated several surrealist texts in which André Breton and Paul Eluard imitate the language of certain mental illnesses. He translated essays such as "Simulation of Mental Debility Essayed" and "Simulation of General Paralysis." [8] Beckett transforms a very precise psychiatric terminology into a new esthetic device.

The spy hole becomes a concrete symbol of the brutal invasion by the outside world into the inner world of the patient, and the patient reacts strongly to this invasion. His gaze is essential in his reaction. It is void of expression as if the outside world did not exist. It is the gaze of someone lost in incommunicable meditations. The individual is alone. His look is not human. At best it communicates a very limited relationship. Murphy has only a chess-player eye for Mr. Endon. The chess game between Murphy, "schizoid spasmophile," and Mr. Endon, "superior schizophrenic," illustrates this lack of contact. Mr. Endon's imperturbability along with his "limpid psychosis" impresses Murphy. Mr. Endon is locked up in his inner world where his "amental system" protects him from the outer world. The chess game symbolizes that closed world; each one is alone in his "monad."

---

[6] Blaise Pascal, *Œuvres Complètes*, Encyclopédie de La Pléiade (Paris: Gallimard, 1954), p. 1138.

[7] Maurice Nadeau, *Histoire du Surrealisme* (Paris: Editions du Seuil, 1964).

[8] Raymond Federman and John Fletcher, *Samuel Beckett, His Works and His Critics* (Berkeley: University of California Press, 1970), p. 93.

Murphy, pursued to the end by his acquaintances, has no friends. He has renounced his "last exile," Celia, whom he had met in a surrealistic encounter in the street; but she will not keep her role of "Ambassadrice du salpêtre" as she does in the poem "Tournesol." [10]

Love, or the caress, is a failure. Neary rejects it: "It does not require even as little as this celebrated act of love, if acts indeed can ever be of love, or love survive in acts, to bid one's neigbour the time of day, the smile and the nod on the way in the evening, the scowl and no nod on the way out at morning, in the way described by Wylie. And to meet and part in my sense exceeds the power of feeling, however tender, and of bodily motions, however expert" (222). The relation between Murphy and the "big world" is expressed by the kick. He wonders if "perhaps there was outside space and time a non-mental Kick from all eternity" (109). Then he adds, "But where then was the supreme Caress?" (109). The whole outside world is a solicitation, an attack against the closed system of the individual. Murphy, "superior schizoid," has not lost any of his quantum: "... his mind was a closed system" (109). This suggests another image: "The horse leech's daughter is a closed system. Her quantum of wantum cannot vary" (57). Murphy has failed in the "big world." He has suffered monstrously from all his human relationships, symbolized in the end by the desecration done to his ashes. Beckett poses clearly the problem of the shut-in and of reduction. For him, "... the cell, blood heat, next best thing to never being born." (44).

To leave the outside world of *quid pro quo* and retire "astir in his mind in the freedom of that light and dark that did not clash, nor alternate, nor fade nor lighten except to their communion" (9). Murphy must annihilate movement and disconnect his mind "from the gross importunities of sensation and reflection" (105). In this zone he finds "the world of the body broken up into the pieces of a toy" (112). In the third zone, the dark, he becomes "but a mote in the dark of absolute freedom" (112). The dark is heaven, and the quest is a Dantesque vision upside down. There is a continual assault between the three zones in Murphy's mind: the light, the grey, and the dark. Even in the dark there remains a yellow spot associated with Celia

---

[9] André Breton, *L'amour fou* (Paris: Editions Gallimard, 1937), p. 64.
[10] Ibid., p. 64.

and the caress in general. This is perhaps a confession that, however latent, the dream of caress always exists.

In the psychastenic society in which Murphy lives, all the patients can suppress the world at one time or another. Mr. Endon is the one who transmits by his gaze the experience of the "gulf" of the encounter with Nothingness. Ticklepenny notices that Murphy's eyes are like those of Mr. Endon, that is, like those of a catatonic. Murphy has reached nothingness in his mind; the body is now ready for disintegration, for reduction by gas into a packet of ashes.

Murphy dreams of a return to chaos but he reflects, "What but an imperfect sense of humour could have made such a mess of chaos. In the beginning was the pun" (65). To state it more positively, perfect humor would save chaos, and it might be the only hope for Beckett as a writer. Humor is the only liberation, the only way man can support the collapsing of the universe in which he feels alienated. The tendency to monstrosity is the image of a physical, corporeal, mental chaos; all three stages are well defined in Murphy's zones.

Murphy is the only one who is not a "puppet." He has experienced nothingness when he looked into the mirror of Mr. Endon's eyes: "Murphy began to see nothing, that colourlessness which is such a rare postnatal treat, being the absence (to abuse a nice distinction) not of *percipere* but of *percipi*" (246).

Objects

Murphy says that objects have been his best friends. The relation of man and object is always challenged. As opposed to the realist novel, one finds very few objects in *Murphy*. They are integrated in the personages, whether it is the rocking-chair or the paralytic chair. Beckett certainly wanted the opposition between the paralytic chair, with its two wheels and levers, and the rocking-chair.

The rocking-chair allows Murphy to achieve oblivion with regard to time and space. Eventually the rocking-chair will be destroyed by fire, its disappearance coinciding to that of Murphy's.

The wheel-chair becomes a source of games for Mr. Kelly, who plays with it while racing in the park.

Cooper's glass eye can also be considered as an essential accessory. Blood-injected, it completes the monstrous portrait.

The personages are also defined by their clothing, which always shows the wear and tear of life. Murphy's suit like the asylum, does not admit the air from the outside world. Finally, Murphy will trade his suit for a hospital uniform, but eventually he will find himself naked in his rocking-chair, rejecting all clothing.

Murphy, unlike other heroes, does not like to wear a hat: "... the memories it awoke of the caul were too poignant, especially when he had to take it off" (73).

An object which plays a crucial role in Murphy's life is the horoscope bought by Celia. Eventually, however, Murphy will renounce it. In the asylum, all the tools are present like torture instruments of the Middle Ages. The most destructive object is the radiator made up of different pieces. Through it, Murphy himself is finally reduced to less than an object, his ashes are "swept away with the sand, the beer, the butts, the glass, the matches, the spits, the vomit" (275).

So Murphy is returned, if not to dust, to the human dirt of the world. Black humor relieves the sadness of the situation, for Murphy appreciates the fatal gas, the "surfine chaos." We are in a shapeless world "when somethings give way, or perhaps simply add up, to the Nothing, than which in the guffaw of the Abderite naught is more real" (246).

At the beginning, Murphy was "one of the elect who require everything to remind them of something else" (63); but at the end he "could not get a picture in his mind of any creature he had met, animal or human" (251-252).

The image of the body as a cart is enhanced by the physical and physiological monstrosity. The mind fights against the body, against the big, outer world. The entire novel, and Chapter VI in particular, is a succession of reductions which eventually leads to a closed-in world. The ultimate reduction is the parcel of ashes, leftovers from Murphy's cremation which "must have weighed well on four pound" (273). The French text adds that this is the average weight of a seven month old fetus.

The juxtaposition of birth-death is constant, as if one was the *sine qua non* of the other. For example, noting that Murphy's wailing at birth was off key, the narrator adds, "His rattle will make amends" (71). Life's extremes are telescoped: "from the spermarium to the crematorium" (78), from the crib to the morgue. Murphy's capillary angioma can be interpreted as "birthmark deathmark" (267).

Literature up to the time of Beckett was a "colossal fiasco:" romantic, realistic, and even Proustian literature require that the writer go beyond what has already been said. True literature is a "reality which refuses to function." Perhaps we should be like Murphy, an enthusiastic "non-reader." But the writer cannot stop from naming; he can only approach nothingness "asymptotically."

There is a mystique of Nothingness. The asylum is like a church, although Beckett warns us against any interpretation. The Word is suffering, and man is but a "morsel of chaos."

In *Murphy*, Beckett has used monstruous reductions of the body and the mind as esthetic devices. Here the pathological is the fundamental condition of man, who is always alienated from himself and from the world, a "monster of humanity and enlightenment, desparing of a world in which the only natural allies are the fools and knaves, a mankind sterile with self-complicity" (170).

NOTE: The author is very thankful to Teresa Dalle of the University of Arizona for her translation.

STATISTICS ON PROPER NAMES IN *MURPHY*

by *William Tritt*

BECKETT'S first novel is remarkable for the frequent occurrences of proper names within the narrative. Sixteen characters appear in *Murphy*, while fifteen additional names created by Beckett are referred to either by the characters or by the narrator. Moreover, *Murphy* contains a considerable number of references (141, including multiple references to a single name) both to real names and to imaginary names which belong to our cultural heritage. These names fall into ten categories, arranged in order of frequency of reference:[1]

    I LITERATURE (32 names):
        A-Writers (20). B-Characters (8). C-Works, author not named (4).
   II PAINTING AND SCULPTURE (22):
        A-Painters (13). B-Sculptors (5). C-Works, artist not named (4).
  III BIBLICAL REFERENCES (19):
        A-Old Testament (10). B-New Testament (9).
  IV MYTHOLOGICAL CHARACTERS (18):
        A-Greco-Roman (17). B-Irish (1).
   V PHILOSOPHERS (15; also Spinoza, paraphrased but not named).
  VI MISCELLANEOUS HISTORICAL REFERENCES (15).
 VII PSYCHOLOGISTS (8).
VIII PHYSICAL AND BIOLOGICAL SCIENTISTS (7):
        A-Physicists (2). B-Astronomers (3). C-Biologists (2).

---

[1] Pages are cited from the English Grove Press edition.

IX MUSIC (3):
A-Composers (2). B-Characters in musical compositions (1).
X CINEMA DIRECTORS (1).

This classification includes only the names which occur in the English version of the novel. In his French translation of *Murphy*, Beckett deleted seventeen names, substituted six names, and added eight others.

TABLE I

NAMES CREATED BY BECKETT IN *MURPHY*

A   Characters in *Murphy* (in the order in which the name appears):

Murphy
Neary
Miss Counihan
Celia Kelly
Willoughby Kelly
Wylie (Needle)
Cathleen na Hennessey
Cooper
Miss Carridge
Vera
Austin (Augustin, Gussy, Gus; p. 94) Ticklepenny
Rosie Dew (and dog Nelly)
Dr. Angus Killiecrankie
Thomas ("Bim") Clinch
Timothy ("Bom") Clinch
Mr. Endon

*Coroner, who is not named

B   Names referred to by the characters or by the narrator (in alphabetical order):

Clarke

Clinch, "Bum"
nee Cox, Ariadne
Dwyer, Miss
Elliman, Flight Lieutenant
Farren, Miss
Few, Sacha
Fist, Dr.
Fitt, Father
Gall of Wormwood, Lord
Kelly, Mr. and Mrs. Quentin
O'Melaghlins
Quigley, Mr.
Suk
West, Mrs.

TABLE II

INDEX OF REAL AND IMAGINARY NAMES CITED IN *MURPHY*

A

Abderite (Democritus) 246
Abraham, Father 48
Ach 81
Adams 280
Apollonian 49
Ariston, son of (Plato) 85
Avercamp 196

B

Balzac 63, 228
Barlach 239
Belacqua 78, 78, 111, 112
Bellini, Giovanni 251
Berkeley 58
Bildad the Shuhite 70, 70
Blake League 70, 71, 71

Boswell 167
Bouvier, Bishop 72
Braque 63
Bühler 81
Burns 261
Busby, Dr. 97

C

Calliope 86
Campanella 17
Canutian 186
Chesterfield, Lord 268
Christ 72
Claude 228
Cleopatra 161
Coleridge-Taylor 215
Cuchulain 42

D

Darwin 218
De Lacey 124
Descartes 140
Dido 195
Dives 48

E

Engels sisters 228, 229
Erato 86
Erebus 175
Esau 23

F

Fabian 187
Fletcher 49
Frankenstein's Daemon 124
Furies 175
Fury 27

G

George II 267
Geulincx, Arnold 178
Griffith 191

H

Harpy Tomb 84, 95
Haydn 195
Hegel 222
Helen 176
Herschel 33, 252
Higgins 184
Hippasos the Akousmatic 47
Hugo 201

I

Io 216
Ixion 21

J

Jacob 23
Jerome 104
Jezabel 199
Job 70, 70
John o'God's 43, 43
Judas 199

K

Kampendonck 196
Koffka, Kurt 48
Korsakow's Syndrome 168
Külpe 80, 81

L

Lazarus (beggar) 48
Lazarus (resurrected) 180
Lena 104, 104
Lilliputian 139
Lot's Road 12, 15
Luke 215

M

Malraux 156
Manichee 104
Marbe 81
Marx Cork Bath Mat Manufactory 74
Matthew 215
Melpomene 86
Mercury 31
Messiah 180
Miller, Joe 65
Milton House 73

N

Narcissus 186
Newtonian motion 113

Newtonian 201
Norwich School 196

O

O'Connor 184
Old Moore 216

P

Pantagruel 120
Parmigianino 101
Penelope 149
Petrouchka 3
Phidias 238
Pilate 170
Prout, Father (F. S. Mahony) 50, 124
Puget 239
Pythagorean 3

Q

Quintilian 17

R

Rima 96, 96
Romiet and Juleo 86
Roussel dummy 14
Russell, George (A. E.) 155

S

Scopas 238
Shelley, Harriet 99

Shelley 99
Simpson's Divan 244
Skinner House 159 *
Socrates 200
Spectator 195
(Spinoza, paraphrased) 107
Steiss 97

T

Tantalus 21
Thalia 86
Tintoretto 140

V

charVenus 37
Vermeer 228
Victoria, Queen 277

W

Watt 81
Watts, G. F. 152
William of Champeaux 81
Wood's halfpenny 170
Wordsworth 100
Wordsworthy 106

Y

Yang Kuei-fei 117

Z

Zophar 70

Table III

INDEX OF NAMES BY CATEGORY

I Literature

A *Writers*

Balzac 63, 228
Boswell 167
Bouvier, Bishop 72
Burns 261
Chesterfield, Lord 268
Fletcher 49
Higgins 184
Hugo 201
Jerome 104

Malraux 156
Milton 73
O'Connor 184
Prout, Father (F. S. Mahony) 50, 124
Quintilian 17
Russell, George (A. E.) 155
Shelley 99
Wordsworth 100
Wordsworthy 106

B *Characters*

Belacqua 78, 78, 111, 112
De Lacey 124
Frankenstein's Daemon 124

Lilliputian 139
Pantagruel 120

C *Works, author not named*

Joe Miller 65
Old Moore 216

Romiet and Juleo 86
Spectator 195

II Painting and sculpture

A *Painters*

Avercamp 196
Bellini, Giovanni 251
Blake 70, 71, 71
Braque 63
Claude 228
Kampendonck 196

Luke 215
Norwich School 196
Parmigianino 101
Tintoretto 140
Vermeer 228

STATISTICS ON PROPER NAMES IN "MURPHY" 207

B *Sculptors*

Barlach 239
Phidias 238
Puget 239

Scopas 238
Watts, G. F. 152

C *Works, artist not named*

Harpy Tomb 84, 95

Rima 96, 96

III BIBLICAL REFERENCES

A *Old Testament*

Bildad the Shuhite 70, 70
Esau 23
Jacob 23
Jezabel 199

Job 70, 70
Lot's Road 12, 15
Zophar 70

B *New Testament*

Abraham, Father 48
Christ 72
Dives 48
Judas 199
Lazarus 48

Lazarus 180
Matthew 215
Messiah 180
Pilate 170

IV MYTHOLOGICAL CHARACTERS

A *Greco-Roman*

Apollonian 49
Calliope 86
Dido 195
Erato 86
Erebus 175
Furies 175
Fury 27
Helen 176
Io 216

Ixion 21
Melpomene 86
Mercury 31
Narcissus 186
Penelope 149
Tantalus 21
Thalia 86
charVenus 37

B *Irish*

    Cuchulain   42

V PHILOSOPHERS

    Abderite (Democritus)   246
    Ariston, son of (Plato)   85
    Berkeley   58
    Campanella   17
    Descartes   140
    Engels   228, 229
    Geulincx   178
    Hegel   222
    Hippasos the Akousmatic   47
    Manichee   104
    Marx   74
    Pythagorean   3
    Socrates   200
    (Spinoza, paraphrased)   107
    William of Champeaux   81

VI MISCELLANEOUS HISTORICAL REFERENCES

    Busby, Dr.   97
    Canutian   186
    Cleopatra   161
    Fabian   187
    George II   267
    John o' God's   43, 43
    Lena   104, 104
    Roussel   14
    Shelley, Harriet   99
    Simpson   244
    Victoria, Queen   277
    Wood's halfpenny   170
    Yang Kuei-fei   117

VII PSYCHOLOGISTS

    Ach   81
    Bühler   81
    Koffka, Kurt   48
    Korsakow's Syndrome   168
    Külpe   80, 81
    Marbe   81
    Watt   81

VIII PHYSICAL AND BIOLOGICAL SCIENTISTS

A *Physicists*

    Newtonian motion   113   Newtonian   201

B *Astronomers*
   Adams   280   Herschel   33, 252

C *Biologists*
   Darwin   218   Steiss   97

IX MUSIC

A *Composers*
   Coleridge-Taylor   215   Haydn   195

B *Characters in musical compositions*
   Petrouchka   3

X CINEMA DIRECTORS

   Griffith   191

TABLE IV

FREQUENCY OF NAMES BY CHAPTER

	1	2	3	4	5	6	7	8	9	10	11	12	13
LITERATURE (32)	—	1	—	2	11	2	4	2	4	4	—	2	—
PAINTING AND SCULPTURE (22)	—	—	—	—	9	—	—	2	—	6	5	—	—
BIBLICAL REFERENCES (19)	—	4	—	3	6	—	—	—	3	3	—	—	—
MYTHOLOGICAL CHARACTERS (18)	—	2	3	2	4	—	—	1	4	2	—	—	—

Philosophers (15)	1	1	—	2	4	—*	—	1	1	4	1	—	—
Miscellaneous historical references (15)	—	1	—	2	4	—	1	—	4	—	1	1	1
Psychologists (8)	—	—	—	1	6	—	—	—	1	—	—	—	—
Physical and biological scientists (7)	—	—	1	—	1	1	—	—	—	2	1	—	1
Music (3)	1	—	—	—	—	—	—	—	—	2	—	—	—
Cinema directors (1)	—	—	—	—	—	—	—	—	1	—	—	—	—
Totals (140)	2	9	4	12	45	3	5	6	18	23	8	3	2

* Chapter 6: Spinoza is paraphrased.
* Skinner House: Since the name *Skinner* has not been identified and classified, only the first occurrence of the name (p. 159) is included in the total of 141 names.

THE ADDENDA TO SAMUEL BECKETT'S *WATT*

by Rubin Rabinovitz

SAMUEL Beckett's novel *Watt* ends with a section called "Addenda," made up of thirty-six fragments of various sorts: poems, bits of narrative, quotations, even a few bars of music. The addenda are introduced with this footnote: "The following precious and illuminating material should be carefully studied. Only fatigue and disgust prevented its incorporation." [1]

At first glance, the "precious materials" appear to be no more than unedited scraps from a writer's notebook, and some commentators on the novel have taken the footnote as Beckett's admission that the addenda are peripheral. But it must be remembered the footnote is written in the passive voice; hence the identity of the speaker can only be guessed at. It is risky to assume that the speaker is Beckett, or that the footnote expresses the author's views: for Beckett — at least since the time he added footnotes to his poem, *Whoroscope* (1930) — has not been overly generous in providing explications for his own texts. The seemingly ironic tone of the footnote, like the fragmentary appearance of the addenda, is not entirely to be trusted. The addenda may appear to be an afterthought, but they are neither artistically inferior to the main body of the work nor structurally isolated from it.

The last point is most easily illustrated by the themes of three poems included among the addenda; all refer to the hero's experiences either directly or obliquely. The poem which begins, "Who may tell

---

[1] *Watt* (New York: Grove Press, 1959), p. 247. Page numbers in parentheses in my text refer to this edition. The Addenda are on pages 247 to 254; where no page number is given for a passage the reference is to this section.

the tale...?" gives a concise summary of Watt's frustrating attempts to determine the limits of nothingness as well as the quantity of human suffering. The first line of the poem also hints at a central problem: the difficulty of locating a consistent narrative voice in the novel.

The poem, "Watt will not..." suggests another important theme: the futility of human inquiry into the incomprehensible and the persistence of inquisitive humanity, which understands the futility but presses on nevertheless. This poem also clarifies two metaphors which are used extensively in the novel. The lines, "dim mind wayfaring / through barren lands," underlines the epistemological nuances of Watt's journey; and the poem's image of a flame about to go out refers to Watt's diminishing mental capacity. The second metaphor also helps to explain Watt's game with the dying coals (pp. 37-39).

The third poem is the descant which was "heard by Watt on way to station (IV)." The reference makes it clear that the descant is a fugitive bit of text; in its proper place in Part IV it would be a symmetrical counterpart to the threne Watt heard on his way from the station in Part I. In each case the choral groups seem similar, for the bass in both the threne and the descant cannot hold back an occasional expletive ("phew!" pp. 34, 253).

The descant, with its theme of spiritual exile and the separation of mind and body ("head awhile darkly apart") comments on the events which occur at the end of the story, when Watt has left Knott behind and is ensconced in his pavilion. The seeming gloom of the descant is a reversal of the apparent cheeriness of the threne, with its spectacle of generations endlessly proliferating.

The monotonous music for the threne is also included among the addenda; it is well suited to its subject matter. In the threne the choir sings a refrain of numbers, the result of the division of 366 and 365 by seven. This attempt to measure time — to determine precisely the number of weeks in a year — leads to a chain of digits generated endlessly, like proliferating humanity.[2] And the threne raises a question which Arsene will explore: what is the purpose of these endless generations, popping so casually and cheerfully into the world? As Watt comes to learn, teleological questions are more easily raised than answered.

In this fashion some of the addenda clarify problems in the text; others add to its mysteries. This is particularly true of a group of fragments which alludes to an earlier draft of *Watt*. For example the phrase, "never been properly born," was used to describe Mr. Knott in the early version; and the second picture in Erskine's room is actually a portrait of Mr. Knott's father, who is never mentioned in the published version of the novel.[3]

Most details of Mr. Knott's family life have been eliminated in the final version; the only remaining trace is an incident among the addenda which tells of an elderly beggar who thinks that Arthur is Mr. Knott and speaks about the times when he "was a fine lovely boy." This indicates that Mr. Knott may have had a childhood, but we do not learn enough about it to understand the original meaning of such fragments. Even so, these allusions to earlier versions of the novel suggest a simpler, more conventional world which the characters once inhabited.

The enigmatic quality of a few fragments rests not in their meaning, but in their application to the events in the main body of the novel. "Her married life one long drawsheet" is clear enough once we discover that a drawsheet is a type of sheet used on hospital beds; but whom does this phrase describe? Is the "thicket flower unrecorded" related to the metaphor of the flowers crushed underfoot (135) or the dimming flowers near Mr. Hackett's bench (22)? Is the wooden table resting on a conical frustrum the same one which Watt marked with chalk a page earlier? Is it Watt — we are told that he is an experienced traveller — who benefitted little from his "frequent departure out of Ireland"? These are things we may never, never know. Like Watt, the reader discovers new obscurities with every elucidatory

---

[2] *Watt*, pp. 34-35. Both the threne and the music have been omitted from the French translation of *Watt*. It should be noted that there is an error in the Grove edition of *Watt*: on page 35, the first line of the second verse reads "Fifty-one point one"; the manuscript version of the novel reads "Fifty-two point one." The number in the manuscript, unlike the number in the Grove edition, is the result of dividing 365 by seven. My thanks to The Humanities Research Center of the University of Texas at Austin, and to Mrs. Sally Leach, Assistant Librarian at the Center, for making the manuscript version available to me.

[3] For a description of earlier drafts of *Watt*, see J. M. Coetzee, "The Manuscript Revisions of Beckett's *Watt*," *Journal of Modern Literature*, 2 (1972), 472-480; on Mr. Knott's father, p. 474. As Richard Coe has pointed out in *Samuel Beckett* (New York: Grove Press, 1964), p. 59, "never been properly born" is similar to the description of a little girl mentioned by Mrs. Rooney in *All That Fall*. Both passages may be based on Dante's description of the "wretches who never lived," *Inferno*, 3:64, or on Revelation 3:1, "thou hast a name that thou livest, and art dead."

detail; this teasing quality of the novel has its roots in Beckett's feeling that enigma and paradox enhance art.

Some fragments challenge the reader to match a description in the Addenda with an incident in the main body of the novel. "Watt snites" may be related to the hero's contemplative nose-picking just after his arrival at Knott's; and it may be after leaving Knott's that Watt looks as though he has been injected with sterile pus. Such fragments serve both to heighten the reader's puzzlement and to hint at earlier drafts of the novel, where such descriptions might actually have appeared in the text.

At times an entire incident is suggested by a phrase in the "Addenda." The fragment which describes Watt marking the positions of Knott's bowl with chalk, for example, conjures up a vision of the hero in his role of indefatigable researcher, still laboring under the delusion that empirical investigation yields significant insights. According to another fragment, "One night Watt goes on roof." Here Watt perhaps assumes that an increase in elevation will lead him to new heights of cosmological awareness.

In a longer fragment Watt is described on a dark plain beneath a dark sky. This passage indicates the richness to be found even in Beckett's starkest settings; its metaphorical quality is suggested when it is called a "soul-landscape." Here, as so often in his later works, Beckett distorts naturalistic reality in descriptions of the outer world in order to create metaphors which deal with inner truths.

There are also metaphorical overtones in the fragment which begins, "dead calm, then a murmur..."; it suggests the beginning and end of consciousness. But speculation about its meaning eventually gives way to admiration of its poetic qualities. And this process illustrates another lesson Watt learns: aesthetic appreciation flourishes best when the need to understand subsides.

For this reason, where the fragments seem designed to deepen the reader's understanding of the work, they often do the opposite. "Note," we are told, "that Arsene's declaration gradually came back to Watt." Purportedly, this is meant to resolve a contradiction: Watt hears little of what Arsene tells him and understands less (80); yet Sam claims that everything in the novel — including Arsene's speech — came to him from Watt verbatim (127). Actually, the fragment is no more than another attempt by Sam, that most unreliable of narrators, to pull the wool over the eyes of the gullible reader. In effect, this is an aspect of Beckett's parody of traditional fiction, which must struggle to preserve narrative integrity even in the face of crumbling verisimilitude.

The technique here is similar to that of the last fragment in the Addenda, which warns: "no symbols where none intended." This short phrase conceals volumes. For while indicating nothing about whether any symbols are included in the work, it promotes the shaky hypothesis that an author controls his material — and his unconscious — to the degree that inadvertent symbolism can be eliminated.

These comments, then, attack traditional ideas of fictional narrative as well as overly assiduous interpretations of a work's literary symbolism. Similarly, the comment "change all the names" undermines interpretations of *Watt* which deal with the what-ness of Watt and the not-ness of Knott. The idea of changing the names of characters lest they become too suggestive — only a threat in this novel — is carried out in *Malone Dies*.

"Limits to part's equality with whole" is a comment which also gives away very little. It refers not only to Euclid's postulate that the whole is greater than any part, but to its antithesis: an argument put forward by Zeno of Elea which demonstrates the illogicality of the part-whole distinction.[4] Applied to the organization of *Watt*, the fragment helpfully suggests that while things may appear to be adding up in some places, they may not add up in other places. It demonstrates the incompatibility of aesthetics and logic: can a work of art be no more than the sum of its parts? When the notes and rhythms of a symphony are added up there are still vibrations that are unaccounted for.

Another fragment purports to elucidate a mystery in the text: "*Watt learned to accept* etc. Use to explain poverty of Part III. . . ." It is clear enough that this fragment refers to a passage on page 80 of the novel. But it hardly explains the poverty of Part III; and, even if it did, the reader still is without an explanation for the poverty in the remaining parts of the novel.

---

[4] W. C. Dampier, in *A History of Science* (Cambridge: Cambridge University Press, 1966), pp. 19-20, summarizes Zeno's argument this way: "A manifold must be divisible to infinity and therefore must itself be infinite, but, in trying to build it up again, no number of infinitely small parts can make a finite whole."

Most of the elucidations and instructions in the novel are therefore not to be trusted: they are not the comments of an author who can leave no portion of his work unclear but caricatures of such comments. Similarly, when Beckett turns to the world of culture and learning, his intentions are usually satiric. This is most obvious in his references to theology. In the "Addenda" he alludes to a number of religious figures; one is Richard Hooker (1554?-1600), an Anglican clergyman, the author of *Ecclesiastical Polity,* known to his contemporaries as "judicious Hooker." Beckett speaks of his heat-pimples.

Another religious writer who is mentioned is Pope Benedict XIV (1675-1758), author of *De Synodo Diocesana.* He, together with a writer named Cangiamila, is given as an authority for the comment, "the foetal soul is full grown." This introduces the idea of prenatal memory, a theme that often comes up in Beckett's fiction. Unlike Benedict, Cangiamila seems to be a made-up figure; his name suggests, appropriately enough, the restrictive and inhibitory nature of much theological writing.[5] These theological references are similar to those in the parody of religious learning in the scene with Mr. Spiro.

There are hints in the novel that Watt was once a scholar; so the various learned references hark back to his early days — and also to the earlier works of Beckett, with their frequent displays of erudition. In addition to theology, there are a number of allusions to art history in the "Addenda." Mr. O'Connery, the painter of the portrait of Knott's father, portrays beads of sweat with an attention to detail that would have done credit to Jan de Heem, the seventeenth-century Dutch still-life painter.

Mr. O'Connery is probably the same as Art Conn O'Connery, mentioned in the second addendum. O'Connery there is called a "product of the great Chinnery-Slattery tradition." As in the earlier reference, O'Connery is connected with artists who painted in a realistic style: George Chinnery (d. 1852), who resided for a while in Dublin during the late eighteenth century, painted portraits and landscapes; John Joseph Slattery was a portraitist active in Dublin between 1846 and 1858.

The author of these addenda obviously has a good knowledge of art history; yet we are told that Watt knew nothing about painting

---

[5] From cang, a wooden collar used in oriental countries for punishment; and the Latin *milia,* thousands. Beckett used the word càng in his poem, "Enueg I."

(129). This again weakens Sam's claim that everything he knows on the matter of Watt and Knott came from Watt himself (125).

Though he may not know about art, Watt is represented as a "very fair linguist" (208); and among the addenda are quotations in four languages: English, German, Italian, and Latin. The quotation in English is the second stanza of James Thomson's poem, "To Fortune." The quatrain fits in well with the mood of the novel; it seems to echo the morose disillusionment which makes *Watt* such a moving work. When the stanza is restored to its original context, however, it becomes clear that its mood is not at all what it seems to be in *Watt*; actually, it is the complaint of an unsuccessful lover:

To Fortune

For ever, Fortune, wilt thou prove
An unrelenting foe to love,
And, when we meet a mutual heart,
Come in between and bid us part;

Bid us sigh on from day to day
And wish, and wish the soul away;
Till youth and genial years are flown,
And all the life of life is gone?

... ...
All other blessings I resign;
Make but the dear Amanda mine! [6]

By putting it into a new context and removing the question mark, Beckett has changed the meaning of the stanza so that it fits in with the theme of his novel.

A quotation from Schopenhauer is similarly altered in its new context: "zitto! zitto! dass nur das publikum nichts merke!" (hush, hush, lest the public notice anything). In the "Addenda," this phrase serves as a challenge to an audience unused to delving deeply into

---

[6] Lawrence Harvey, in *Samuel Beckett, Poet and Critic* (Princeton: Princeton University Press, 1970), p. 391, first noted that the stanza is by Thomson. I have quoted only the first two stanzas and last two lines of the poem; it has four stanzas. The poem may be found in *The Complete Poetical Works of James Thomson*, edited by J. L. Robertson (London: Oxford University Press, 1908), pp. 427-428.

fiction. For Schopenhauer it was part of a tirade against German academicians who, he felt, suppressed his works out of fear that he would find overwhelming support among those outside the academy.[7]

An Italian quotation, "parole non ci appulcro" (I will add no more words to embellish it), is from one of Beckett's favorite writers, Dante.[8] It underlines the purposeful silences in the work, and hints that reticence and hiatus can be powerful literary tools. But the phrase is also used ironically, for Beckett does add a few words of commentary after the quotation.

In the *Inferno* Virgil utters this phrase to indicate that he will not waste his breath describing the corruption of the popes and cardinals who were guilty of avarice. But he cannot resist adding a few words even after he has promised to remain silent: he lectures Dante on the vanity of a life wasted in the pursuit of worldly goods. This speech fits in with the novel's mockery of bourgeois life as well as with its critique of materialism and a belief in the reality of the things of time and space.

A Latin quotation "pereant qui ante nos nostra dixerunt" ("death to those who used our words before we did") is from Aelius Donatus, a grammarian of the fourth century. This again is ironic: for Beckett is in a sense cursing Donatus, the originator of the quotation. But more than this, it comments on the use of the other quoted material in the "Addenda," and endorses Beckett's method of incorporating others' phrases into the texture of his own work.

When he quotes directly, Beckett relies on the context to add an ironic twist which enhances the meaning of the quotation for the novel. But in some instances, when he borrows material from other writers Beckett likes to improve on it. For example, he takes the phrase "die Erde hat mich wieder!" (the earth has me once more) from Goethe's *Faust*, adds a letter, and transforms it into a witty macaronic: "die Merde hat mich wieder."[9]

---

[7] The quotation is from Schopenhauer's *Über die vierfache Wurzel des Satzes vom zureichenden Grunde* (Hamburg: Felix Meiner, 1957), p. 66. This translation, like translations of other passages, is my own.

[8] *Inferno*, 7:60. The source of this quotation was first noted by Susan Senneff, "Song and Music in Samuel Beckett's *Watt*," *Modern Fiction Studies*, 11 (Summer, 1964), 143.

[9] *Faust*, line 784. I am grateful to Matthew and Uta Winston, of Columbia University, for locating the source of this quotation. I suspect that another German phrase in the Addenda, "das fruchtbare Bathos der Erfah-

Another phrase which alludes to Dante is "sempiternal penumbra." The *Paradiso* ends with a brilliant vision of celestial light, the "rosa sempiturna" (eternal rose). The splendor of the vision, by the time it reaches *Watt*, is considerably diminished; but Beckett's shadowy eternity is as appropriate to his way of seeing the world as a luminous rose was to Dante's.[10]

Equally gloomy is a Latin phrase which parodies a line from the missal, "Agnus Dei, miserere nobis" (Lamb of God, have mercy on us). In the "Addenda" this has been changed to "causa causarum miserere mei" (cause of causes, have mercy on me). The speaker's appeal is to a scholastic version of the Aristotelian deity, the unmoved mover. The speaker seems, like Watt, to have suffered the agony of watching causal chains recede towards infinity with no sign of a beginning; so there is also an entreaty to a first cause to make itself known and end the frustrating search. The speaker has not left the intellectual battlefield unscarred; as he says, "I entered this world in filth; I lived in it uneasily; in confusion I leave it."

A similar issue comes up in another fragment, "the maddened prizeman." The phrase contains a pun which refers to the Madden Prize, a fellowship award at Beckett's University, Trinity College, Dublin.[11] Beckett referred to a "Madden prizeman" once before, in an early unpublished story, "Echo's Bones."[12] The pun — which suggests that a surfeit of learning leads to madness — aptly applies to Watt who, we are told, was very likely a university man (23).

Some of the puns in the "Addenda" are simple, like the Laurel and Hardy joke ("made merry with the hardy laurel"); others are ingenious and intricate. An example of the latter is the phrase, "Watt's Davus complex (morbid dread of sphinxes)." Davus is the name of

---

rung," may similarly be a quotation Beckett has altered; but I have been unable to find its source.

[10] Dante uses the phrase "rosa sempiturna" twice: *Paradiso* 30:124 and 12:19.

[11] The Madden Prize is named for Samuel Madden (1696-1765), who left a bequest for the award, a cash prize to scholars who place well in fellowship examinations. See Sidney Lee in *DNB* s.v. Madden, Samuel; and Constantia Maxwell, *A History of Trinity College Dublin, 1591-1892* (Dublin: The University Press, Trinity College, 1946), pp. 154-156.

[12] I wish here to express my thanks to the Baker Memorial Library at Dartmouth College, and to Mr. Walter Wright, Chief of Special Collections at the Library, for supplying me with a copy of the manuscript of "Echo's Bones."

a slave in Terence's comedy, *The Lady of Andros*. One of his quips which has survived from antiquity is "I am Davus, not Oedipus"; he says this when he pretends to be ignorant about amorous matters. [13]

Since Davus is linked in this fashion to Oedipus, the Davus complex may be considered an analogue of the Oedipus complex. Like Oedipus, Watt prefers older women; even more important is his dread of sphinxes. This reverses the situation of Oedipus: the Theban sphinx had reason to dread him since he was to cause her to die by solving her riddle. Watt, however, solves few riddles; and eventually he comes to dread sphinxes — in the sense of persons or things of an inscrutable nature — like Knott. Arsene has warned him about the dangers of plumbing too deeply into the mysteries of Knott's establishment; but Watt, like Oedipus stubbornly demanding to hear about his origins, cannot give up his need to know. Only towards the end of the story is Watt reconciled to not knowing, even to accept "that a nothing had happened." But then, as we are told, "it was too late" (80). All of this is consistent with Beckett's view that paradox and enigma — the sphinxes a rationalist cannot tolerate — enhance art.

Beckett stresses this point in a review of the poetry of Denis Devlin. Art, Beckett says, has always been "pure interrogation, rhetorical question less the rhetoric — whatever else it may have been obliged by 'social reality' to appear...." Great art incorporates "the need to need"; but, because this negative quality has never been understood, much that is significant in modern art has been called obscure and dismissed. [14]

Beckett first mentioned "Davus" and "the morbid dread of sphinxes" in this review, while inveighing against a public with no patience for the enigmatic in art: "the gogetters, the gerrymandlers, Davus and the morbid dread of sphinxes, solution clapped on problem like a snuffer on a candle, the great crossword public on all its planes...." [15]

Davus in this review is not only an alternative to Oedipus but also a blend of Dives and Lazarus: a few lines down Beckett speaks of the "Dives-Lazarus symbiosis, as intimate as that of fungoid and

---

[13] "Davos sum, non Oedipus," Terence, *Andria*, line 194. The Latin spelling is Davos, but many translations render the Latin version Davus in English (e.g., the Loeb edition). The remark is famous enough to be listed in *Bartlett's Familiar Quotations* (14th ed.).

[14] "Denis Devlin," *Transition*, 27 (April-May, 1938), 289-290.

[15] "Denis Devlin," 290.

algoid in lichen...." The rich man, Dives, like Lazarus, the beggar on his doorstep, is caught up in a need for worldly goods; neither one can pause long enough in his acquisitive preoccupation to recognize the artistic "need to need." Yet rich man, poor man, and artist have this in common: they are all motivated by need. The Davus complex is an intolerance for paradox which interferes with the appreciation of art; it affects both Watt and readers who are impatient with need and obscurity in art.

Another phrase in the Addenda is equally complex: "the Master of the Leopardstown Halflengths." Leopardstown is the name of a racecourse outside Dublin, not far from Foxrock, Beckett's birthplace. There are a number of hints in *Watt* that Mr. Knott's house is in Foxrock; and Watt, on his way to Mr. Knott's by train, sees a racecourse and remembers that he must soon disembark (29). It is probably the Leopardstown course that he sees.

But the Master of the Halflengths is not, as one might suppose, a minor racing official; the phrase refers to the Master of the Female Halflengths, a sixteenth-century artist whose name is lost (the designation is based on one of his favorite subjects). In an earlier draft of *Watt*, the Master of the Leopardstown Halflengths is mentioned as the artist who executed a portrait of Knott's mother.[16] The phrase is also reminiscent of Dante's epithet for Aristotle, "the master of those who know."[17]

The halflengths of the Leopardstown Racecourse also suggest one of the paradoxes of Zeno of Elea, "The Race Course," which attempts to demonstrate the impossibility of motion. To complete a given course, Zeno argues, a runner must first cross half of it; then half the distance remaining; and then half of every remainder, ad infinitum. The racecourse can be divided into an infinite number of halflengths, each of which must be traversed. The runner, faced with the task of completing an infinite number of operations in a finite span of time, cannot traverse the course.[18]

---

[16] Coetzee, p. 474. Beckett parodies this convention for unnamed artists in *More Pricks than Kicks* (New York: Grove Press, 1970), p. 44, where he speaks of the "Master of the Tired Eyes." Beckett himself followed in the tradition of the Master of the Female Halflengths when, in *Happy Days*, he immersed Winnie up to her waist in a mound.

[17] *Inferno*, 4:131: "vidi 'l maestro di color che sanno."

[18] My summary of the paradox is based on an article by Gregory Vlastos, "Zeno of Elea," in *The Encyclopedia of Philosophy*, Paul Edwards, editor-

Zeno's version of "The Race Course" did not survive from antiquity; it is known because Aristotle discusses it in the *Physics*. This provides a link between Aristotle, master of those who know, and the halflengths. Aristotle is one of many philosophers who have proposed refutations of the paradox. He argues that if a runner must traverse an infinite number of half-units of length, he has an infinite number of half-units of time in which to complete his task. [19]

But Aristotle's double-negative solution never laid the matter to rest; there have been a number of modern attempts to refute the paradox. One argument, put forward by Henri Bergson, denies that space and time can be divided into units. [20] Most twentieth-century refutations utilize a number of recent mathematical innovations, notably Georg Cantor's theory of varying orders of infinity. This is the approach of Bertrand Russell and other thinkers who favor an empirical or positivistic point of view. [21]

The most radical approach of all is the raison d'etre of Zeno's entire collection of paradoxes: a denial of the ultimate reality of time and space. There is a good deal of evidence in *Watt* to suggest that this is the favored alternative; like other allusions to antimaterialistic philosophers in the Beckett canon, this reference is part of a critique of the empirical view of reality. [22]

But even more important than the ideas here is the technique: in a single phrase, as compressed and suggestive as a line of poetry, Beckett touches on issues as far-ranging as Greek philosophy, the history of art, and Irish horse-racing; yet all are related to themes in the novel. More than clever devices to tease a crossword puzzle public, these addenda contribute to the novel's structure.

---

in-chief (New York: Crowell Collier and Macmillan, 1967), vol. 8, pp. 372-74. Aristotle's refutation of Zeno's paradox is discussed by Schopenhauer in the same book where Beckett found the "zitto! zitto!" phrase, *Über die vierfache Wurzel...*, pp. 118-121.

[19] Aristotle's summary of the paradox is in the *Physics*, 239b 11-13 and 263a 4-11; the refutation begins at 263a 12.

[20] See Dampier, p. 463.

[21] This argument is too intricate to be summarized here; see Vlastos, p. 372 and ff. For Russell's views on the question see his *A History of Western Philosophy* (New York: Clarion, 1967), pp. 828-830.

[22] A more comprehensive version of this argument will be found in my essay, "*Watt* from Descartes to Schopenhauer," in *Modern Irish Literature*, ed. by Raymond Porter and James Brophy (New York: Twayne, 1972), pp. 261-287. Beckett alludes to Zeno's paradox, "The Millet Seed" in *Endgame* (New York: Grove Press, 1958), p. 70.

For example: when the reader comes to the end of the story, he thinks the novel has ended; the Addenda indicate that this is not so. For in this novel — unlike most novels — the story is only a minor component. Urged on by the Addenda, the reader returns to the important issues raised in *Watt*. He formulates problems, tracks down clues, makes discoveries, and soon is ready to launch a major interpretation. He may not notice that he is also slipping into a bog of paradoxes; he is too involved with his hypotheses. At this moment he is no longer reading about the protagonist of *Watt*; he has taken over this role for himself. [23]

When the reader speculates about alternatives and imagines incidents suggested by fragments in the Addenda, he begins to play an authorial role. Beckett's writing recognizes that the ultimate arena of literature is not the printed page but the mind of the reader; and that each person's experience of a work must be idiosyncratic. Beckett's novels may be thought of as collections of materials for a mental drama, designed so that a repeat performance will be no less entertaining than the first. And this literary figured-bass device is a reason why *Watt* continues to give pleasure even after many rereadings. The Addenda are no less important in this scheme than any other portion of the work; as the footnote recommends, they are precious, illuminating, and deserving of careful study. [24]

---

[23] See Beckett's comment on Joyce's writing in *Finnegans Wake*: "His writing is not *about* something; *it is that something itself.*" Samuel Beckett and others, *Our Exagmination Round his Factification*... (London: Faber and Faber, 1972), p. 14. H. P. Abbott discusses this technique of Beckett's, which he calls imitative form, in *The Fiction of Samuel Beckett* (Berkeley: University of California Press, 1973), p. 61 *et passim*.

[24] I wish to record my gratitude to the National Endowment for the Humanities for a research grant which made the completion of this essay possible.

A MYTHIC READING OF *MOLLOY*

by Angela B. Moorjani

IN *Molloy*, Beckett stages the fragmentation of a unity into two opposing parts. Whether approached from a narrative, rhetorical, or thematic perspective, the text is seen to mediate between complex, intertwined oppositions. According to Claude Lévi-Strauss, it is the role of mythical thought to grapple with the basic contraries of existence. *Molloy*, of course, is not a myth, but develops in a manner analogous to the mythical production of meaning. Like much of modern literature, however, the novel's production and exploitation of mythic material is ultimately ironic, for at the end, Beckett undermines the intricate mythic network constructed in the novel.[1]

The puzzling relationship between the narrators of *Molloy* illustrates the symmetries and dissymmetries of the novel. Although one usually speaks of two narrators in *Molloy*, a close reading reveals three. The first narrator opens the book with "Je suis dans la chambre de ma mère." He speaks in the first person, muses about his activities

---

[1] For Lévi-Strauss's conclusions on myth, see particularly the "Aube des mythes" and "Finale" chapters of *L'Homme nu* (Paris: Plon, 1971), the final volume of *Mythologiques*. In his last chapter, moreover, Lévi-Strauss hypothesizes that with Bach and Frescobaldi music inherited the formal symmetries of myth, whereas the novel, at the same time, took over myth's non-formal residue (p. 583). From what follows in this paper, it would appear that in *Molloy*, Beckett adopted both the formal symmetry and the residual material of mythical thought. It is interesting to note as well that Beckett prefers musical terms when speaking of the production of his works and when commenting on certain of its repetitions.

On the other hand, *Molloy* shares many of the aspects of what Northrop Frye terms "ironic myth" and applies to Kafka and Joyce in *Anatomy of Criticism* (Princeton Univ. Press, 1957), pp. 40-43.

as author, but fails to name himself. His Preamble to the book is followed by two symmetrical first person narrations of equal length, one by Molloy, the second by Moran.

Although all three narrators speak in the present tense of writing in a room, the Preamble follows the other parts chronologically. On a different level than the two narrations, the Preamble presents previously written texts to the reader. At the beginning of the book, we are, as the narrator tells us, almost at its end: "C'était le commencement, vous comprenez. Tandis que c'est presque la fin, à présent" (p. 8).[2]

Who then is the narrator of the Preamble? While sharing the first person pronoun and the fictional present tense with Molloy and Moran, he speaks of his mother like Molloy, of his son like Moran. Within the mother's room, Molloy's destination, he writes under the orders of Moran's master(s). It follows that he cannot be identified exclusively with either Molloy or Moran. To the contrary, the relationship among the three narrators is best expressed by the formula: one and one make one.[3] The two narrators, Molloy and Moran, make up one author. And this author, instead of producing a unified text, has splintered it into two, just as he has split his persona of author into two narrators.

In a spiraling progression, furthermore, this implicit author divides not only into two narrators/characters, but each character in turn subdivides into two parts (called A and B in Molloy's French narration), each of which again separates into two. Indeed, Molloy after staging the fading of the senses ("Tout s'estompe" [p. 9].), announcing the fraying of a path into the psyche ("La route, dure et blanche, balafrait les tendres pâturages..." [p. 10].), begins the description of what he calls his unreal journey (p. 22) with the experience of disjunction. Perched on an elevation, Molloy sees A and B move toward each other, meet, and continue on in opposite directions. This episode clearly figures the character watching two parts of himself come together in a brief encounter and separate. Having stated that he distinguishes himself from A and B only with difficulty ("Il passe des gens aussi, dont il n'est pas facile de se distinguer avec netteté"

---

[2] The page numbers in parenthesis refer to the French edition of *Molloy* (Paris: Editions de Minuit, 1951).

[3] In Jean-Paul Sartre's play, *Les Séquestrés d'Altona*, which like *Molloy* echoes many of the themes of the Oedipus story, these words stand out during the concluding soliloquy: "Un et un font un, voilà notre mystère."

[p. 9].), Molloy is tempted to join each of them. Moreover, while identifying with B, he imagines B's contemplating a divided soulscape (p. 11) just as Molloy is doing himself. Likewise, in the second narration, after his hallucinatory encounter with A and B, Moran sees A become disjointed (p. 234). The narrations of Molloy and Moran thus mirror each other as well as the novel as a whole. The author/narrator's mediating position between two opposing parts of himself is duplicated by each narrator/character's experience with two uncoupled selves.

Beckett switched to this ternary configuration at the time he turned to French. In *Watt,* the character is still an inner mirror image of the narrator. At the beginning of *Mercier et Camier,* on the other hand, the anonymous narrator tells of his relationship to a double persona: "Le voyage de Mercier et Camier, je peux le raconter si je veux, car j'étais avec eux tout le temps." With the adoption of a different language, the author distanced the two parts of the persona from the narrator. Through the introduction of a lengthy description of a knife-rest into Molloy's narration, Beckett gives the reader a model of the complex ternary and dual configurations of the text. For the knife-rest figures a mediating third term between two doubly dual terms: X——X

The text, however, mirrors itself both horizontally and vertically: Molloy and Moran and their narrations are not only in symmetrical opposition to each other, but as in *Watt,* one is contained within the other. Molloy is shown attempting in vain to translate an inner text, "quelque chose de changé dans le silence" (p. 135). The inadequate translation Molloy is writing, however, figures in turn the inner discourse Moran must learn to recognize as his own. As such, Molloy's story is present in Moran's although unrecognized. And the implicit author of the Preamble as well speaks of pages, written by him in the past, marked with signs he can no longer decipher. We have then an archaic text (1) within Molloy, whose text (2) is contained within Moran, whose text (3) is contained within the author. The author, like the largest external figure of nested dolls, envelops the other three. The three texts are thus simultaneous versions at different levels of an identical story imprinted in the past. And up the spiral, each narrator fails to decipher the texts accurately. We are left with two faulty translations of one text.

This ultimate text, of course, is the same one represented by Malone's notebook, which he calls his life, and of which he can decipher only a part. *L'Innommable* seems to be an attempt to stage the functioning of this discourse in itself. In *Comment c'est*, on the other hand, the narrator again quotes fragments from the primal text. The way, then, in which this illusive text functions in Beckett's works, brings to mind Lacan's definition of the unconscious: "L'inconscient est cette partie du discours concret en tant que transindividuel, qui fait défaut à la disposition du sujet pour rétablir la continuité de son discours conscient." [4]

Because of the multi-layer construction of *Molloy*, the vertical paradigm of the bee's dance may be said to complement the horizontal figure of the knife-rest. A bee dances at several heights — three or four, Moran specifies — but performs intricate variations in hum and figure on the various levels (pp. 261-62). Since both Molloy and Moran fail to grasp the function of the two figures they describe at length, the reader is invited to puzzle over these paradigms of the horizontal and vertical symmetries of the novel.

When one examines the different temporalities of the text, one notices that just as the first person pronoun is shared three ways by the author, narrators, characters, three different present tenses operate in the text. To the present tense of the author and of the narrators must be added Molloy's mythological present (p. 37), for it, not the literary past, appears to be the proper temporality for the character's story.

Each of the two long narrations begins and is pervaded by the present tense indicative of the writing activity. The character's journeys, however, are chronicled in the literary past tense reserved for representative writing. The present of the writing runs parallel to the past of the story and points to its fictional modality. Or better, the narrations tell both the fiction of the writing and the fiction of the story. In addition, the present contests the past tense, for Molloy clearly does not chronicle a past journey, but rather, the traces it left in the psyche. He consequently tends to slip into the mythological present, a tense indicating the present as repetition of the past.

The following passage at the beginning of Molloy's narration (pp. 9-10) illustrates the oscillation among the three different temporalities found in the text:

C'*était* sur une route d'une nudité frappante, je *veux*
   (fictional past)   (present of enunciation)

---

[4] Jacques Lacan, *Ecrits* (Paris: Seuil, 1966), p. 258.

dire sans haies ... car dans d'immenses champs des vaches

mâchaient.... J'*invente* peut-être un peu, j'*embellis*
(fictional past)   (present of enunciation)

peut-être, mais dans l'ensemble c'*était* ainsi. Elles
                      (fictional past)

mâchent, puis *avalent,* puis après une courte pause *appellent*
(mythological present)

sans effort la prochaine bouchée.

By means of the mythological present, the narrator indicts the literary past for its failure to translate the psychic material bearing in the present the traces of the past.[5]

The disjunctions apparent in the narrative structure are repeated by intricate thematic variations from one part to the other and within each part. We have seen that the characters are two opposite parts of one persona. Their journeys, then, best told in the mythological present, each lasting a full turn of seasons, each suggesting a regression/progression to womb and tomb, are but one journey staged at different psychical levels. Molloy's quest, under the sign of the mother, is duplicated by Moran's, under the dictate of the father.

Richly illustrated through cosmic symbols and mythological figures, the mother/father, female/male polarities are joined by the basic life/death duality. The two parts of the novel pose the questions: Am I my mother or am I my father? Am I alive or am I dead? Where do I find Being?

For Molloy, the mother-figure is all encompassing. She is the origin of life (and therefore of death) and the one who sustains him (she supplies him money); he variously describes her as his sexless, undifferentiated equal (p. 23) or merges her with Rose - Eros, his one experience with love; with Loy-Lousse, a representation of the law; and with the image of the old hag, an androgynous, monstrous sphinx (p. 89). She is both mother and not mother (Mag), self and other, desired and feared, positive and negative, goal and obstacle.

---

[5] For more detailed studies on the performative and metalinguistic aspects of *Molloy,* see Véronique Boulais, "Samuel Beckett: Une écriture en mal de je," *Poétique,* No. 17 (1974), pp. 114-32; and Dina Scherzer, "Quelques manifestations du narrateur-créateur dans *Molloy* de Samuel Beckett," *Language and Style,* 5 (1972), 115-22.

The only mention of his father occurs when Molloy voices the suspicion that his mother takes him for his father: "Moi je la prenais pour ma mère et elle elle me prenait pour mon père" (p. 23). Further echoes from the Oedipus myth are sounded throughout Molloy's story. Once on the way to his mother, he is impeded by obstacles, foremost his crippled leg (later legs) and various personifications of the law. Accordingly, the first encounter with the policeman and the sergeant stages the frightening ambiguity and inconsistencies of the law, recalling the ancient oracle, and more recently, Kafka's nightmares, for the law both demands and obstructs Molloy's quest. Repeated references to a sacrificial victim or *pharmakos* (pp. 38; 41; 51) reinforce Molloy's identification as victim of the law.

On the other hand, the beating of the charcoal-burner reenacts the myth's fatal meeting at the crossroads. The man in the forest first arouses Molloy's filial love (p. 128). Like all encounters with father-figures and the law in *Molloy*, however, the meeting soon degenerates into misunderstanding. Finally, when the man tries to stop Molloy on the way to the maternal city, the episode ends in the predictable violence.

The personifications of the law are then replaced by an equally ambiguous voice that goads and impedes. This voice, together with the other obstacles, prevents Molloy from reaching his destination. He ends in the ditch awaiting transfer to the maternal room. Once he reaches the room, as we know from the Preamble, instead of finding his mother, he takes her place. Was his then a journey to life or death? The ditch and the room suggest the tomb and the womb, leaving Molloy simultaneously dead and unborn. His journey has both regressed and progressed to the womb/tomb mother. Instead of finding Being, he is, as it were, reabsorbed into the mother, is yet unborn.

The discussion of the lengthy Lousse episode has been purposely set aside until this point. For this central episode combines the various mythic threads into an emblem (or *mise en abîme*) in the middle of the narration. Molloy's narration, staging a descent into the psyche, here proceeds into a further *descente en enfer*. In Jungian terminology, which seems appropriate here, Lousse's closed-off garden represents the innermost region of the psyche, the mother's realm. Accordingly, the complex figure of Sophie Loy-Lousse takes on all possible roles, both positive and negative. As ambiguous as the male representations of the law, she appears to be a chthonian mother-goddess, a lunar deity, the law (Loy) and ruler of a matricentric realm, and finally the sphinx. That she has usurped the place of the father-god is indicated by the death of Teddy. For Teddy's death at Molloy's hands and his name ("Theodore" contains "gift" and "god"), recall the archaic death of the father-god. Teddy's death causes Molloy to fall (a constant of the death-of-god motif in Beckett) and to enter the paradisiacal realm of the mother. Indeed, Lousse asks Molloy to take Teddy's place (p. 70). She combines the three fundamental images of the mother; she is the oedipal mother, the oral mother (she feeds Molloy), and the primitive, uterine mother. While Molloy is captive in her garden, he merges with the cosmos in an experience of immanence, alike to womb and tomb (p. 73).

Although paradisiacal (there are further allusions to Dante's earthly paradise) Lousse's realm is also a prison. Lousse keeps Molloy captive in her enchanted encirclement. (The allusions to Circe and Ulysses have been caught by many.) Lousse, however, as obstacle also recalls the sphinx. After wondering if she is not perhaps a man or at least androgynous (p. 84), Molloy finally agrees that a woman could have stopped him on the way to his mother. For most importantly, although in Lousse's garden Molloy has reached the stage of immanence in the realm of the mother, it is not the end of his journey. A voice tells him to be on his way. The journey does not end, but spirals on: the answer to Being is not to be found in the mythic pole of the mother or in the negative Nirvana of a return to the womb.

Moran's journey, on the other hand, is under the sign of the father. And instead of a mother-deity we have a father-god, instead of immanence, transcendence. The biblical exile from Eden is reenacted, or better, is parodied, when Gaber-Gabriel transmits Youdi-Yahweh's order for Moran to leave his garden-paradise. Whereas Molloy is a son-figure (who compares himself to Christ, the son-god) and merges with Loy-Lousse, Moran identifies with the father-representation of the law. As Youdi commands him, Moran commands his son: "Tu laisseras tes deux albums à la maison... Pas un mot de reproche, un simple futur prophétique, sur le modèle de ceux dont usait Youdi. Votre fils vous accompagnera" (p. 168). Youdi's orders, moreover, turn into an inner voice of conscience, reminiscent of the super-ego (p. 204).

As already pointed out, Molloy's story is a figuration of what goes on within Moran; the two characters share one story told at different levels. Together they show the self divided by opposite poles, by ambiguous laws that both order and forbid what they command. In a striking analogy to the structure of *Oedipus Rex,* Moran is consciously like the father (as demanded by the law) and simultaneously the son who killed the father and joined with his mother (in imitation of the father, yet forbidden). And like Oedipus, Moran is both the seeker and the sought; as narrator, the teller and the told. Like the odyssey of many modern writers, his journey, moving from a mystified consciousness of the self to the recognition of his identity with the other, progresses like the psychoanalytic path of the Oedipus tragedy.[6] Telling the kind of detective story of which the Oedipus tale is considered the prototype, Moran must search out Molloy, both absolutely other, "tout le contraire de moi" (p. 175), and an inner image of himself. And yet again, although Moran sets out on this path, he does not follow through to the end. Beckett, as it were, plays with the mythical material, substituting uncertainty and discontinuity for the mediating solutions of mythical thought. (Interestingly enough, when Robbe-Grillet based his detective novel *Les Gommes* on the Oedipus theme, perhaps with the ironic intention of erasing the myth, only Beckett immediately noticed the presence of the myth in the novel.)[7]

Like Oedipus, then, Moran considers himself powerful and innocent. Yet, he is simultaneously his opposite, Molloy, whom he fails to recognize in himself, but projects on all around him. Consequently, the events in Molloy's story, which the reader already knows, serve to demystify the illusory attitudes in Moran's. For example, Moran, portraying himself as meticulously religious (while projecting on his son his actual impiety), nevertheless repeats the death-of-god episode in Molloy's story through his loss of faith. In relation to his son Moran appears to incarnate the law; in relation to Youdi, he is its victim like Molloy. And after suspecting his son of wanting to kill him, in a repetition of Molloy's encounter with the charcoal-burner, Moran hallucinates the murder of the part of himself most closely mirroring his conscious identity of father.

---

[6] See René Girard, "De l'expérience romanesque au mythe œdipien," *Critique,* No. 222 (1965), pp. 899-924; and "Symétrie et dissymétrie dans le mythe d'Œdipe," *Critique,* No. 249 (1968), pp. 99-135.

[7] Bruce Morrisette — "Clefs pour *Les Gommes,*" in Alain Robbe-Grillet, *Les Gommes* (Paris: Union Générale d'Editions, 1962), p. 311, n. 4 — indicates: "Seul Samuel Beckett, d'après Robbe-Grillet, a remarqué tout de suite que *Les Gommes* était basé sur le thème d'Œdipe."

Cosmic symbols further illustrate the relation between the two parts: fire and water, light and dark alternate like the father/mother orientations of the two characters. For instance, Moran prefers the light of day, Molloy the dark of night. And Moran's time around the campfire corresponds to Molloy's time in the cave at the seashore, a maternal place. Even more strikingly, Moran imagines himself a burning torch next to his fire (p. 228), whereas Molloy envisions putting out to sea never to return (p. 104). Throughout, the father-figures are fire-related: Molloy calls the man in the forest a charcoal-burner because he sees smoke; both A and Moran carry lit cigars. The cosmic symbols underline both the repetitions and the oppositions of the two narrations.

After hallucinating the death of the father or of his own egotistical part, Moran experiences great inner metamorphoses and begins to resemble Molloy. Molloy, correspondingly, after killing the charcoal-burner physically disintegrates and mingles with the earth and the forest. The spiraling movements take them in the direction of Being. During Moran's return journey, then, as in Molloy's, darkness, water, physical decay, and confusion predominate. (His circular journey from garden to garden covers the regression/progression to womb and tomb.) And yet, Moran continues nevertheless to be the opposite of Molloy: he bullies his son, is mistaken for the butcher among the lambs (p. 246) — Molloy is taken for a sacrificial victim (p. 41) — is recognized as Moran.

From our reading, it is clear that Moran does not "become" Molloy, since Molloy is at all times a disjointed part of Moran. During his travels Moran has come to the borderline of Molloy's territory, the zone between consciousness and the unconscious, has recognized the movements, the strange forces within this region, without, however, reaching them: "Et cet Obidil [anagram of libido] ... que j'aurais tellement voulu voir de près, eh bien je ne le vis jamais..." (p. 251). Still separated, if less so, from the other part of himself, Moran remains Moran and Molloy simultaneously, two, not one.

Consequently, Moran hears both the voice of conscience (Gaber delivers the order to return home) and the mysterious voice heard by Molloy speaking at first an unrecognizable language: "J'ai parlé d'une voix qui me disait ceci et cela.... Elle ne se servait pas des mots qu'on avait appris au petit Moran, que lui à son tour avait appris à son petit. De sorte que je ne savais pas d'abord ce qu'elle voulait"

(p. 272). This ambiguous voice represents an exteriority from the self; it indicates the direction in which the quest must proceed once freed from the mythic mother/father poles that tie the characters to their identity and to violence.[8] Accordingly, at the end of his narration, Moran wonders whether he is perhaps more free.

What then is the end of the quest? Moran searches for Molloy, Molloy for his mother. And yet since we already know of the identity of Molloy with his mother, repeated by the Molloy/Mollose — Loy/Lousse parallel, the quest is the same. (Moran perceives this Molloy-mother identity [p. 173].) We also know, however, that Molloy's quest does not end with the mother, but spirals on. Moran, as well, speaks of his quest as ultimately impersonal: the first apparition of what he later reluctantly names Molloy surfaces without name, sex, or age (pp. 175-76). (Correspondingly, namelessness, bisexuality, timelessness recur throughout Molloy's narration.) The one quest moves beyond personal identity in the direction of Being. One wonders, though, if "Being" does not betray the end of the quest as much as do the Molloy/mother appellations. For from *Watt* through *Comment c'est*, both origin and end are manifested ultimately as absence.

And so both narrators undermine their mythical versions of the journey: they are lies, not truth, they contend. Molloy's narration is but a faulty translation of what he calls the "quelque chose de changé quelque part" or the "quelque chose de changé dans le silence" (p. 135). His narration is but a game for Moran, the kind a child plays when making objects come and go, appear and disappear, in order to master the fear of absence. After having written a story, called meaning into the presence of a text, Moran makes it all disappear with his final words: "Alors je rentrai dans la maison et j'écrivis, Il est minuit. La pluie fouette les vitres. Il n'était pas minuit. Il ne pleuvait pas." Each narrator thus disassociates himself from his text and from his character. The characters are abandoned in the third person at the end of each narration: the I of narrator and character are not one. Finally, it is suggested that each character remains unborn.

The Preamble, of course, introduced the simultaneity of beginning and end, of birth and death. At the beginning of the novel we are also at its end. And the author-narrator identifies birth and death:

---

[8] The concept of exteriority comes from Emmanuel Levinas, *Totalité et infini: Essai sur l'extériorité* (The Hague: Martinus Nijhoff, 1971).

"Moi je voudrais... finir de mourir" (p. 7). Each character, consequently, as we have seen, follows a simultaneous movement to birth and death. (The reading of the text similarly regresses and progresses to the beginning and end, the point at which the text annuls itself.) And yet, being unborn suggests the possibility of a birth, and since we know from the Preamble that the novel does not end, only nears the end, there is a simultaneous possibility of an ending. At all levels, the book remains open-ended. The quests for origin and end — the two directions illustrated through *Molloy*'s mythic mother/father polarities — will be replayed throughout Beckett's subsequent works.

In the meantime, all the disjunctions in *Molloy* are retained: there is no continuous text but discontinuous versions of an illusive discourse. No mediation appears possible between the oppositions illustrated both through the narrative structure and the mythic content. And ultimately we are invited to view the novel as a brilliant game where nothing takes place. Yet, this is a game vitally worth playing, for by acting out our desires and fears, it frees us for a while through its play.

THE COUPLES IN *COMMENT C'EST*

by Hannah Case Copeland

IN the novel *Comment c'est*, as in many of his other works, Samuel Beckett reveals two primary concerns: the human condition and the plight of the artist. In fact, he strips the traditional novel form of its diverting, illusion-creating characteristics (and even of its customary punctuation) in order to portray more directly than ever the misery of mankind and the tormented existence of the human creator. The protagonist inhabits an infernal, endless swamp through which he must crawl naked and panting in the dark. At regular intervals he tortures a fellow creature and is tortured by another. To slake his thirst, he swallows portions of the slime which surrounds him. Little wonder that he has no appetite for the fishy contents of the tins he carries in his sack or that he longs for the mud to open and engulf him. He is doubly condemned, however, for not only must he travel indefinitely through mud and darkness; he is also compelled to *tell* of the various stages of his journey. As narrator-hero, his fate is grim. Like his predecessors Molloy, Malone, and the Unnamable, he must recount unceasingly the story of his life. More especially he must describe "how it is" with him at the moment of composition; that is, what it feels like to express himself. But his means of expression are still more limited than those of the Unnamable, who could not lift his hand from his lap. The nameless protagonist of *Comment c'est* murmurs his tale breathlessly to the mud in a muted voice, driven to do so by a mysterious inner mandate. He is aware of his own expressive activity only because he can feel his jaw moving. Perhaps worst of all, he knows that he is alone and that no one hears him. He affirms and reaffirms from beginning to end his essential solitude, yet to speak of himself he relies upon images of couples. Let us consider first how he uses this kind of image to portray the human condition. Later we will discuss how couples illustrate the dilemma of the artist.

The traditional romantic couple appears in Parts I and II but does not convey the customary message. Even though man continually seeks happiness in a love relationship, sentimental bliss always eludes him. Indeed, his futile pursuit of it can have tragic consequences. The narrator-hero expresses the need for a loving companion when he speaks early in Part I of his relationship with the sack he carries: "je le prends dans mes bras lui parle y fourre ma tête y frotte ma joue y pose ma bouche m'en détourne avec humeur m'y presse de nouveau lui dis toi toi."[1] By recalling here both the positive and negative feelings which intimacy occasions, the protagonist heightens the pathos of his real solitude. Even though companionship can never be perfectly blissful, he seems to prefer it to loneliness. Further on, when the presence of the sack fails to fill the emptiness of his existence, he turns to memories of the past. In particular, he has a vision of himself as an adolescent strolling hand in hand with a young girl through an ideal pastoral landscape complete with sheep: "vieux songe de fleurs et de saisons au mois d'avril ou de mai" (35). But, like Belacqua and Winnie of Beckett's early short story *Fingal*, the hero and heroine here fall far short of the romantic ideal both in their physical characteristics and in their emotional relationship. All that is said of the girl is that she is "moins hideuse" seen from the front; the true enormity of her ugliness is left to our imagination. As for the boy, the narrator's former self, he appears awkward and gangly with a repelling figure and complexion and the look of an imbecile. The emotional rapport between these two young lovers is depicted as a comically mechanical synchronization. As they walk, their heads move together "comme reliées par un essieu" (37). Even their love-talk is perfunctory and mechanized. Although unfeeling, however, it is efficient — for it is combined with eating — and equitable — for each partner receives equal time. While one bites his sandwich and chews, the other swallows and emits a cliché:

> nous mangeons des sandwiches à bouchées alternées chacun le sien en échangeant des mots doux ma chérie je mords elle

---

[1] (Paris: Editions de Minuit, 1961), p. 21. Hereafter, page references to the text will appear in parentheses after the quotations.

avale mon chéri elle mord j'avale... mon amour je mords elle avale mon trésor elle mord j'avale. (37)

In short, then, their feelings for each other are little more than appetites, which are appropriately expressed in a mere routine. Romantic relationships can scarcely be satisfying if they are carried out much as one devours a sandwich. Beckett further undercuts the traditional idyll by giving the couple a dog as companion. Referring repeatedly to its genitals, he suggests that the two young people must sooner or later seek sexual gratification as well as companionship and affection from one another. In fact, his treatment of the animal makes it seem at least as worthy of our sympathy as the couple, if not more so. It is on a leash (36) and has no strength left (37). There is little difference between man and dog here and, thus, small hope for human fulfillment through love. This becomes undeniably clear when the narrator-hero, painfully aware that the happiness sought by the lovers is illusory, cries out to his former self: "plaque-la là et cours t'ouvrir les veines" (37). There is no use trying, he seems to say; death, not love, offers the only possible escape from the anguished solitude of the human condition.

In Part II, the search for happiness through love appears even more futile. To begin with, mutual affection simply cannot exist, even though beings still want to cling to one another: "trouver quelqu'un que quelqu'un vous trouve enfin vivre ensemble collés ensemble s'aimer un peu sans être aimé être aimé un peu sans pouvoir aimer" (91-92). The little loving possible is inevitably one-sided, so that there can be no common joy. Worse, as Pim's story reveals, the despair that accompanies failure to attain the romantic ideal can be fatal. Pam or Prim (Pim cannot even remember his wife's name) chooses to die rather than endure the prolonged disintegration of a once intense love life:

> Pam Prim on s'aimait tous les jours tous les trois puis le samedi puis comme ça par-ci par-là pour se débarrasser essaya de relancer par le cul trop tard elle tomba de la fenêtre *ou se jeta* colonne brisée. (94, my emphasis)

As intercourse (commonly thought to be the greatest source of mutual satisfaction in marriage) gradually becomes mechanical and, finally, impossible, it steadily undermines the rapport between Pim and Pam and in the end precipitates Pam's attempted suicide. Afterwards, when she is hospitalized, Pim takes flowers to her, dutifully performing the role of the fond husband. Once in her hospital room, however, he gazes at the furniture and not at his beloved: "l'amour voir les meubles des autres et pas l'être aimé avouez" (95). Even the flowers, which should serve as a link between the two persons, actually separate them: "les fleurs entre nous le visage à travers" (95); and Pim ends his visit by counting them: "elles étaient bien une vingtaine" (95). When Pam begs for holly to enliven the whiteness of her room, Pim struggles for the words to explain why he cannot find any (96). The difficulty of the simplest communication between man and wife confirms the ultimate disillusion of love. Pim and Pam's union exists in name only. For them, as for so many Beckettian couples, the quest for fulfillment through mutual love leads but to a deeper awareness of every individual's essential, impenetrable loneliness.

Because they have suffered such disappointments in the past, one may well wonder why Pim and the narrator continue to seek companionship in their present state. Still, from the first, the narrator-hero announces that Pim will come and, in fact, orients his story according to the alternating absence and presence of his fellow creature: "comment c'était... avant Pim avec Pim après Pim comment c'est trois parties" (9). Later he accounts for this state of affairs by declaring that the encounter with another is built into his present existence: "l'ordre naturel le voyage le couple l'abandon" (24). The "natural" order of things makes it inevitable that either one exists alone, or one has a partner. This becomes evident in Part III where the hero describes an infinite procession of creatures like himself and Pim, who spend one half of their time as solitaries and the other half in the company of a fellow being (131ff.). However, as one might expect, togetherness is not a happy state. Sharing a stifling intimacy, the partners act as victim and tormentor and thus find themselves "deux par deux agglutinés pour les besoins du tourment" (140). As we learn in Part II, the torturer scratches, jabs, and thumps his victim in order to extract certain replies from him. But, since justice requires that the tormentor be tormented in turn, the narrator conceives of a fourth part to his story in which he casts himself (the former torturer of Pim) as the victim of a third character named Bom: "celui qui pour moi pour qui moi ce que moi pour Pim Pim pour moi" (75). To be with another, then, is to suffer or to cause suffering. The "training" of

Pim is accomplished and repeated endlessly so that the narrator envisions himself performing over and over again the same apparently pointless and cruel acts: "le mortel suivant me coller contre le nommer le dresser le couvrir jusqu'au sang de majuscules romaines me gaver de ses fables nous unir pour la vie" (77). His victim's stories divert him, but all the while he knows that his partner will not remain with him forever and that he in turn will be forced to tell of his life when Bom arrives on the scene. It seems that the only reason for this cycle of torture is to reassure oneself that one's life is still going on: "la voix extorquée quelques mots la vie parce que ça crie c'est la preuve il n'y a qu'à enfoncer bien profond un petit cri tout n'est pas mort on boit on donne à boire bonsoir" (148). No joy of comradeship comes from this give and take; only the feeble assurance that life goes on and the fleeting pleasure of inflicting pain: "tant il est vrai qu'ici on ne connaît son bourreau que le temps de le subir sa victime que celui d'en jouir" (146).

One does not even get to know one's partner in spite of the painful intimacy that is shared: "ici personne ne connaît personne ni personnellement ni autrement" (149); and should the same persons meet and interact a million times, they would still be strangers: "et ces mêmes couples qui éternellement se reconstituent d'un bout à l'autre de cette immense procession que c'est toujours à la millionième fois ça se laisse concevoir comme à l'inconcevable première deux étrangers qui s'unissent pour les besoins du tourment" (146-147).

Since, then, one cannot know another or be known by another, friendship is an illusion, but the *need* for friendship is real enough. In fact, the conflict between this basic human desire and the impossibility of gratifying it causes constant suffering. It seems both ludicrous and pathetic when the hero near the end of his stint as tormentor asks Pim: "M'AIMES-TU CON" (110). The very tone of the question anticipates a negative reply; yet by asking it the narrator restates his need to be loved. Unfortunately for him, as for humanity, companionship produces more pain and misunderstanding than joy. For this reason, the narrator's vision of the best possible world excludes the couple entirely: "un [monde] peut-être il s'en trouve un peut-être assez miséricordieux pour abriter de tels ébats où personne n'abandonne jamais personne et personne n'attend jamais personne et jamais deux corps ne se touchent" (172). It would be better, he suggests, to free oneself from the slightest hope of realizing meaningful interpersonal rapport than to pursue an ever unattainable goal. As it is, he sees the world filled by men who, solitary and unknowable, make endless attempts to escape the bounds of solitude so as to love and be loved. Repeated, dolorous failure does not quell the desire for a satisfying relationship to be achieved further on in life.

While demonstrating through images of couples the frustrating isolation which the human condition imposes, the narrator-hero tells too of the even more agonizing solitude which he must endure as an artist, for he is actually quite alone throughout his story. As he acknowledges definitively at the end, it is he who all along has imagined Pim and Bom as well as the other personae which people his tale: "moi seul responsable de cet inqualifiable murmure" (173). Visions, sacks, couples — he declares them all "foutaise" (175), thus condemning their artificial nature and reaffirming his solitude. As early as Part II he suggests that both he and his creatures are only masks. Portraying himself as the prime mover or original persona in the story, he says: "le premier est toujours moi ensuite les autres" (108). Pim and Bom are but "frères imaginaires" (139) and the tale as a whole but an "orgie de faux être" (85). Even though he would like to believe from time to time that others besides himself inhabit the mud, the conclusion which he reaches in the beginning remains the only possible one: "conclusion non moi seul élu" (17). It is, then, to escape his loneliness that he turns to his imagination. By creating fellow beings to fill the void of existence, he hopes to find diversion from his misery. Like so many other Beckettian creators, he speaks of others so as to forget himself. Boasting of his ability to do this, he says: "sans moi il ne serait jamais Pim," and "je sais m'effacer derrière ma créature" (65). But, ironically, the disguises he puts on only serve to betray his own true condition and to make him ever more mindful of it. Apparently speaking of others, he in fact describes himself. As he says of the chain of numbered beings which he creates in Part III: "si le 814 336 décrit au 814 335 le 814 337 et au 814 337 le 814 335 il ne fait en définitive que se décrire soi-même" (146). Essential isolation excludes the possibility of all but self-description. Thus, Pim and the narrator are one and the same, as the latter frankly admits: "jamais été que moi moi Pim" (127). Still, although he clearly indicates that he must claim Pim's portrait as his own, at the same time the author-hero retains the image of the couple which Pim's presence establishes from the first. Developing in a logical fashion the previously cited statement of identity with Pim, he gives revised titles to the three parts of his tale: "comment c'était avant moi avec moi après moi" (127). Absolutely alone, he yet experiences life as though accompanied by a double or alter ego. The couples which haunt his narrative reveal in effect his dual personality, source of the ceaseless creative agony he endures.

Like those artist-heroes before him, the protagonist of *Comment c'est* relates his story compulsively. If he could be silent, he would not speak. But the compulsion to express himself is felt as the unbearable pangs of unending torture. Like Pim tormented, the hero cannot resist; he must speak out. He tells his tale in the hope that suffering will cease once his story has been told. At the same time, however, he can honestly see no end in sight — neither to pain nor to story-telling. The pair of couples formed by the narrator, Pim, and Bom vividly illustrate the terrible dilemma faced by the artist: he must say something — create — in spite of his scant ability to do so. In particular, he must speak of his life regardless of its ever more circumscribed nature: "ma vie ici avant Pim avec Pim comment c'était le peu que j'ai eu ... ce peu vite donc le peu qui reste" (120-121). With apprehension, the hero anticipates the anguish he would have to endure were Bom to arrive: "le moment où sans le pouvoir j'aurais à dire" (131). That he is in fact continuously possessed by the creative compulsion appears very early in statements such as "mon Dieu avoir à murmurer ça" (30) and "ce mot qu'il faut entendre murmurer" (48). In his distress he even appeals to the muse of comedy: "Thalie par pitié une feuille de ton lierre" (46). Furthermore, in the story of Pim he indicates clearly the true source of his own inspiration: "la part d'invention énorme assurément ... une chose qu'on ignore la menace le cul à sang les nerfs à vif on invente" (89). Only martyrdom (72 and passim) and the torments of hell (44 and passim) provide an accurate idea of the creator's agony. Worst of all, like that of the damned, the artist's suffering seems eternal. Pim imagines that the narrator will remain "collé contre lui ... à le martyriser ... éternellement" (120), while the hero refers directly to his *douleur* as "laquelle entre toutes la profonde hors d'atteinte" (40). Death would bring relief, but it will never come. Alluding to Atropos (the third Fate, who cuts the thread of life), the author-hero laments: "grands ciseaux de la vieille noire ... clic clac clic clac deux fils à la seconde cinq toutes les deux jamais le mien" (129). Compelled to express himself continuously even though he has nothing to say, he cannot go on, yet he cannot do otherwise. Like the Unnamable, the protagonist here complains: "on ne peut continuer on continue la même chose pourra-t-on s'arrêter c'est là plutôt on ne peut continuer on ne peut s'arrêter arrêter" (110). Thus, he struggles on, trying to say enough to satisfy some unspecified requirement: "un peu de sang quelques cris quelques mots... pour la paix" (153). Still, what he strives for is in truth "une paix inexistante" (173). Like the search for happiness in love, the artist's quest for relief from compulsive creation is doomed to fail from the outset.

To better comprehend the precise nature of his painful compulsion and the reason for self-portrayal, let us consider another couple which demonstrates the creator's duality. Mentioned anonymously as early as the second page of the novel, this pair presents simultaneous perception and transcription of a message: "quelqu'un qui écoute un autre qui note ou le même" (10).[2] The suggestion that the two duties could be performed by one being confirms that the couple here represents the condition of a single creator who both perceives his artistic vision (as an Evangelist receiving the Holy Word) and must at once transcribe it. In his *Proust,* Beckett refers to this dual nature as follows: "The artist has acquired his text: the artisan translates it."[3] But from where does the artist obtain his inspiration, and how does he give form to it? For answers to these questions we must pursue the narrator's tale of Kram and Krim.

Almost from the beginning of his story, the hero imagines that he is followed about through the mud by a witness who, in the darkness, constantly shines lights upon him: "toute ma surface visible plongée dans la lumière de ses lampes" (22). Later we learn that the lamp image is a metaphor for eyes, and that the witness needs good ones: "il lui faudrait de bons yeux au témoin... de bons yeux une bonne lampe" (54). In Part II this observer receives the name of Kram and is accompanied by a scribe named Krim (98). It is here that their rapport with each other and with the narrator becomes clear. Kram must keep the hero under constant surveillance while informing Krim

---

[2] Cf. the rapport between Watt and Sam in Beckett's *Watt* (New York: Grove Press, 1959), pp. 156-158, and the image of Matthew and the angel in his *Murphy* (New York: Grove Press, 1957), p. 215, and in his *L'Innommable* (Paris: Editions de Minuit, 1969), p. 28.

[3] (New York: Grove Press, 1957), p. 64.

of his subject's every move. Krim in turn must write down all that is dictated to him by Kram. For the protagonist, this close observation is both excruciatingly painful and ceaseless. Kram's description of him reveals his distress: "baignant dans la lumière de mes lampes à en avoir la peau en eau il marmonne d'obscurité" (101). Like an actor laboring beneath a merciless spotlight,[4] the hero seems almost overcome by the intense heat which the "lamps" produce. Further, he imagines generations (98), even dynasties (102), of Krams and corresponding Krims who watch over him and record his words and deeds. Kram and Krim seen separately and as one are his constant companions and his only audience:

> murmure mal quelques mauvaises bribes pour Kram qui écoute Krim qui note ou Kram seul un seul suffit Kram seul témoin et scribe ses feux qui m'éclairent Kram avec moi penché sur moi jusqu'à la limite d'âge puis son fils son petit-fils ainsi de suite
>
> ... d'âge en âge leurs feux qui m'éclairent. (161)

More than ever it seems evident that the hero, creator of this couple, can speak only of his own life and, in particular, of his experiences as an author. Kram is simply an incarnation of his inner self-perception — a painful, continuous sensation which, because it is so dolorous, demands expression. Similarly, Krim represents the narrator's creative faculties which are compelled to give to the artistic vision of existence some ordered, and here, verbal form. As if to confirm this interpretation, the hero, after denying the reality of Kram and Krim (103), yet applies the perception-transcription process to himself at least twice, saying: "on dit la chose qu'on voit" (106) and "sous les feux de l'observateur idéal la bouche soudain qui s'agite" (117). He contains within himself both witness and scribe, perceiver and transcriber.

In fact, from the start he repeatedly calls attention to his duality with the refrain "je cite" (9 and passim), the phrase "je le dis comme je l'entends" (23 and passim), and repeated references to an inner voice which dictates to him all he must say (9 and passim). These expressions become fully comprehensible only after the Kram-Krim episode. Even the nature of the artist's agony (first presented by the

---

[4] Cf. the characters' situation and activity in Beckett's play *Play* (London: Faber and Faber, 1964).

narrator and Pim) gains clarification here, for the enormous difficulty of the creative act is evident when Krim complains that Kram's reports are often rapidly and ineffectively conveyed: "à peine s'il bafouille encore... j'en perds les neuf dixièmes ça part si soudain sonne si faible va si vite dure si peu je me précipite c'est fini" (99). (Compare the narrator's complaint: "j'entends mal ou la voix dit mal," 140.) Kram's message eludes him in spite of his diligent efforts to seize it. The transformation of artistic inspiration into words appears virtually impossible; and to show his impatience with Kram, Krim insults him with the epithet "fou" (101, 102). The difficulty which the artisan encounters seems, then, due to the nature of the artist's perception. Dominated by a consciousness of self which is uniquely lucid and totally uncompromising, the hapless creator finds that his inner vision defies formulation. He is compelled to respond to this unspeakably intense self-perception and is forever unable to do so. At the end he resorts to primeval howls of pain — the only adequate expression of the torment caused him by his dilemma.

The Kram-Krim story helps, too, to explain the rapport between the hero, Pim, and Bom. We can see now that the tormentor acts as Kram, relaying violent self-consciousness to his victim. The latter, overcome by the pain this brute data imparts, attempts to frame it in words. All three couples show the creator's experience of self-awareness to be the equivalent of systematic torture which can end only with an unattainable death.

Finally, the story of Kram and Krim reveals the reason for the creator-hero's series of self-portraits: with his mental faculties declining, he can provide nothing else. We first learn of this cerebral poverty when, addressing a prayer to sleep, which would bring an end to anguished consciousness, the narrator implores: "viens éteindre ces deux vieux charbons qui n'ont plus rien à voir et ce vieux four détruit par le feu" (44). In the light of Kram's death wish — "mes phares que mes phares s'éteignent" (102) — the hero's meaning is clear. Lit by the fires of his inner eyes, his mind is conscious only of its own reflection. Having consumed memory and imagination in vain attempts to evade the truth, the narrator finds that tormenting self-awareness alone remains active. At the beginning of Part III he places himself within his skull and describes its emptiness in a way that recalls Beckett's short piece *Bing*: "tout ça presque blanc qui fut si orné quelques traces c'est tout" (126). In the same passage he complains of a waning imagination: "l'imagination qui décline étant au plus bas" (126), and links his own diminishing existence to it: "je baisse baisse c'est trop dire plus de tête imagination à bout plus de souffle" (125). Were he finally unable to imagine anything more to say, he would cease to exist.

In the end, bereft of matter and means for expression, the creator-hero yet acknowledges the most agonizing aspect of his condition: the need to keep up his murmur. Although he longs for the peace of silence, for the right to say no more, he frantically clings to words, depending upon them for his very existence: "pour des comme nous ... plus de nourriture dans un cri voire un soupir arraché à celui dont le silence est le seul bien ou dans la parole extorquée ... que n'en offriront jamais les sardines" (173). For the artist, to create is to live, even though the demands of intense self-consciousness constantly beset him. Here the hero's creative effort, evident in his continual panting, is his only "gage de vie" (160): "un halètement dans le noir la boue à ça que ça aboutit le voyage le couple l'abandon" (155). His story terminates in a description of how it was told. Appropriately, the narrator answers with formless cries a series of self-imposed questions like those which he scratched into Pim's back. Both interrogator and interrogated, torturer and victim, he presents *sans masque* the creative dilemma and his feelings about it: "QU'EST-CE QUI S'EST PASSE hurlements bon" (174). The question signals self-perception, and the cries of pain the attempt to give expression to it. The judgment "bon" confirms the paradoxical need to go on expressing. [5]

The artist's loneliness is, then, much harder to bear than that of the ordinary man. No one hears what he has to say, and no one diverts him from the infinite pain of self-awareness. Even his personae betray him, since he inevitably creates them all in his own image. Still, although he yearns to be done with his tale, the end of storytelling can come only with his unimaginable death. As the stories of couples show, the artist is compelled to create continuously; to conclude one work means to begin the next. For this reason, the pun of the final words, which echo the title, closes the novel with the certitude that the teller of tales can never say "the end."

---

[5] For a detailed and comprehensive analysis of the Beckettian artist, see my *Art and the Artist in the Works of Samuel Beckett* (The Hague: Mouton & Co., 1975).

HOW IT IS

by Howard Harper

IN Samuel Beckett's early essay on *Work in Progress,* he announced that Joyce's "writing is not *about* something; *it is that something itself.*"[1] Although this can be — and sometimes has been — dismissed as a youthfully pretentious pronouncement of doubtful value as criticism, it does seem consistent with the principles and the practice of Beckett's own art. The careers of both Joyce and Beckett, in fact, illustrate how the meanings of truly original works can remain hidden from audiences schooled in more traditional forms — yet why, when we discover those meanings at last, they seem so right and so necessary that we feel that we have always known them: they emerge with the force of revelation. A similar view of the evolution of art is implicit in Picasso's feeling that a truly new thing is always "ugly" because the artist creates it out of his own bafflement and anguish; later his followers, who can see it from the outside, more objectively, can discover its rules and can use them to create things that are "pretty."[2]

This evolutionary process is also exemplified, of course, by the history of critical responses to the artist. In the case of Beckett, it is most evident in the criticism of his drama, as Martin Esslin has pointed out:

---

[1] "Dante... Bruno. Vico.. Joyce," in *An Exagmination of James Joyce* (1929; Norfolk, Conn.: New Directions, n.d.), p. 14.

[2] Gertrude Stein, *The Autobiography of Alice B. Toklas* (New York: Harcourt, Brace, 1933), p. 28. Stein's way of putting it is delightful: "as Pablo once remarked, when you make a thing, it is so complicated making it that it is bound to be ugly, but those that do it after you they don't have to worry about making it and they can make it pretty, and so everybody can like it when the others make it."

When "Waiting for Godot" opened in London in 1955, most of the local critics dismissed it as incomprehensible; when the play was revived at London's Royal Court Theater 10 years later, it was most respectfully received by the critics (the same ones in many cases) except, it was now said, the play had one fault; its symbolism was too open, too obvious, too easy to get. There could be no more telling proof of the intensity with which the substance of "Waiting for Godot" had been pondered over, discussed and absorbed into the very fabric of the mythology, the living imagery, of our epoch.[3]

The meanings of Beckett's fiction are emerging more slowly than those of his drama; obviousness is not yet a frequent complaint against *How It Is*. Still, as time passes and as the audience for Beckett's fiction grows in size and in sophistication, the nature of his achievement is becoming better defined and its influence on other writers more apparent.

Nevertheless, especially with the later works, the reader needs all of the help he can get. Most important, perhaps, is a sense of the evolutionary development, the coherence and continuity, of the *œuvre*, the lifework. Emerging into Beckett's consciousness in a "natural order" which he himself does not fully understand, this strange procession of books, plays, etc., seems astonishing, amusing, fascinating, puzzling, and frustrating to the author as well as to his audience.[4] But as the process goes on, its structural principles become more evident to both author and audience: later works illuminate earlier ones, in ways which at first seem unexpected but later seem inevitable; individual works are revealed in new perspectives as the horizons of the *œuvre* develop. The longer the process goes on, the more apparent becomes its fidelity to certain laws: Each new work must be a truly new thing, but must emerge naturally out of everything which has gone before. The new work must go beyond everything in the canon, and at the same time subsume that canon. It is as if Beckett writes

---

[3] *New York Times*, 24 Sept. 1967, p. D3.

[4] "Beckett himself occasionally speaks of his œuvre as though it has taken place in his absence; or as though he were a resonator for works that speak through rather than from him. He feels that the root of each of his works lies in a previous work, and he is sometimes puzzled by the order in which the works come to him," says Ruby Cohn, *Back to Beckett* (Princeton: Princeton Univ. Press, 1973), pp. 270-71.

in order to discover the necessity of his writing. It is a continual discovery of meaning — of the lifework, of the life, of all life — a process in which personal experience is transfigured into myth, a myth that must become constantly more inclusive as its horizons expand.

The notion of expanding horizons seems at first glance to contradict the pattern of development of Beckett's fiction. From novel to novel, as well as within each one, his incarnations move toward more undifferentiated forms of existence, more attenuated levels of energy.[5] Protagonist, place, knowledge, language — everything diminishes, dwindles, declines, descends, decays. In their successive incarnations Beckett's grotesques blur into flickering projections of the same confused and dying imagination:

> he feels me in him, then he says I, as if I were he, or in another, let us be just, then he says Murphy, or Molloy, I forget, as if I were Malone, but their day is done, he wants none but himself, for me, he thinks it's his last chance, he thinks that, they taught him thinking, it's always he who speaks, Mercier never spoke, Moran never spoke, I never spoke, I seem to speak, that's because he says I as if he were I, I nearly believed him....[6]

---

[5] This tendency is reflected in the succession of narrative techniques, which lose one linguistic capability after another, abandon fictional conventions and structural principles, etc. This degeneration is reflected in an absurdly literal way in the deteriorating physical states of the protagonists. Murphy's body is more or less ignored until its end (unlike his girlfriend Celia's), but we are tempted to assume that its is "normal"; if it were not, Beckett surely could not have resisted describing it. But when the figure of Watt first appears, "it was scarcely to be distinguished from the dim wall behind it. Tetty was not sure whether it was a man or a woman. Mr Hackett was not sure that it was not a parcel, a carpet for example, or a roll of tarpaulin wrapped up in dark paper and tied about the middle with a cord." In the trilogy the degeneration continues. In *Molloy* Molloy begins on crutches, ends prostrate in a ditch; Moran, sent to search for him, begins in a less advanced state of entropy, but ends by becoming indistinguishable from Molloy at the beginning. In *Malone Dies* Malone is bedfast, but still manages to deteriorate by losing his pencil and various other possessions. In *The Unnamable* the protagonist is beyond writing, and leads a cerebral existence, trying — and failing — to give himself incarnation in one imagined character after another. In *How It Is* the existence is cerebral also, and the possibility of fictional creation is denied in advance — though contradicted, in a sense, by the creation of Pim et al. Still, the suspension of disbelief is suspended; we know all along that the "ten yards fifteen yards" through the mud is nothing more than "ten words fifteen words."

[6] *Three Novels by Samuel Beckett: Molloy, Malone Dies, The Unnamable* (New York: Grove, 1965), p. 403.

Here, toward the end of *The Unnamable*, the narrative incarnations seem to have entered their endgame; the narrative consciousness seems unable to discover a new incarnation which can survive at this lower level of energy and in this less differentiated form. After attempts to claim an existence in the fleeting, unstable identities of Mahood and Worm, the voice goes silent at last with the famous assertion that "you must go on, I can't go on, I'll go on."

Thus the trilogy seemed to be the culmination of Beckett's regressive fictions. In it the nature of the *œuvre* becomes clear at last: it has turned out to be the story of a consciousness engaged in compulsive story-telling — the definitive literary "expression that there is nothing to express, nothing with which to express, no power to express, no desire to express, together with the obligation to express." [7] This, Beckett's classic description of the work of the painter Tal Coat, appeared at a time when Beckett himself was finishing a portrait of such an artist; in the final volume of the trilogy we see a consciousness reduced inexorably — beyond the state where "writing" is still possible — to an unnamable, disembodied voice, which goes silent at last.

With the end of *The Unnamable*, then, Beckett's fiction reached the famous "impasse" in which he came to feel that "There's no way to go on." [8] *Texts for Nothing* and *From an Abandoned Work* issued from this impasse but did not break it; Beckett recognized both as abortive efforts. But in *How It Is* he discovered a way to go on, a way to both fulfill and advance the *œuvre*, to move beyond the realization that human essence is unnamable, to enlarge and deepen the meaning of the obligation to express. Because it is both a truly new thing and the product of all its predecessors, *How It Is*, beneath its often amazingly "lyrical" [9] surface, is a very dense work — perhaps impossible to read unless one can approach it at first from the direction that Beckett himself did, through the earlier work. Yet for the reader

---

[7] Samuel Beckett and Georges Duthuit, "Three Dialogues," in *Samuel Beckett: A Collection of Critical Essays*, ed. Martin Esslin (1949; Englewood Cliffs, N.J.: Prentice-Hall, 1965), p. 17.

[8] Interview with Israel Shenker, "Moody Man of Letters," *New York Times*, 6 May 1956, p. X3.

[9] Ruby Cohn says that Beckett's fiction after *The Unnamable* moves "into a fourth dimension of prose, where a fusion of words sometimes borders on confusion, and where the meaning seems buried in the melody" (p. 220). These works she calls "lyrics of fiction."

who is willing to make the effort, its meanings are there, in the words themselves, in the larger structures of the book, and in the still larger context of the lifework.

> how it was I quote before Pim with Pim after Pim how it is three parts I say it as I hear it
>
> voice once without quaqua on all sides then in me when the panting stops tell me again finish telling me invocation [10]

The reader of *How It Is* knows at once that he has entered a unique world of language which, as Hugh Kenner has said, is "paced and cadenced like elegiac *vers libre,* though the reader, sharing the protagonist's vigil, must detect for himself the boundaries of the phrases and reconstitute the muted *bel canto.*" [11] Following Kenner's suggestion, we can modify the typography of the opening of *How It Is* to explore its topography:

```
1   how it was
    I quote
        before Pim
        with Pim
        after Pim
    how it is
        three parts
    I say it
        as I hear it

2   voice
        once without
            quaqua on all sides
        then in me
            when the panting stops
    tell me again
    finish telling me
    invocation

3   past moments
    old dreams
```

---

[10] *How It Is* (New York: Grove, 1964), p. 7. Subsequent references are to this edition, and page numbers are given in parentheses in the text.

[11] *A Reader's Guide to Samuel Beckett* (New York: Farrar, Straus & Giroux, 1973), p. 139.

```
            back again
            or fresh
                like those that pass
        or things
            things always
        and memories
        I say them
            as I hear them
        murmur them
            in the mud
```

This arrangement is the conventional one in which phrases on the primary grammatical level are arranged at the left, the first-order modifiers are indented once, the second-order twice, etc. If this arrangement helps us to define the boundaries of the phrases and to survey their conventional grammatical topography, it also brings us up against the limits of that grammar. We realize that other orders are possible, and the longer the story goes on, the more apparent becomes the tension between the complexity of its thought and the limitations of its form. Yet within the limitations imposed, the narrative consciousness chooses and orders the words in ways which become meaningful and which at times achieve a power, a precision, and an elegance which can only be called poetic.

Beckett forces us to learn to read all over again. This task is especially frustrating because we are confronting materials we had thought were familiar, but which now seem to be used in totally new ways. The struggle which the reader goes through tends to merge with that of the writer himself — to fulfill the obligation to express, using what is at hand (mostly worn-out tools and second-hand materials) to create something entirely new.

In *How It Is* there is no punctuation, and conventional rules of syntax are largely ignored. Various terms have been used to describe the groups of words between the silences in *How It Is*; let's call them paragraphs. And if a sentence is still to be understood as a group of words containing a subject and a predicate then there are seven sentences, at least, in the first seven paragraphs:

```
        I say it as I hear it
        tell me again
        finish telling me
        I say them as I hear them
            murmur them in the mud
```

> we follow the natural order
> I hear it
> I learn it

(In these last three "sentences" there are additional words — predicate appositives and descending chains of modifiers.)

Although the logical relationships between phrases and paragraphs are ambiguous enough to allow a wide variety of interpretations, this strange language is in some ways unmistakably clear. All of these opening "sentences" are concerned with storytelling, and especially with the *process* of storytelling. This turns out to be a major theme, perhaps *the* theme: the attempt to say how it is to try to say how it is.

The basic unit of expression in the book seems to be the phrase; of meaning, the paragraph. Although sometimes one phrase or even one word constitutes a paragraph,[12] most paragraphs consist of a series of phrases. Since Beckett provides no stage directions or notes, each reader must direct *How It Is* for himself, determining the timing and emphasis to be given to each paragraph or burst of speech, and to each silence. An interesting approach to the reading might be to give equal time and emphasis to each paragraph; this would emphasize the ironic quality of the work by reducing the longer flights of fancy of the narrative consciousness to a rapid, almost blurred whisper which only momentarily delays the engulfing silence. With each reading of the book, as with each performance of a Beckett play, the silences between the bursts of speech become more meaningful. Beckett's great achievement is to make us aware of silence, absence, distance, to make us aware of the vast emptiness which surrounds, isolates, and ultimately engulfs every man and each human achievement. The literary ambition of Beckett's archetypal hero, Belacqua, expressed more than thirty years earlier, comes close to realization in *How It Is*:

> The experience of my reader shall be between the phrases, in the silence, communicated by the intervals, not the terms, of the statement, between the flowers that cannot coexist, the

---

[12] The very short paragraphs, by increasing the ratio of silence to words, produce a feeling similar to that of the pauses in Beckett's plays. And as in the plays, conventional communication theory seems to be inverted: silence becomes meaning while words are revealed as "noise."

> antithetical (nothing so simple as antithetical) seasons of words, his experience shall be the menace, the miracle, the memory of an unspeakable trajectory.[13]

Out of the human experience of silence comes the yearning for a voice; out of the experience of absence, the longing for touch and communion. The tension between the ideal and the actual produces the unspeakable trajectory which Belacqua foretold.

Tension is also created by the structuring of the book. As Beckett himself has explained, the tension between form and chaos challenges the artist, who must somehow make room in his imagination for both light and darkness, and create something that is truly and simultaneously expressive of both.[14] Then there are the many antithetical poles which define the force fields of the *œuvre* and create the "paradoxes" so dear to the commentators ("nothing so simple as antithetical," Belacqua murmurs, still waiting). There are structures within structures within structures in *How It Is*.

The largest structure may be the *frame*, if that is indeed the function of the "I quote" in the first paragraph and the "end of quotation" in the last:

> how it was I quote before Pim with Pim after Pim how it is three parts I say it as I hear it (p. 7).

> good good end at last of part three and last that's how it was end of quotation after Pim how it is (p. 147).

Between the "I quote" and the "end of quotation" is every word in the book, except for "how it was" and "after Pim how it is." From the very beginning the book is announced as a literary artifice, and in that sense it is already "how it was," a literary artifact of the past, and synonymous with "after Pim how it is." The placement of "I quote" after, rather than before, "how it was" in that first paragraph, however, makes it much more ambiguous than if the book had begun with the words "I quote." The frame, if that is what it is, can easily

---

[13] Quoted by Ruby Cohn (p. 17) from the unpublished *Dream of Fair to Middling Women*.

[14] Interview with Tom F. Driver, "Beckett by the Madeleine," *Columbia University Forum*, IV, 3 (Summer 1961), 21-25. Beckett said that "If there were only darkness, all would be clear. It is because there is not only darkness but also light that our situation becomes inexplicable" (p. 23).

go unnoticed. And that is how it should be, for despite Beckett's constant reminders that this is all artifice, that its only reality is on the page, we are still taken in by it, still participate in it imaginatively, still look for the "paradoxes" and the "answers" in spite of what we know. A lesser writer might have framed only the ending;[15] Beckett tells us at the beginning that it's only a story, and dares us to believe it anyway.

He does something similar with the three-part structure. Between the opening and closing paragraphs of the book, there are well over a hundred references to its three specific parts, as well as some mention of other possible forms which the story could take. The reader, reminded constantly of the structure, of the three parts into which this odyssey is divided, is invited to question the structure as it develops. Certainly the narrative consciousness questions it: in the relentless catechism near the end of Part 3 the narrative denies its own validity:

> all these calculations yes explanations yes the whole story from beginning to end yes completely false yes (p. 144).

But Part 3 survives the catechism which brings it to a close, and of course all three parts survive in the artifact which is the book itself. It seems idle to argue, as the reviewer for the *Times Literary Supplement* and many later critics have argued, that the structure of the book "collapses" or is "swept away" or "falls into ruins" or is "destroyed" at the end.[16] Its validity is denied, but whatever the strength or conviction of the denial, the structure itself continues to exist — along with its denial. Both the structure and its denial are realities and because of this, Beckett would say, the "situation becomes inexplicable."[17]

The center of the structure is Part 2, which describes the encounter "with Pim." The structure thus reflects the centrality in human experience of the need to get in touch with, to become aware of, and communicate with, some reality outside the self; Part 1 anticipates this encounter, and Part 3 meditates upon it, so that the encounter itself is framed between two long stretches of solitude. The narrative

---

[15] The novels of William Golding, for example, often end this way, with the entire story suddenly shifted into a new perspective.
[16] *Times Literary Supplement*, 21 May 1964, p. 429.
[17] See note 14.

voice tells us that life is a series of such encounters, in the first of which the individual takes the role of tormentor, in the next the role of victim, etc., alternately, ad infinitum, with a stretch of solitude between each encounter in which he either searches for his victim or awaits his tormentor. Theoretically, then, the narrative voice "proves" in an exhaustive analysis of the possible permutations of tormentors and victims, that the encounter and the solitude should be given equal time — but the book itself reveals that the theory is wrong, and that solitude is the overwhelming reality in which we exist, a solitude filled only with yearning for encounter, and for meaning.

In a comment prophetic of his own work, Beckett said that in Proust "art is the apotheosis of solitude." [18] In *How It Is* the central encounter, anticipated so longingly, meditated upon so exhaustively, is disclosed at last as the apotheosis of solitude, a purely literary encounter. There are hints from the very beginning that Pim is a figment of the narrator's imagination: "I quote," the emphasis on "images" in Part 1, on "words," various comments (e.g., "my life last state last version ill-said") which could mean that the only story to be told is that of the narrator's own imagination. Even in Part 2 itself the narrator fleetingly reveals an awareness that Pim is a fiction — e.g., "how I can efface myself behind my creature" (p. 52), "a human voice there within an inch or two my dream perhaps even a human mind" (p. 56), and the vaudeville comedy of names: "I too Pim my name Pim," "me too I feel it forsaking me soon there will be no one never been anyone of the noble name of Pim,"

> the one I'm waiting for oh not that I believe in him I say it as I hear it he can give me another it will be my first Bom he can call me Bom for more commodity that would appeal to me m at the end and one syllable the rest indifferent (p. 60)

Overshadowing such specific verbal indications of the unstable identity and uncertain existence of the "other" in the encounter is the grotesque comedy of the abortive incarnation:

> good a fellow-creature more or less but man woman girl or boy cries have neither certain cries sex nor age I try to turn him over on his back no the right side still less the left less

---

[18] *Proust* (1929; New York: Grove, n.d.), p. 47.

still my strength is ebbing good good I'll never know Pim
but on his belly (p. 54)

The narrator is delighted to discover a rationalization for limiting the scope of his creation, and as the incarnation continues, various other physical attributes of the creation are imagined only to be abandoned, hopelessly confused, or forgotten. The creative process degenerates into an increasing preoccupation with the self; it becomes increasingly an interrogation of the creation by the creator, but because it is a creation of solitude it can yield nothing more than echoes.

As in the films of Chaplin and Keaton which Beckett loves, much of the comedy arises from the discrepancy between the dimensions of the protagonist's awareness and the dimensions of the reality in which he exists. Single-minded, relentless, endlessly resourceful, Beckett's absurd heroes, too, move in a world whose laws and complexities always seem just beyond their grasp. The audience, seeing and understanding more of the world, sees the analogy between that situation and its own, and is reassured. Chaplin once said that the long shot is for comedy, the close-up for tragedy. In Beckett's successive novels we see the protagonist in tighter and tighter close-ups, but always against an implied horizon or background of a much larger world. This larger world is usually created by condensation from the earlier work, so that in the latest fiction single symbols come to stand for much more extensive structures of meaning.

Part 2 of *How It Is* represents the artist's encounter with his creation. Although this creation contains its own antithesis, and at last gives way to it, during Part 2 words are in the ascendant. Compared to Parts 1 and 3, it contains the most words and the fewest paragraphs (hence the fewest silences). In it Kram and Krim, the witness and the scribe, find their incarnation; a series of three notebooks is described; flashes of literary history intrude. Relentlessly the creator interrogates his own creation until he lapses into silence. This, too, seems to typify Beckett's vision of the creative act — an objectification, elaboration, exploration of the artist's own consciousness until its possibilities are exhausted. As Beckett says of the work of Proust, "The only fertile research is excavatory, immersive, a contraction of the spirit, a descent." [19]

---

[19] Ibid., p. 48.

In the sixth paragraph of the book we first glimpse "someone listening another noting" (p. 7). In Part 2 these latent identities are brought to life and named:

> all alone and the witness bending over me name Kram bending over us father to son to grandson yes or no and the scribe name Krim generations of scribes keeping the record a little aloof sitting standing it's not said yes or no samples extracts (p. 80)

Ruby Cohn has pointed out that these names pun on the German *krimkram*, or junk.[20] So it is ecologically as well as linguistically satisfying that they are first reduced to Kram (rubbish, trash, etc.) in Part 3 (p. 133) and then removed altogether from the book. But while they are there, they seem fairly important in the narrative consciousness. In the passage in which they first appear, the idea of generations of scribes and witnesses is rather striking, and it is reiterated in at least half a dozen other passages. The narrative voice says that "I'm the thirteenth generation" (p. 83). Beckett's preoccupation with that number is well known: it is associated with his birth on Good Friday the thirteenth, with his favorite thirteenth letter of the alphabet, with the thirteen poems of *Echoes Bones*, the thirteen *Texts for Nothing*, etc. But why the preoccupation with generations? Is it, perhaps, a cryptic reference to Beckett's own work? If we try to trace the generations of Beckett's books, and if we omit the translations and his plays, we find that *Comment c'est* is his thirteenth published book.[21] The only two other references to specific generations of Krams in *How It Is* make the pattern unmistakable.

> Kram the Seventh at his last gasp perhaps his face whiter than the pillow-slip and me still a shitty little chit can it be the end at last... (p. 82)

---

[20] Cohn, p. 237.

[21] Beckett's "generations" (exclusive of plays and translations): 1) *Whoroscope* (1930), 2) *Proust* (1931), 3) *More Pricks Than Kicks* (1934), 4) *Echo's Bones* (1935), 5) *Murphy* (1938), 6) *Molloy* (1951), 7) *Malone meurt* (1951), 8) *Watt* (1953), 9) *L'Innomable* (1953), 10) *Nouvelles et Textes pour rien* (1955), 11) *From an Abandoned Work* (1956), 12) *Poems in English* (1961), 13) *Comment c'est* (1961). If these works were listed in the order of their composition, *Watt*, written in 1942-44, would come after *Murphy*.

The "seventh generation" of the lineage of *How It Is* would be *Malone Dies,* an assumption clearly borne out by the context. The other specific reference to generations seems equally clear in some ways, though obscure in others:

> dreamt of the great Kram the Ninth the greatest of us all up to date never met him more's the pity grandpa remembered him raving mad before the limit brought up by force trussed like a faggot Krim vanished never seen again (p. 83)

Kram the Ninth, if our hypothesis is correct, would represent *The Unnamable,* which many critics — perhaps Beckett himself — would agree is still "the greatest of [them] all up to date." The words "never met him more's the pity" could be an ironic reference to the "impasse" which followed *The Unnamable* and to the struggle in *How It Is* to "go on" meaningfully beyond the earlier novel. This interpretation seems strengthened by the final words of the paragraph, "Krim vanished never seen again": after *The Unnamable* it seemed that Beckett's scribe had indeed deserted him. The "grandpa" referred to here would be *From an Abandoned Work,* which "remembered" *The Unnamable* by trying to carry the œuvre beyond it, but succumbing instead to Beckett's sense of artistic *deja vu.* The other phrases are more ambiguous. The "raving mad before the limit" could refer to either *The Unnamable* or *From an Abandoned Work,* but probably to the former, since the phrases following seem to refer to it too, and since that book is probably the major subject of the paragraph as a whole. Perhaps the reference is to the culmination of Beckett's effort, in the trilogy, to transcend all of the existing limits for fiction. This would also explain the "brought up by force," which could also refer to the force-feeding of the unnamable one (or his surrogate Mahood) in the pot outside the Paris restaurant. The "trussed like a faggot" may refer to this pot too. Let's hope so. At any rate, it seems likely that the references to generations of witnesses and scribes are a new way of incorporating the moribund *m*'s into *How It Is.*

The scribe writes in three notebooks — blue, yellow, and red — "simple once you've thought of it" (p. 82). The first is "for the body" (p. 81), the "second for the mutterings verbatim," and the "third this for my comments" (p. 82). Should we see the notebooks as analogous to the three parts of *How It Is*? If so, there may seem to be "something wrong there," for the third notebook is at hand in Part 2, which should be the province of the second notebook. But if the whole story is already over, there is "nothing to emend there" and the third notebook is the right one. (We may recall, perhaps, that the narrator has told us in Part 1 that "it is over I am in part three after Pim" [p. 20].) Blue is appropriate for a notebook dealing with Part 1, which contains the "images" of childhood and innocence, and the feelings of nostalgia, anticipation, and longing. Blue is the color of the skies ("heaven's azure") of youth, of the mountains on that lost horizon, of the virgin's cloak. The word itself becomes a symbol: "the childhood the belief the blue the miracles all lost never was" (p. 70). Its last use before it is mentioned as the color for the first notebook is in connection with the narrator's memory of his wife, who fell — or more probably jumped — from a window, broke her spinal cord, and died a lingering death (p. 77). In the narrative consciousness blue has become identified with youth, with love, with all that is irrecoverably lost. It appears more frequently than any other color,[22] and acquires great symbolic force. The life of the body which the blue notebook contains, however, is only a memory and a longing in *How It Is*.

The second notebook is "the yellow book that is not the voice of here" (p. 83). Aside from the two references to the yellow notebook, the word *yellow* is used only twice in *How It Is*: as the color of the

---

[22] The precision of this study of the text of *How It Is* would have been impossible without a computer-prepared index designed by Barbara Snider and produced by the Computation Center at the University of North Carolina at Chapel Hill.

Blue appears 31 times, *bluey* once, and *azure* three times. *White* and its variants appear 30 times, *black* 24 times. Other words denoting colors appear much less frequently. In *How It Is* color is a phenomenon of the world "above in the light" before the fall into mud and darkness. It is something that the narrative consciousness tries to recapture, but by Part 3 we have reached the point where there is "no more blue the blue is done" (p. 106). The white is not exhausted, but its meanings are reversed from Part 1, where it is the clouds in the wind, the lambs, the blossoms, etc. — along with blue, the color of nostalgia: "the white there was then" (p. 45), to Part 3, where it is associated always with death, or at least with the degeneration of physical life into a wholly cerebral life. The "eight planes bone white" (p. 128) could enclose either a corpse or a mind, and Beckett seems to suggest that there isn't much difference. The reversal of meaning takes place very dramatically in Part 2, where white is suddenly the color of the wife's death (p. 77). All of this in *How It Is* is further compressed into the "blue and white in the wind" of *Ping* (1967), perhaps.

narrator's boots and of the potted crocus which a disembodied hand keeps in the sun. Both of these scenes are "images" of "life in the light." The word *golden* is used five times, *gold* twice, always to refer to a golden age above in the light. Yellow, then, seems inappropriate for a notebook containing "mutterings verbatim" — unless we realize that Part 2, "with Pim," is the effort of an imagination to somehow create a new golden age. In that sense, the voice of Part 2 "is not the voice of here," but the voice of us all, comforting ourselves with fictions.

The red notebook is "for my comments." Like yellow, red is a primary color — but not in the universe of *How It Is*. Aside from its mention for the third notebook, red is mentioned only three times in the book: it is the color of the tiles of the veranda where the narrator prayed with his mother, of his face when he wore his yellow shoes, and of the gilt edges of his mother's Bible — all associated with life in the light. *Rose* (or *rosy*) is mentioned nine times; twice in connection with the life "above," elsewhere ironically (Kram and Krim argue over the possibility of rosiness in the mud). Part 3 does, of course, contain the narrator's "comments," which are predictably and amusingly inadequate as they become involved in the higher arithmetic of thousands and hundreds of thousands of pilgrimages, couplings, and abandonments. The final catechism, however, does succeed in entering the silence — or should one say, as Beckett did to an interviewer, in *admitting* the silence? [23]

Perhaps the three notebooks also serve symbolically to absorb the earlier work into *How It Is*. Perhaps the search "for the body" of the first notebook is an implosion of *Molloy*; the "mutterings verbatim" of the second, an ultimate condensate of *Malone Dies*; the "comments" of the third, an essence of *The Unnamable*. Perhaps Beckett had grown weary of calling his old protagonists by their given names as they appeared to him once again, demanding death and transfiguration. Perhaps now they could be reduced still further, to lost generations of rubbish, to undecipherable notes in fading grey hidden beneath primary colors.

Permeated by meaninglessness, *How It Is* becomes more meaningful. The dynamics of the story grotesquely symbolize the creative process of art. In the beginning the artist considers his own situation

---

[23] Interview with Driver, p. 23.

and begins to objectify his feelings about it — hence the mud, the dark (relieved now and then by flashes of "images"), the limited possessions, the spasmodic movements exhaustively elaborated, etc. We watch the creation of a world which, despite its seemingly endless elaboration, succeeds only in revealing its own pathetic limitations. But at the same time its origins are convincingly human. For example, the "ten yards fifteen yards" which is the endlessly reiterated measure of the narrator's progress through the symbolic primordial mud appears first in the extended "image" of a woman who looks up at the narrator, grows anxious, and "suddenly leaves the house and runs to friends" (p. 11). In Part 3, yards are transfigured into words:

> an image too of this voice ten words fifteen words long silence ten words fifteen words long silence long solitude once without quaqua on all sides vast stretch of time then in me when the panting stops scraps (p. 126)

and then into time:

> all that once without scraps in me when the panting stops ten seconds fifteen seconds all that fainter weaker less clear.... (p. 132).

This very complex chain of rhythms and words (the "ten... fifteen..." pattern appears forty-six times in the book) originates in the narrator's "image" of a woman:

> she sits aloof ten yards fifteen yards she looks up looks at me says at last to herself all is well he is working (p. 10).

One is tempted to call these "images" memories, especially since some of them are very clearly images of Beckett's own memories,[24] but the narrator resists that temptation — and so should we. Their major importance is as images, which weave the rich poetic reality of *How*

---

[24] See, for example, Michael Robinson, *The Long Sonata of the Dead: A Study of Samuel Beckett* (London: Rupert Hart-Davis, 1969), p. 217; G. C. Barnard, *Samuel Beckett: A New Approach* (New York: Dodd, Mead, 1970), pp. 69-70; and Kenner, pp. 139-40, who calls attention to the fact that the language of the images differs from that of the struggle in the mud: "Though unpunctuated these are formal sentences, the book's convention for such memories" (p. 139).

It Is. The single thread that we have unravelled here contributes something to the texture of the whole; it serves, almost subliminally, to link the grotesque, spasmodic struggle in the mud to the human experiences of love, concern, compassion, anxiety, absence, and loss, of the yearning for speech and touch but the failure to speak and touch. And the original image here reveals something, perhaps, of the pathological self-consciousness of the narrator; it is finally not so much an image of the woman who loved him as it is of his consciousness of her love for him. The loneliness which the book expresses becomes almost overwhelming.

Although the narrator's analysis of his predicament is elaborated to absurd extremes, the *process* itself, which parodies the process of art, seems very real. In Part 1 the narrator tries to find his story, tries to find his voice. His "past moments old dreams" are examined for "images" which he denies are "memories," but which, as we have seen, may provide the horizons against which the colorless story itself is seen. At last the possibilities of his state of solitary anticipation are exhausted; the narrator is reduced to postulating the existence of God:

> or a celestial tin miaculous sardines sent down by God at the news of my mishap wherewith to spew him out another week (p. 48)

In the next paragraph the narrator discovers the promised land: "instead of the familiar slime an arse two cries one mute end of part one before Pim that's how it was before Pim." The arse and the audible cry are Pim's; the mute cry is the narrator's; not a moment too soon, he has succeeded in losing his voice.

In Part 2 the narrator brings his discovered fictional creation to life, or rather, to an obscene parody of life arrested in the anal stage. In a vaudeville version of the struggle of the poet with his muse and his material, the creator attempts to make his creation "sing," but the only sounds possible in this primordial solitude are echoes. The fictional creation will not yield its secrets; Part 2 concludes with a relentless catechism in which the answers are echoes too — and at last even those are lost in the silence.

Then the meditation on the failure must begin:

> here then at last I quote on part three how it was after Pim how it is part three at last and last towards which lighter

> than air an instant flop fallen so many vows sighs prayers without words ever since the first word I hear it the word how (p. 103)

The "first word," *how* — the logos of the world of this book, and perhaps of Beckett's phenomenological universe. In Part 3 the narrator meditates on the phenomenology, the *how*, of his being. And after more exhaustive — and perhaps exhausting — parody, the narrative consciousness enters into a final catechism.

Even though the narrative consciousness asks the questions knowing that there can be no answers, only echoes from the vast surrounding silence, the questioning process itself is not merely an exercise in futility. Beckett's books contain series after series of exquisitely erudite questions and answers which seem to mock the absurdity of man's questioning and questing. Yet the process itself is important. Even though each catechism frustrates our hunger for revelation, it also reveals the hunger itself and, in a sense, feeds it — because the literary process itself is so rich and artful and alive.

The context from which the final catechism emerges reveals the desperate need

> to have done then at last with all that last scraps very last when the panting stops and this voice to have done with this voice namely this life
>
> this not one of us harping harping mad too with weariness to have done with him
>
> has he not staring him in the face I quote on a solution more simple by far and by far more radical
>
> a formulation that would eliminate him completely and so admit him to that peace at least while rendering me in the same breath sole responsible for this unqualifiable murmur of which consequently here the last scraps at last very last (p. 144).

This phrase "not one of us" first appears in the book fairly late in Part 3:

> ...one life all life not two lives our justice one Kram not one of us there's reason in me yet his son begets his son leaves the light Kram goes back up into the light to end his days (p. 134)

We have already seen how, in Part 2, the lineage of Kram seems to be cryptically — even cryptographically — related to the generations of Beckett's own books. Now, with the generations of Kram (Krim the scribe has just been merged with Kram the witness), "Kram alone witness and scribe his lamps their light upon me Kram with me bending over me till the age-limit then his on his son's son so on" (p. 133) and "their books where all is noted" are there overtones (with the imagery of lamps, books, son's sons "from age to age," scribes and witnesses, ascents into the light, etc.) of a post-Biblical epic, an abortive attempt at witness in this wasteland of mud and darkness, where the only story possible is a gospel according to Kram?

The religious overtone becomes almost explicit in the next appearance of the phrase "not one of us," which emerges from a context in which the narrative voice is talking of "our justice" and our need to perceive some higher power that is sensitive to our hungers. This need of ours is spoken of as the

> ...need of one not one of us an intelligence somewhere a love who all along the track at the right places according as we need them deposits our sacks (pp. 137-38).

In the next appearance of the phrase, the "not one of us" is spoken of in almost conventional religious terms — but without being specifically named as God, of course. And now the "not one of us" is given a role in the narration itself:

> there he is at last that not one of us there we are then at last who listens to himself and who when he lends his ear to our murmur does no more than lend it to a story of his own devising ill-inspired ill-told and so ancient so forgotten at each telling that ours may seem faithful that we murmur to the mud to him (p. 139)

This third appearance of the phrase is linked to the second through a chain of six paragraphs in which various aspects of our need for "one not one of us" are revealed. But even in this context, "there he is at last that not one of us" comes as a surprise; it is like a sunrise over this sea of mud and darkness, and the whole paragraph, with its vaguely Biblical cadences, rings with joy and conviction. This moment of communion with the timeless cannot be sustained. This new faith must be elaborated, and a comprehensive system of "justice" created, and under the weight of all this the faith itself is soon submerged in the mud and darkness once more. But the *need* and the religious dimension of the quest are sustained realities which survive beyond the end of the book. Like most other positive values in Beckett's work, they are created as latent values, expressed indirectly. But they are *there* nonetheless.

The catechism begins, then, as an effort "to have done at last" with this foreign reality, this "one not one of us" which haunts the narrative consciousness. The catechism itself denies the truth of

> all these calculations yes explanations yes the whole story from beginning to end yes completely false yes (p. 144)

Yet the next paragraph shows that these replies are merely a reflection of the mood of the questioning consciousness:

> that wasn't how it was no not at all no how then no answer how was it then no answer HOW WAS IT screams good (p. 144)

The "screams good" which ends this paragraph also ends three later ones. In each case the narrative voice has asked a question which has elicited "no answer"; the question is then repeated in a scream (indicated by capitalization). Why are the screams good? Perhaps because they provide a momentary relief from the mere echoes which "answer" the other questions. As the capitalization indicates, the screams are a departure from the gray homogeneity of the existential world of this narrative. Perhaps the screams "represent the perilous zones in the life of the individual," as Beckett says in *Proust*, "when for a moment the boredom of living is replaced by the suffering of being." [25] The penultimate paragraph of the book ends in a scream:

> so things may change no answer end no answer I may choke no answer sink no answer sully the mud no more no answer the dark no answer trouble the peace no more no answer the silence no answer die no answer DIE screams I MAY DIE screams I SHALL DIE screams good (p. 147)

It is this scream which enables the narrative voice to enter the silence, the consummation it has so devoutly wished. Now, in achieving this awareness of its own mortality, it has finally said how it is.

---

[25] *Proust*, p. 8.

Although this discovery of the anguish of mortality enables the narrative to reach the "end of quotation" and at last permits the silence to speak,[26] we should not reduce it to a "key" to *How It Is*. The book has tremendous density, and even though we can isolate one element or another for analysis, we can't really comprehend the work as a whole — we can only enter into it imaginatively. The previous discussion of its structural dynamics may have uncovered some of its aspects which have not been discussed before, but, as Beckett himself would say, "What is more true than anything else?"[27] The ending of *How It Is* emerges in its full meaning only when we have reached it as Beckett himself did — by way of the long struggle through every word.

The struggle involves not only this particular book, but the lifework as a whole — whose rules Beckett discovers as he goes along. In writing each work he discovers why it is necessary and why, in retrospect, it was inevitable. His discovery of his vocation as an artist and of his work as a lifework seems to coincide with his period of great creativity, from 1946 to 1950. In the masterwork of this period, the trilogy, there is an increasing tendency for his earlier works to surface again and again in the narrative consciousness. This growing awareness of the unity of the *œuvre* and of its thematic and formal necessities led to the "impasse": Beckett felt that he could not go on without merely repeating himself. But after a decade devoted to plays, translations, and two major false starts in fiction, he discovered in *How It Is* authentic ways in which to recapture his previous work within an even more powerful gravitational field.

One is tempted to use such cosmic metaphors for Beckett's work because of the austere elegance of its laws.[28] His heroes seem to move according to a literary second law of thermodynamics: trapped in a

---

[26] As Isak Dinesen has written, "Where the storyteller is loyal, eternally and unswervingly loyal to the story, there, in the end, silence will speak." "The Blank Page," *Last Tales* (New York: Random House, 1957), p. 100.

[27] Interview with Driver, p. 22.

[28] Cosmic metaphors have some precedent in Beckett's own work. "So they drift past, Oriane and the Duc de Guermantes, Rachel and Bloch, Legrandin and Odette, and many others, carrying the burden of Saturn towards the light that will rise, towards Uranus, the Sabbath star" (*Proust*, p. 59). Then there is the famous passage in *The Unnamable* where the earlier "characters" pass in review, like planets, through the narrative consciousness (*Three Novels*, pp. 292-93), the astrology in *Murphy*, etc. In the later works, there are the coffined microcosms of *Imagination Dead Imagine*, *Ping*, and *The Lost Ones*.

closed system, they degenerate continually toward lower levels of organization and energy. The books themselves and the laws which govern their succession seem analogous to the creation of the "black holes" which astrophysicists are now speculating about — realms of space in which gravitational force becomes so concentrated that atomic structures themselves are crushed and transformed to "anti-matter," stars so dense that no light can escape from them. Of the works published after *How It Is*, *Ping*, especially, seems to achieve even greater density as well as an even more strange and haunting lyrical beauty.[29]

One could say of the later work what Beckett said of the *Wake* in progress: it is not *about* something; it *is* something. Like all great art, it is finally inexplicable because it contains its own implicit criticism — the darkness shining within the brightness, in Joyce's words. Relentlessly, exhaustively, it questions both its own validity and the larger human context in which it exists. Ultimately, there may be, for the consciousness unwilling to ignore its own limitations, only one honest answer to these questions — the answer that Joyce expressed at the end of the catechism in Ithaca, where the narrative itself has reached an interstellar distance from the human life it questions:

That is the realm into which Beckett's fiction is constantly collapsing.

---

[29] Beckett has called some of these works "residua," a term which he "explained" to Brian Finney, '*since how it is*': *A study of Samuel Beckett's later fiction* ([London:] Covent Garden, 1972), p. 10, as meaning works which "are residual (1) Severally, even when that does not appear of which each is all that remains and (2) In relation to whole body of previous work."

Ruby Cohn closes her recent book by saying that these later works contain "the traces of thirty years of rich reference — people, things, ideas, emotions, rhetorical patterns, a cultural heritage. The traces have had to earn their right to spareness — 'only just almost never.' The traces are the residue of basic human experience, distilled into phrases that resist paraphrase so that we must go back to the words of Beckett" (p. 272).

WORKING WITH BECKETT

by Alan Schneider

THROUGH twenty theatrical seasons, I have happily carried a typescript by Samuel Beckett with me to rehearsals through more than that number of productions — in Washington or Texas or San Francisco, in New York's off-Broadway, and twice even on to Broadway itself. On three occasions, those scripts had never before been performed —*Happy Days* (1961), *Film* (1964) and *Not I* (1972). On four others —*Waiting for Godot* (1956), *Endgame* (1958), *Krapp's Last Tape* (1959), *Play* (1964) — the scripts were receiving their first production in English and/or in the United States. And more than a dozen other times, I have carried these same or other scripts of his through a proscenium arch, onto the thrust stage, or out directly into the middle of an audience — something Mr. Beckett had neither expected nor entirely understood. In these twenty years, there have been few times when I had not just finished directing one Beckett work or another, or was not actively planning to do another one.

Did I gravitate to Sam at once, immediately recognizing his dramatic genius? Truthfully, I'm not sure. When I first read *Endgame* in manuscript, I told Barney Rosset, Beckett's American publisher, that it seemed to me like a combination of *Oedipus* and *King Lear*. This was before either Jan Kott's book or the Brook-Scofield production, so I must have had the correct sympathetic vibrations. But did I recognize it then as a major work of the twentieth century? And that first time I watched *Godot* at the Babylone in Paris back in 1954, without catching more than a portion of its French dialogue, I did at least respond emotionally enough to its stage directions to try — at that time unsuccessfully — locating the playwright to have him translate it into English for me. One year later, when I first read the English text, I remained equally intrigued and baffled, trying to figure out which one of those two fellows was which. But when a producer happened to offer the play to me to direct, I at once accepted. Even though at that time, as now, I had serious reservations about both the producer and the play's viability for Broadway audiences. But the moment I started to work on the text itself, I was hooked, as I have been on every one of them ever since.

Which of the almost dozen different plays of his which I've directed, I am always being asked, do I prefer? That's like asking a parent to pick out a favorite child. Or making a mountain climber name his favorite peak. All I can really say is that they've all spoiled me for the lowlands. I tend to prefer the Beckett play I'm working on at whatever moment I'm asked. Though, perhaps, *Krapp* and *Happy Days* seem to be most human and moving. Or *Endgame*. Or *Godot*, which is no longer a play but a condition of life. Let's just say: the one I favor is the one I'm going to be working on next. On all of these working occasions, with the one exception where Beckett was told that the shooting of a very unusual filmscript absolutely required his physical presence, my favorite playwright has never wanted to venture forth from his Parisian privacy to face the periods of production à l'Americaine. So that, in a real sense, this present account of my experiences with his plays might more accurately be labeled "Not Working With Beckett"; or "Working With Beckett's"; or, perhaps most exactly, "Working on Beckett."

Sam's continued reluctance to cross the Atlantic to be with me in rehearsal is no proof that he is the shadowy recluse pictured by his interviewers. Actually, he remains the most accessible of men and authors — though only to his friends. He has, after all, taken an active role in most of his French productions; and he has even managed to cross the Channel in order to be of assistance to directors George Devine and Donald McWhinnie. And he has regularly journeyed to Berlin himself to direct new productions of his plays at the Schiller Theater. Why then never to New York except for *Film?* Does he trust me or mistrust me so much? Is he not interested enough in the American theatre's attempts at his plays, in contrast to his feelings about what the European stage does with them? Does it take Buster Keaton to get him over here?

Sam could answer those questions better than I can. But my own impression is that the truth, as always with Beckett, is much simpler. New York is just too far away and noisy; the job of getting here too demanding. Nor does he especially favor either press conferences or cocktail parties, occupational hazards he has discovered to be endemic to the American production process. Nor, I am supposing, have his early publishing experiences (prior to Grove Press) with American commercialism and commercial Americans endeared him generally to our jangled rhythms and demands. He prefers to stay away if he can, gently but firmly declining all manner of invitations, whether they come from Harvard or the neighborhood of Washington Square.

Not that I've been content to have him stay away. In the theatre, I agree with my friend and Sam's, the late Jackie McGowran, that we most of the time seem to be trying to keep the author out but with Beckett we feel just the other way round: we want him in. To hold our hands through the darkness. To illuminate the dots, interpret the ellipses, and explain the unexplainable. To hover and fume (though he'd never let us see). So although he'd never actually been there, I've always rehearsed as though he were in the shadows somewhere watching and listening, ready to answer all our doubts, quell our fears, and share our surprises and small talk. Sometimes, without sounding too mystical or psychotic, I've felt that he was indeed there, and that I might easily be talking with him. Once we all did talk to him, when we nicknamed the light that flicked from urn to urn in *Play*, "Sam."

In work then, all of his texts — and that word includes both dialogue and stage directions — have always been "Sam's" to me, a marriage in absentia, in which I have loved, honored, and obeyed as though he were always with me. Every actor and actress cast by me for a Beckett production, every designer of setting and costumes and lighting — and posters — every producer and would-be producer has had to deal with me on this one fundamental premise: we're doing Sam's play more or less in the way he'd want it to be done; "at least insofar as I as the director can understand that and transmit it to you." Whatever else may be happening, we're not trying to put anything over on Sam.

Having Sam actually at rehearsals, however, would have made my problems easier. At least, deciding what he really wanted or meant at any given moment would have been immediately possible, without anyone's taking or not taking my word for that. Resolving all those inevitable differences of opinion or interpretation of each word and each moment. And clearing up his specific technical demands, all those complications that those simple little Beckett plays with one or two characters and hardly any scenery, manage to be loaded with: undersized ashcans and oversized urns, parasols that burn up on cue but not before, carafes that fly without twisting slowly slowly in the wind, a Mouth that floats unsupported in space, and a Figure with head and arms lit up but with feet invisible.

And, best of all, with him there, it would have been more possible to adapt and change something. Because like the rest of us, whenever Sam goes to work on a given production, he understands its uniqueness and special problems. Something for some reason (whether acting or technical) doesn't seem to be working, or might be more interesting with some slight variation. A line doesn't sound exactly right coming from that particular actor, or the actor cannot deal properly with a certain prop. When, for example, I wanted to add an overhead lamp to Krapp's den, it took me some weeks to get up the nerve to ask Sam. Had he been there, he would have seen the pool of light that such a lamp at once created and agreed at once — instead of getting a description and a request from me and answering back, "Yes, of course." When I wrote to explain that "weir" was too unfamiliar a word for us, suggesting "dam" as an alternative, Sam came back with "lock." As well as, years later, Erskine for Arsene, which was too specifically French. How much more leeway we would have always had if only he had been with us day by day!

I have always held to the old-fashioned belief that a first production — certainly of a living author, especially of an author as clear and as explicit in his directions to all concerned as Beckett has always been (and is increasingly becoming more so) — should try to bring to stage life the author's play. Should a director disagree, significantly or violently, he shouldn't be doing that play. Nor do I believe that the creative ego has necessarily to feed on the principle of contradicting the author, or trying to substitute for, elaborate upon, evade or elude the author's own point of view, or to use the text as simply the starting point for the director's virtuosity. Interpretation is one thing — like *Hamlet, Godot* will always be different when filtered through a director's temperament and the imponderables of casting — but interpolation is quite another, not to mention extrapolation, and the intrusion of a subtext that clearly distorts instead of illuminating its text.

Not too immodestly, I hope, I admit that my directorial mind is quite capable of conceiving *Godot* with an all-female cast (and, in fact, had one such in an acting class I once supervised long enough ago to have included several performers since elevated (?) to stardom. Nor am I any longer appalled at the idea of Vladimir and Estragon as homosexuals — but reject it as I have thousands of other ideas equally unrelated to the play. Let's say the idea of having the two playing Cat's Cradle with string all through the graveyard scene. I've seen (or myself used) *Godot*'s tree bedecked in the second act, with the greenest of ribbons, balloons, rubber bands, even spaghetti, even leaves (real or stylised); but the idea (which graced a recent highly praised version) of not having the tree onstage at all is not one I can immediately respond to, even in theory. Nor do I yet understand why having Hamm and Clov ad lib a hodge-podge of pop-art songs and slogans, not to mention having Clov sit and Nell and Nagg pop in and out like box puppets at various times not even suggested by the text, or opening the play with Nelson Eddy and Jeanette MacDonald singing away on a gradually running-down record, is necessarily preferable to honoring the lines and pauses by trying to discover why Beckett put them there in the first place — and doing something theatrically interesting with that knowledge. Shakespeare, of course, is being done (including sometimes by myself) in everything from bathing suits to cave-man outfits with all the concomitant details. I once did *Macbeth* with six witches (though I am now embarassed to admit that only three appeared to the audience at any given time, the others were doubles who made the witches seem to be able to fly through space). And Beckett will one day be performed in 17th century armor or space suits with *Godot* as an extra-terrestial intelligence, as well as set to music (*Godot* already has been). But in the blessed meantime, at least within the author's own span of life and awareness, I utterly reject the "colored lights" school of production and favor an author's inalienable right to the relative satisfaction of his own intentions, limited as they may be.

I got into my very first troubles with a Beckett production early in the game, on my first *Godot,* when I actively resisted Bert Lahr's open desire to be "top banana," with Tom Ewell as "second banana." Very simply, Bert wanted to relegate the role of Vladimir to that of straight man. In the instance of Lucky's speech, he wanted to cut it out entirely "since nobody understood it anyway"; at the very least, since I would neither cut it nor let him go offstage during the speech, he insisted on doing lots of comic business all through it so that no one would have to listen and be bored. After all, they had come to see Bert and not the actor playing Lucky, whoever he was. And to hear Bert repeat his familiar "Onnnggg-onnnggg" in response to his recurrent realisation of his fate instead of Mr. Beckett's simpler and very ordinary (but how extraordinary) "Ahh." The fact that Bert was superbly eloquent in many of his own manifestations of Estragon's character didn't make my choices easier. Eventually, another director more willing to accept and deal with Bert's insecurities took the play to New York — and away from Beckett.

When the original off-Broadway producers of *Endgame* at the Cherry Lane wanted to bring a gag-man in to amplify Sam's (and my) lack of humor, or when one of the actors who replaced our original Clov wanted to explore less conventionally than had the author what the character might be doing in the play's opening sequences instead of climbing up to look out those two windows, I demurred both times. On the play's own stated premise that nothing is funnier than unhappiness. And when Buster Keaton wanted to keep sharpenning the end of a broken pencil until it got smaller and smaller and eventually disappeared, a "bit" he told me he had always used successfully, I explained — quietly I trust — that we were only doing what was in the shooting script, funny or unfunny as it happened to be. All the way down to someone's repeated suggestion while we were doing *Not I* to blow up the Mouth on to a giant full-stage color TV screen so that the audiences at the Lincoln Center Forum would be able to see and understand the play better. Not I, said I.

Which attitude on my part, by the way, has not prevented a few of my not-so-friendly neighborhood critics, who feel that I have somehow hypnotised Sam into giving me a stranglehold on his work, from accusing me of seriously distorting his plays. I shudder to think what such non-gentlemen of the press would have said about me had I actually tampered with Beckett's texts and intentions even a fraction of the extent to which certain recent productions (some not authorised and sometimes not paying royalties) have done — in the process being praised for transmitting the author's "true" intentions. One leading critic has even blamed me for adding bananas and other extraneous business to my most recent version of *Krapp's Last Tape*. The revisions in some of Krapp's pantomime were the result of Sam's own experiences in Berlin, which of course the critic had no way of knowing about. The bananas, however, are quite apparent in the text. What such critics do not at all understand is that I didn't have to hypnotise Sam. He's just been burnt too many times elsewhere by too many people in too many ways.

With all of my Beckett productions, then, I have been more faithful than the Pope himself often required. And since Rome (or in this case, Paris) has never except for that once come to me, I have always gone to Paris, to get the full benefit of the author's "stutherings," as he once described them. Before each production, including that first one, I've sailed or flown or trained or driven at the production's expense, if possible, if not on my own — to spend whatever time with Sam he could give me. Punctual as a churchbell, he always comes first to my hotel, the Boulevard Raspail's modest L'Aiglon, which I found by accident of fate back in 1949 on my first pre-Beckett visit and have stayed in ever since, later to discover it was around the corner from Sam and an old favorite of his. I sit with him in his favorite cafés and restaurants, sometimes in his apartment around that corner. We eat, drink, wander through the Luxembourg Gardens or elsewhere in Montparnasse. I badger him with all the questions and problems that I've jotted down or that occur to me as we walk and talk. Sometimes, we don't even mention the play, although we do get into everything else — from the state of the damnation to my daughter's schooling. He is fond of her, remembering her as a little girl playing in front of the L'Aiglon. When he speaks with the waiters, Sam always seems completely French to me — and to the waiters; when he talks with me, he's very Irish.

As much as possible, those conversations are like ones we would be having if he were in New York at rehearsals, and the atmosphere is very like that of the Village although somewhat more pleasant because we're in Paris. Naturally, it's impossible to anticipate even a fraction of what may happen during production or actually does. But while such preliminary meetings cannot be as valuable as the real day-by-day give and take of rehearsals, they are not without benefits, or concrete results.

Over the years, the benefits have increased and the results intensified. While the meetings between us have mellowed from that first formal conference he so grudgingly granted to "the American director" of *Godot,* whose name he didn't know. My questions have gotten less general and silly, more carefully thought through and phrased. The answers have come more willingly, even if they have not always been complete ones. And I have been able to interpret them more precisely because I have understood the pauses as well as the words.

That very first time, I asked Sam who or what Godot was, though luckily not what it "meant"; and he told me, after a moment of deep reflection in those seemingly bottomless blue-grey eyes, that if he had known, he would have said so in his play. The last time, I came over to talk about a production, it was to encourage him to write a companion piece to Hume Cronyn's rendition of *Krapp's Last Tape,* bringing along the companion-lady in question to inspire him. It turned out that Sam liked the lady and happened to have something in his trunk, or in his desk, that if he could do a bit of work on it, it might fit her nicely. He did, it did, and we did it; after a few days of questions and thoughts and wanderings and cafés. On all the visits in between, I've always asked him everything I could think of, and Sam has always tried to answer as fully and as specifically as he could. And at the end of it all, after he's delivered me in his rusty tin buggy of a Citroen to L'Invalides air terminal or the Gare du Nord, he always has sent me homeward with the same farewell:

"Do it anny way you like, Alan; anny way you like."

Once, Sam came over to join me in London, where we went together to see the original English *Godot,* then playing at the Criterion. It had just transferred from a successful run at the Arts although the theatre was not full and people were walking out all during the performance, sometimes loudly venting their British spleen. Sam sat next to me in various sections of the stalls for four or five nights in a row, staring in somewhat stunned amazement at the proceedings on stage and in the audience, occasionally leaning over to whisper to me: "They're doing it ahl whrang." Referring to what was taking place on the stage. One evening, while we were backstage in the absence of the director, who happened to be the youthful Peter Hall, I had to prevent Sam firmly from giving out an array of written notes to the actors. Under the mistaken assumption that I was part of the opposition to his production, I'm afraid, Peter Hall has never forgiven me.

But at least I did learn what Sam considered to be "ahl whrang." So that I could eventually go back and do it "anny way" I liked. As if I actually could.

But even after I've gotten back each time, there have always been afterthoughts, new questions, new explanations. Never has there failed to be a further exchange of ideas and problems between us, a dialogue via airmail. Continued and regular cross-currents of air-letters, postcards, or just little pieces of paper, typed or printed, or scrawled so unintelligibly as to challenge the top cryptographer for the CIA. Over the years now, seemingly hundreds of them, suddenly part of theatre history though once read and re-read and studied and cherished for their apt responsiveness to a particularly crucial confusion.

Since that brief initial inquiry into the cosmic nature of *Godot,* Sam has never wanted to discuss with me (or anyone else) the metaphysical backgrounds or symbolic meanings of any of his plays; nor have I pressed him in this direction. As Beckett himself once wrote about Joyce, Sam is after all basically "not writing about something, he is writing something." His plays are not about things, they are themselves things. His work is a "matter of fundamental sounds," he once explained, with the pun intentional; and the overtones should be let fall where they may without being verbalised or pinned down at every turn. Nor does he want to try to tell me something already either obvious or not there.

Not that my reluctance to pursue philosophical trails with him means that I am totally uninterested in intellectual matters, or don't enjoy these pursuits. Especially away from valuable rehearsal hours and with people who don't have to act them all out on stage on opening nights. Besides which, Sam is enough of a theatre man himself to understand more and more the futility of trying to act out abstract themes on stage. Explanations of philosophical meanings provide marvelously satisfying speeches with which the director can impress his actors but very little practical help for them. How does one, after all, play "the end of history," or "the decline of Western values"? One has to sit in a certain way against the mound, or turn over a certain way over a certain shoulder at a certain time with the spectacles held in a certain hand. Theatrical truth, as Brecht said and Beckett knows, is concrete.

And when it comes down to concrete matters, our trans-oceanic message service has never failed to function so as to further illuminate the plays. How long should one those famous "pauses" really take? In relation, say, to a "long pause" or, when it gets there, a "maximum pause"? Sam could give me the actual counts if I would ask him — though I never did — and although he doesn't own a stop watch. But then he doesn't own a tape-recorder either, and look what he figured out for Krapp to do! It's a matter of his own innate sense of rhythm. Should Winnie's glasses be on or off at this or that point in the play? Would it be better for her to be holding the toothbrush in her left hand or her right — so that she can take care of other required matters with her other hand? And so on.

When Sam was directing *Happy Days* in Berlin a season or so ago, he carried all those answers, and a few thousand others, with him in a completely detailed cross-lined notebook, practically Cartesian in its organisation of information and insight. But even before that notebook existed, it was all down logically in his head — and not only for *Happy Days* — and quite willingly shared with me whenever I was able to ask the proper questions.

The literal meaning of a line that seemed unclear, the source of a quotation, a desirable pattern of behavior or movement — these were all not mysteries but knowledge to be shared. The pace of *Godot* should always be kept light and quick, he feels; in fact that is a basic rhythm, a common denominator for most of his plays. The "Tree" is, of course, not to be a representation of the tree on stage at all, with hands outstretched as it usually is for the branches, but one of the basic positions of yoga: the sole of one foot placed directly alongside the calf of the other, with the two hands clasped together as if in prayer. That makes infinite sense — and not just comic nonsense — of Estragon's next line: "Do you think God sees me?" Sam once even drew a small diagram to show me exactly what he meant. And I have hidden away somewhere some lovely and even more detailed pen-and-ink sketches from him outlining Willie's exact optimum path around the mound when he comes visiting Winnie. If Beckett hadn't become a writer, he could have quite well found other uses for his pen.

Nor is Sam unwilling to discuss his characters as people, although he's more concerned with their external than with their internal qualities. And never with their symbolic significances or "meaning." Yes, Vladimir is more or less restless and roams around the stage; Estragon is more or less still and sits down a lot. The Mouth is "on fire" and must keep on talking in short rapid bursts (separated by those perennial dots, of course) because she has to. The Mouth is totally unaware of where she is or of a Figure watching her. The Figure is aware of and sees the Mouth but has no effect on it. No, there's nothing in the text to indicate whether the Figure is male or female. And Krapp looks at his watch at regular intervals not just because he is bored or wants to know what time it is but because he wants to see if enough minutes have gone by for him safely to have another drink. Then he goes for that other drink anyhow. And that clink of glass without the siphon is telling us that he's saying the hell with it here and taking the last shot straight up instead of with soda, as he should, to dilute the alcoholic content. (How many otherwise intelligent drama critics have talked about the "wine" Krapp is drinking!) As Jackie always called it, Sam's "underlying simplicity" is never simple — but it's there if one only looks for it.

Once, when my entire cast of the first off-Broadway *Endgame* insisted that I write to Beckett to find out why Hamm's and Clov's faces were red while Nell's and Nagg's were white, the answer came back like a slap: Why is Werther's coat green? In other words, because the author had decided that he liked that particular color. Or colors. Or when Sam thought that both Jessie and I were asking too many foolish questions about the birth, life experience and physical circumstances surrounding that solitary floating Mouth, he finally decided that enough was enough: "I no more know where she is or why than she does," he wrote. There was only the text and the stage image, both of which he had provided for us. "The rest is Ibsen." Or, as I used to tell Jessica Tandy when I felt that she wanted to probe too hard into recesses that didn't have actual existence, this was Samuel Beckett and not Arthur Miller. If one once started to worry about where Winnie got her groceries or how she managed to discharge her bodily functions, one could get into a lot of unanswerable questions. And into another play.

Oh yes, those inquisitive *Endgame* actors, not pacified, decided among themselves that Nell and Nagg, being older, had less efficient circulatory systems so that the blood couldn't get to their faces so easily. This without informing Sam — who would have been eminently surprised at this revelation. And Hamm and Clov had high blood pressure — though luckily neither Sam nor our audiences needed to know that.

The key to my directing of Beckett, then, may be described as that of dealing simultaneously with what I have come to call "the local situation" (in contrast to that other more cosmic one) and his rhythmical and tonal structure, his specific style or "texture." In principle, that is no different than when I am directing Shakespeare or Chekhov; in practice, one is more concerned in Beckett with the juxtaposition of specific sounds and silences, movement and speech, instead of with, say, the handling of iambic pentameter and Elizabethan footwork. The needed intertwining of comedic and serious tones in Chekhov is matched by a parallel necessity in Beckett, though framed in a more formal and less naturalistic pattern. Although *Krapp* to me has always seemed almost Chekhovian in its blend of emotional colors; Krapp himself is both Trofimov and Pischchik — and, perhaps, Epihodov as well.

Dealing with "the local situation" simply assumes that I try to concern myself primarily with who the characters are as human beings, and what their human situation is. What are they doing, wanting, getting, not getting in a given scene? How do they change or not change? What happens to them in the play? How do they affect their own situation, and the other characters? What is their awareness of and reaction to the various events of the play? (It is not, for instance, the "significance" of the burning of the umbrella in *Happy Days* that can be acted but Winnie's reaction to that burning.) Most importantly, what is their physical, their sensory, reality?

Of course, examining the "local situation" also means that I have to consider how the characters got there, or even perhaps why. Is Clov that same small boy whom the father, crawling on his belly, brought to Hamm years ago? What happened to the Mouth in April in that field? But not in the same manner or to the same extent that I explore those questions of background and motivation in Ibsen or in Chekhov. How, after all, did Winnie get into that pile of sand in the first place? The answer is that she's always ("the old style") been there. The sand, though "real" to her, is to Beckett a stage world only, a theatrical metaphor, a stage image. The sand, that mound into which she eternally sinks — why? — is simply the condition of her existence. Just as, in some other type of drama, a character's job or position in society is given to us. Or just the character's happening to be there in order to fulfill a function or complete a relationship. All of those seemingly accidental but necessary and unquestioned coincidences that make possible even the entrances and exits in any supposedly realistic play.

I accept Winnie's dominating presence in the mound, the literal absence of legs in the first act and of anything below her neck in the second as I accept Picasso's lady with several faces or Dali's bent watch. Though in spite of a century of non-representational art, we are still more familiar and more comfortable with the most outrageous juxtaposition of circumstances masquerading as "reality" than we are with the simplest and most direct of metaphors: let us say, our inevitably vanishing existences, for example. But we don't have to go on being uncomfortable, and the plays of Sam Beckett, I am pleased to know, have moved us a few miles up the road towards understanding of that.

Metaphor or not, though, it is the sensory reality with which the director must be primarily concerned. Winnie should be hot as well as cosmically happy and unhappy. It has never mattered who Godot really is, although we keep on asking and those convicts at San Quentin have always known. Nor even who told Vladimir and Estragon that they had to wait for him. It's the two hours of their lives and of our playing time that count. It's how they wait. Clov cannot sit down, for whatever reason; and a generation of American actors have, within my experience, offered up various answers: from arthritis through gonorrhea to hemorrhoids — although their audiences were not always able to diagnose those exact causes. So long as they were interesting and theatrical, I don't mind — and I'm sure Sam wouldn't have. Nagg and Nell are elderly, cold, hungry, sleepy, somewhat deaf, not so good at seeing, without legs, and feel a certain way about their son Hamm keeping them cooped up in those ashcans. These qualities can be acted, while the concept of the "older generation discarded" or the "dead past put onto the garbage heap" or "the flower of French civilization" cannot. Even though Sam tell us very clearly that they lost their shanks at a special time and place, Sedan, which has a distinctive echo of meaning for the French nation although the rest of us have forgotten what happened there.

At the same time, every Beckett play — from the extremely formal *Not I* to the extremely informal *Krapp's Last Tape* — posseses its own specific tonality, its special texture. That which distinguishes it from anyone else's work. Almost any page of Beckett can be immediately identified as his. Because of his particular vision of the universe and of mortal man's frail fate in it. But also because of his specific technique of organizing and orchestrating the formal elements involved. The sparseness and simplicity of his language, juxtaposed against its passages of poetic musicality. The balance and tension of its various rhythms and sounds and images. His repetition of words and phrases. The constant interplay of parallel and opposing ideas and themes: counterpoint, auditory and visual. The carefully worked-out opposition of lines and the inter-relating of opposites. And other notes of dramatic music.

As the Royal Court's George Devine, one of the earliest and most loyal of Beckett's supporters and interpreters, once explained his own view of the Beckett terrain: "One has to think of the text as something like a musical score wherein the 'notes', the sights and sounds, the pauses, have their own inter-related rhythms; and out of their composition comes the dramatic impact."

It is only through constant attention to both Beckettian "texture" and the "local situation" that his plays can be presented faithfully. For the repetition of three dots contains a specific clue to both character reality and dramatic meaning. And I have always tried to deal with both these aspects without distortion or distraction. Through whatever means. I have talked or not talked with my actors, before or during the work. I have both demanded and given way, read them portions of Beckett's letters to me or kept them to myself. I have gone up on stage to demonstrate a special move or piece of business I wanted done in a certain way, or waited for the actors to come up with their own version — as with the choreography of Vladimir's song about the dog. Helped by Beckett's own pauses, I have always worked out the "beats" in the text — with the proper intentions, adjustments, circumstances, and other standard underpinnings. Most of all, I have tried to cast only those actors whom I felt to be suitable and agreeable to Beckett's world — and not cast those who would deny or destroy that world.

* * *

After all these years, there are a number of actors (and directors) who still do not respond to Beckett, or avoid doing his plays. They feel he limits them too severely as artists, removes their creativity and individuality, constricts them too rigidly in their physical and vocal resources. They tell me that he must hate actors because he denies them the use of their own impulses, as well as more and more of their physical selves. After all, if they cannot move freely about the stage, cannot use the full range of their voices and bodies — their very means of reaching their audiences — what are they but impersonal or even disembodied puppets of his will? Now he's even down to strapping them into some sort of medieval torture chamber, closing off their faces, including their eyes — the windows of the stage souls — in order to leave only a mouth visible on stage. What's next, they ask me, the uvula alone, pinpointed on a darkened stage? And no words for them to speak?"

I do not agree. Nor did Jackie. Before his recent death, Jackie told an interviewer that Beckett's "feeling for precision in inflection, rhythm, and movement seems almost severe, but not for a moment does he restrict the imagination or inventive feeling of others except if it is outside the framework of what is being interpreted. He creates a freedom in working which actors do not often enjoy in the theatre today, and that freedom is always the bedfellow of true discipline."

How right Jackie was and yet how difficult it is still to explain to those actors who do not want to understand that it is precisely because Sam so admires them and so respects their abilities that he trusts them to be extraordinarily effective even with certain of those abilities confined or even removed. We have known for centuries that an actor can hold us and move us when he has full range on stage. But that he can reach us as powerfully or more so with only his face or his eyelids or his mouth, or with lips and teeth and voice alone, that is fantastic. And theatrical. And worth exploring further.

After all, do we think that Beckett hates or despises the English language because he uses so many simple one or two-syllable words instead of availing himself of its entire range of syllabification and richness? Does he deny that language its strength and virtues because he has gone in the opposite direction from Joyce or Giraudoux or Yeats towards greater and greater selection and bareness? Is he uninterested in language itself because he makes use of only a small portion of those possibilities he knows it possesses? Of course not.

Yet even this sort of analogy has not and does not satisfy his critics on the stage and in the audience. They still complain or get angry when Beckett doesn't cater to their expectations or fit in with their past habits, though they can no longer accuse him so readily of heresy or hoax. They do continue to avoid him or in praising him not bother to read his plays or attend his productions. Years ago, Ralph Richardson turned down the part of Estragon because Beckett was unable to inform him adequately of the exact extent of Pozzo's holdings (although Richardson later had the good grace in his autobiography to confess his error). Everybody turned down Hamm for me once, as well as Krapp. In fact dozens of actors, those of the first rank and others, have in the past turned down Beckett roles; today, more and more star names have begun to think of the plays as stage or screen vehicles for themselves to be manipulated towards their own personalities or purposes. In Paris, Madeleine Renaud and Jean Louis Barrault have been doing *Happy Days* for years; over here, I tried in vain once to interest Lynn Fontaine and Alfred Lunt. Eventually, the last time around, I did get Jessica Tandy and Hume Cronyn, though I had a hard time talking him into doing Willie. And even the gracious Miss Tandy, if I'm not giving away too sheltered a confidence, despaired nightly of the various restraints, literal and metaphorical, placed upon her by author and director in *Not I*. She could not wait to be forever free of its head clamp, blackened makeup, and stichomythic pace.

As to my own feelings of confinement, I have none. When a limit my imagination to the boundaries set for me by Sam, I feel with Jackie that I am not so much limiting as freeing myself. Just as a sonnet writer who has something he wants to express may not be bound tighter but actually guided into greater complexity by the demands of its rhyme scheme. Or any artists always is by the specific limitations of his materials. When I direct Shakespeare or Brecht there are also limitations involved, though in those cases they are inherent, thus perhaps seemingly more flexible, than imposed. When I direct Beckett, I know and trust him and respond to him so directly that I can allow my own impulses and imagination to flow through his pulse-beats. Even though some of the critics may still say that I am abdicating my directorial responsibilities, that I am betraying Beckett by being too loyal.

Once I did put a bowler hat instead of a toque on my Hamm, but I did not consider that a betrayal of Beckett, just a practical adjustment to the fact that the actor playing the role simply did not look right in any toque we could find or make. Only once have I myself felt that I actually did betray Sam's real intentions. When we were doing the first production of *Play,* whose text is constructed so as to be spoken twice, the preview audiences at the Cherry Lane seemed to resent the repetition, sitting there stony-faced and bored the second time around, instead of offering up greater attention and more laughs. At the same time, our actors didn't relish the idea of speaking the lines the first time as rapidly as both Beckett and I wanted them to. They felt that the audiences didn't have a clue as to what was going on, and that they were losing their laughs. (The same conflict took place, by the way, during rehearsals of the original London production; it was eventually resolved — in Sam's presence — by a rearrangement of the repetition, but with the actors both times speaking so rapidly that, Rosemary Harris told me, they could hardly catch their breaths.) After continued urgent requests by our producers and against my better judgement and previously held position, I wrote to Sam explaining that perhaps New York audiences were more sophisticated (or jaded) than all others and were actively resenting this supposed slur upon their intelligence. I asked him if he would mind if during a few of the previews we experimented with playing the text through only once and spoken a bit more slowly just to see how it would go. He wrote back his approval, without making apparent his underlying tone of sadness and disappointment.

We tried it only once through in the rest of the previews, where it seemed to be getting more of a response, and eventually in performance. Not that the change saved us. In spite of reasonably favorable notices, the production ran only a few weeks, which it would probably have done anyway, even had we played it as originally intended. They just were not ready for the play. But I realised as I have so often, before and since, that I should have stuck to my instinctive guns, done the show the way the author had conceived it. By distorting his writing we diluted his play and still did not "succeed." Doing it his way, we might also have "failed" him but at least on our own terms. Nor has that play always been successful when performed elsewhere. But at least its quality and dramatic audacity has now been accepted.

It was not until many years later, and most indirectly because he would never tell me himself, that I learned how hurt Sam had been by my decision. By then I had learned my lesson.

Those theatre people who are not willing to trust, not ready to go along on a production or part of a greater equilibrium than that provided by their reflexes — or ego — cannot understand my pleasure and gratitude and joy at having been associated with Samuel Beckett's work. Not because of his fame but because of his quality. For Sam's feeling for precision, for order, has always been for me a most uncategorical imperative. His rhythms, his insights, his vision of the theatre have rarely, if ever, restricted my own. On the contrary, he has deepened my own experience as a working director more than any other playwright — perhaps more than anyone outside of my own immediate family.

Without, I hope, waxing overly sentimental, I must confess that I have always felt both privileged and inspired to have worked so long and so often with him. If not as directly as I would have chosen had not a particular accident of geography intervened yet no less fully or richly. To quote the words of Sam's favorite French publisher, Jerome Lindon, "I have never met a man in whom co-exist together in such high degree, nobility and modesty, lucidity and goodness." Sam has not only changed my life, both professionally and personally, but become part of it. From that moment, almost a quarter-century ago but still seeming as though yesterday, when he first wrote to me that "the Miami fiasco does not distress me in the smallest degree, or only in so far as it distresses you," there has not been a day when I did not think of him or feel him present in my work and life. There is nothing I would not do for him, on stage or off.

Last season, while substituting for Zelda Fichandler as a somewhat inadequate Producing Director at Washington's Arena Stage, I had one of my few satisfactions in bringing into being an extraordinary production — on the order of accomplishment, I believe, of Peter Brook's *Marat/Sade* or *Dream* — by a leading Romanian director, Liviu Ciulei, of Georg Buchner's *Leonce and Lena*. Written circa 1830, the play had never been professionally presented in this country; yet it was as contemporary in feeling as though it had been written today. While we were in previews, a sizeable portion of our subscription audience walked out in high dudgeon that we could inflict this particular pain on them, then proceeded to bombard both Zelda and myself with letters expressing their keen resentment of such "trash" (Although by the time we opened — and the favorable notices came out — they were a little less sure.) I thought once more of Samuel Beckett and of Miami Beach, circa 1956, and realised once more how little had actually changed in the theatre. It was Harold Hobson, writing in the London *Sunday Times* not so long ago, who best expressed my feelings: "This complacent inability to recognize the highest, this apparently natural enmity towards the exaltation of the spirit... checks one's heart."

My heart, I am well aware, has been checked often throughout my theatre life. As has everyone's, although the causes always differ. But it is Sam Beckett's exaltation of the spirit that has taught me the one basic truth, that in spite of everything or whatever, one goes on. With or without sand in those bags. That in the theatre as in all of art the only thing which counts is the work itself; the need to go on with that work at the highest possible level. Not to be distracted or disturbed by success or failure, by praise or blame, by surface or show, analysis or abstraction, self-criticism or the criticism of others. Especially when that work is of Beckett's order of magnitude, possessed of Beckett's sublimity, his degree of compassion, his eloquent understanding of the potentialities both of the stage and of human frailty. After twenty years of working with him, I can only be grateful that whatever theatrical fates that be have put me into the same universe of possibility with him.

NORTH CAROLINA STUDIES IN THE ROMANCE LANGUAGES AND LITERATURES

I.S.B.N. Prefix 0-88438

Recent Titles

CHARLES NODIER: HIS LIFE AND WORKS, by Sarah Fore Bell. 1971. (No. 95). *-895-6.*
RACINE AND SENECA, by Ronald W. Tobin. 1971. (No. 96). *-896-4.*
LOPE DE VEGA. "EL PEREGRINO EN SU PATRIA," edición de Myron A. Peyton. 1971. (No. 97), *-897-2.*
CRITICAL REACTIONS AND THE CHRISTIAN ELEMENT IN THE POETRY OF PIERRE DE RONSARD, by Mark S. Whitney. 1971. (No. 98). *-898-0.*
THE REV. JOHN BOWLE. THE GENESIS OF CERVANTEAN CRITICISM, by Ralph Merritt Cox. 1971. (No. 99). *-899-9.*
THE FOUR INTERPOLATED STORIES IN THE "ROMAN COMIQUE": THEIR SOURCES AND UNIFYING FUNCTION, by Frederick Alfed De Armas. 1971. (No. 100). *-900-6.*
LE CHASTOIEMENT D'UN PERE A SON FILS, A CRITICAL EDITION, edited by Edward D. Montgomery, Jr. 1971. (No. 101). *-901-4.*
LE ROMMANT DE "GUY DE WARWIK" ET DE "HEROLT D'ARDENNE," edited by D. J. Conlon. 1971. (No. 102). *-902-2.*
THE OLD PORTUGUESE "VIDA DE SAM BERNARDO," EDITED FROM ALCOBAÇA MANUSCRIPT ccxci/200, WITH INTRODUCTION, LINGUISTIC STUDY, NOTES, TABLE OF PROPER NAMES, AND GLOSSARY, by Lawrence A. Sharpe. 1971. (No. 103). *-903-0.*
A CRITICAL AND ANNOTATED EDITION OF LOPE DE VEGA'S "LAS ALMENAS DE TORO," by Thomas E. Case. 1971. (No. 104). *-904-9.*
LOPE DE VEGA'S "LO QUE PASA EN UNA TARDE," A CRITICAL, ANNOTATED EDITION OF THE AUTOGRAPH MANUSCRIPT, by Richard Angelo Picerno. 1971. (No. 105). *-905-7.*
OBJECTIVE METHODS FOR TESTING AUTHENTICITY AND THE STUDY OF TEN DOUBTFUL "COMEDIAS" ATTRIBUTED TO LOPE DE VEGA, by Fred M. Clark. 1971. (No. 106). *-906-5.*
THE ITALIAN VERB. A MORPHOLOGICAL STUDY, by Frede Jensen. 1971. (No. 107). *-907-3.*
A CRITICAL EDITION OF THE OLD PROVENÇAL EPIC "DAUREL ET BETON," WITH NOTES AND PROLEGOMENA, by Arthur S. Kimmel. 1971. (No. 108). *-908-1.*
FRANCISCO RODRIGUES LOBO: DIALOGUE AND COURTLY LORE IN RENAISSANCE PORTUGAL, by Richard A. Preto-Rodas. 1971. (No. 109). *909-X.*
RAIMOND VIDAL: POETRY AND PROSE, edited by W. H. W. Field. 1971. (No. 110). *-910-3.*
RELIGIOUS ELEMENTS IN THE SECULAR LYRICS OF THE TROUBADOURS, by Raymond Gay-Crosier. 1971. (No. 111). *-911-1.*
THE SIGNIFICANCE OF DIDEROT'S "ESSAI SUR LE MERITE ET LA VERTU," by Gordon B. Walters. 1971. (No. 112). *-912-X.*
PROPER NAMES IN THE LYRICS OF THE TROUBADOURS, by Frank M. Chambers. 1971. (No. 113). *-913-8.*
STUDIES IN HONOR OF MARIO A. PEI, edited by John Fisher and Paul A. Gaeng. 1971. (No. 114). *-914-6.*
DON MANUEL CAÑETE, CRONISTA LITERARIO DEL ROMANTICISMO Y DEL POSROMANTICISMO EN ESPAÑA, por Donald Allen Randolph. 1972. (No. 115). *-915-4.*
THE TEACHINGS OF SAINT LOUIS. A CRITICAL TEXT, by David O'Connell. 1972. (No. 116). *-916-2.*
HIGHER, HIDDEN ORDER: DESIGN AND MEANING IN THE ODES OF MALHERBE, by David Lee Rubin. 1972. (No. 117). *-917-0.*
JEAN DE LE MOTE "LE PARFAIT DU PAON," édition critique par Richard J. Carey. 1972. (No. 118). *-918-9.*
CAMUS' HELLENIC SOURCES, by Paul Archambault. 1972. (No. 119). *-919-7.*

Recent Titles

FROM VULGAR LATIN TO OLD PROVENÇAL, by Frede Jensen. 1972. (No. 120). *-920-0.*

GOLDEN AGE DRAMA IN SPAIN: GENERAL CONSIDERATION AND UNUSUAL FEATURES, by Sturgis E. Leavitt. 1972. (No. 121). *-921-9.*

THE LEGEND OF THE "SIETE INFANTES DE LARA" (*Refundición toledana de la crónica de 1344* versión), study and edition by Thomas A. Lathrop. 1972. (No. 122). *-922-7.*

STRUCTURE AND IDEOLOGY IN BOIARDO'S "ORLANDO INNAMORATO," by Andrea di Tommaso. 1972. (No. 123). *-923-5.*

STUDIES IN HONOR OF ALFRED G. ENGSTROM, edited by Robert T. Cargo and Emmanuel J. Mickel, Jr. 1972. (No. 124). *-924-3.*

A CRITICAL EDITION WITH INTRODUCTION AND NOTES OF GIL VICENTE'S "FLORESTA DE ENGANOS," by Constantine Christopher Stathatos. 1972. (No. 125). *-925-1.*

LI ROMANS DE WITASSE LE MOINE. *Roman du treizième siècle.* Édité d'après le manuscrit, fonds français 1553, de la Bibliothèque Nationale, Paris, par Denis Joseph Conlon. 1972. (No. 126). *-926-X.*

EL CRONISTA PEDRO DE ESCAVIAS. *Una vida del Siglo XV,* por Juan Bautista Avalle-Arce. 1972. (No. 127). *-927-8.*

AN EDITION OF THE FIRST ITALIAN TRANSLATION OF THE "CELESTINA," by Kathleen V. Kish. 1973. (No. 128). *-928-6.*

MOLIÈRE MOCKED. THREE CONTEMPORARY HOSTILE COMEDIES: *Zélinde, Le portrait du peintre, Élomire Hypocondre,* by Frederick Wright Vogler. 1973. (No. 129). *-929-4.*

C.-A. SAINTE-BEUVE. *Chateaubriand et son groupe littéraire sous l'empire.* Index alphabétique et analytique établi par Lorin A. Uffenbeck. 1973. (No. 130). *-930-8.*

THE ORIGINS OF THE BAROQUE CONCEPT OF "PEREGRINATIO," by Juergen Hahn. 1973. (No. 131). *-931-6.*

THE "AUTO SACRAMENTAL" AND THE PARABLE IN SPANISH GOLDEN AGE LITERATURE, by Donald Thaddeus Dietz. 1973. (No. 132). *-932-4.*

FRANCISCO DE OSUNA AND THE SPIRIT OF THE LETTER, by Laura Calvert. 1973. (No. 133). *-933-2.*

ITINERARIO DI AMORE: DIALETTICA DI AMORE E MORTE NELLA VITA NUOVA, by Margherita de Bonfils Templer. 1973. (No. 134). *-934-0.*

L'IMAGINATION POETIQUE CHEZ DU BARTAS: ELEMENTS DE SENSIBILITE BAROQUE DANS LA "CREATION DU MONDE," by Bruno Braunrot. 1973. (No. 135). *-934-0.*

ARTUS DESIRE: PRIEST AND PAMPHLETEER OF THE SIXTEENTH CENTURY, by Frank S. Giese. 1973. (No. 136). *-936-7.*

JARDIN DE NOBLES DONZELLAS, FRAY MARTIN DE CORDOBA, by Harriet Goldberg. 1974. (No. 137). *-937-5.*

Symposia

LOS NARRADORES HISPANOAMERICANOS DE HOY, edited by Juan Bautista Avalle-Arce. 1973. (No. 1). *-951-0.*

When ordering please cite the *ISBN Prefix* plus the last four digits for each title.

Send orders to:
University of North Carolina Press
Chapel Hill
North Carolina 27514
U. S. A.

The Department of Romance Studies Digital Arts and Collaboration Lab at the University of North Carolina at Chapel Hill is proud to support the digitization of the North Carolina Studies in the Romance Languages and Literatures series.

www.ingramcontent.com/pod-product-compliance
Lightning Source LLC
Chambersburg PA
CBHW030611230426
43661CB00053B/1933